PRAISE FOR *LET'S TALK ABOUT DEI*

"Shaun Harper shows what it looks like to live one of our deepest American values: to engage in respectful civic discourse with those who disagree. This book brilliantly captures the conversations of this moment, and pushes for deeper engagement across difference."

—**Na'ilah Suad Nasir**, President, Spencer Foundation

"This is the perfect book for any educator, trainer, or leader looking to kick-start courageous conversations in classrooms and workplaces. Harper models what constructive disagreement looks like on some of the nation's hardest problems."

—**Khalil Gibran Muhammad**, Professor of African American Studies and Public Affairs, Princeton University

"With our democracy in the balance, Dr. Harper offers a path forward for us to find common ground, inviting us to consider others' viewpoints while co-constructing learning across perspectives. This book is a must-read for all who care about our democracy and each other."

—**Patty Perillo**, Vice President for Student Affairs, University of Maryland

"In these divisive times, *Let's Talk About DEI* is a poignant call to engage across difference with respect, courage, and intellectual honesty. Dr. Harper and his students offer a powerful model for moving beyond polarization toward deeper understanding. This book is both a practical resource and a vital reminder that respectful disagreement and robust exchange across difference are not only possible, they are essential to a healthy democracy."

—**Angel B. Pérez**, CEO, National Association for College Admission Counseling

"A balanced and timely exploration of an acronym many weaponize, but few fully understand. Dr. Harper reflects on how individuals and students experience DEI differently and directly addresses anti-DEI rhetoric. This is a must-read for those committed to transformative change beyond this moment in history."

—**Cheryl Holcomb-McCoy**, CEO/President, American Association for Colleges of Teacher Education

"Educational leader Shaun Harper has dynamic exchanges with students holding opposing viewpoints on DEI. With a willingness to experiment and challenge assumptions, Harper offers us this unique collection, which encourages discussion and leaves readers with plenty to consider."

—**Prudence L. Carter**, Sarah and Joseph Jr. Dowling Professor, Brown University

"Timely. Inspiring. Necessary. Harper provides a master class in managing difficult conversations, a blueprint for how we might navigate increasing polarization and revive meaningful conversations across difference."

—**Jonathan M. Cox**, Vice President, Congressional Black Caucus Foundation

"Grounded in research, this provocative book models how to agree to disagree while centering civility, humanity, and possibility. In a time of divisiveness, this book helps us move closer to true democracy."

—**H. Richard Milner IV**, Cornelius Vanderbilt Professor, Vanderbilt University

"Shaun Harper offers a timely guide for engaging in uncomfortable, yet worthwhile conversations. From classrooms to boardrooms, Harper empowers faculty to learn from and with students and facilitators to inclusively engage their teams."

—**Maisha T. Winn**, Excellence in Learning Graduate School of Education Professor, Stanford University

"Dr. Harper's approach to productive disagreements arrives at a critical time in our history. With 40 student counterpoints, he offers a unique and exceptionally nuanced approach to intellectual critique and deepening conversations."

—**Jason Pina**, Senior Vice President for University Life, New York University

"The point/counterpoint approach provides a rich and nuanced take on a broad range of DEI topics. As such, this book helps readers understand what's at stake and appreciate others' perspectives."

—**Robert E. Thomas**, Charles M. Hewitt Professor of Business Law and Ethics, Indiana University Kelley School of Business

"*Let's Talk About DEI* is essential reading for this moment. Dr. Harper and his students discuss timely issues and controversies related to DEI. In reality, we are all students grasping to understand these evolving issues. Believing we already know it all is a fatal error, and resources like this one that will help each of us to express, confront, examine, and productively debate divergent opinions on DEI are of the utmost importance."

—**Areva Martin**, Civil Rights Attorney and Disability Advocate

"By welcoming all voices into sociocultural exchange, Harper debunks the rhetoric that this space seeks to silence conservative voices. Offering his own writings as the prompts, engaging the genius of his students in reaction to those prompts, and honoring their offerings with respectful responses that sometimes stand firm, at other moments capitulate, and occasionally redirect, Harper audaciously opens a space for constructive dialogue on compelling and entertaining issues of the day."

—**Denise B. Maybank**, Vice Chancellor for Student Affairs, The City University of New York

MULTICULTURAL EDUCATION SERIES
James A. Banks, Series Editor

Let's Talk About DEI: Productive Disagreements About America's Most Polarizing Topics
Shaun Harper

Why Historically Black Colleges and Universities Matter: 25 Years of Historical Research for Justice
Marybeth Gasman

Hidden in Blackness: Being Black and Being an Immigrant in U.S. Schools and Colleges
Chrystal A. George Mwangi & Adaurennaya C Onyewuenyi

"To Remain an Indian": Lessons in Democracy from a Century of Native American Education. 2nd Ed.
K. Tsianina Lomawaima and Teresa L. McCarty

From Foster Care to College: Navigating Educational Challenges and Creating Possibilities
Royel M. Johnson

Achieving Equal Educational Opportunity for Students of Color: Disrupting Structural Racism—An American Imperative
Richard R. Valencia

Critical Multicultural Education: Theory and Practice
Christine E. Sleeter

Race and Media Literacy, Explained (or Why Does the Black Guy Die First?)
Frederick W. Gooding, Jr.

Whiteness in the Ivory Tower: Why *Don't* We Notice the White Students Sitting Together in the Quad?
Nolan L. Cabrera

Culturally Sustaining Policymaking in Indigenous Communities: Partnering to Promote Lasting Change
Aprille J. Phillips

Educating for Equity and Excellence: Enacting Culturally Responsive Teaching
Geneva Gay

Speculative Pedagogies: Designing Equitable Educational Futures
Antero Garcia & Nicole Mirra, Eds.

Seeing Whiteness: The Essential Essays of Robin DiAngelo
Robin DiAngelo

Becoming an Antiracist School Leader: Dare to Be Real
Patrick A. Duffy

The Hip-Hop Mindset: Success Strategies for Educators and Other Professionals
Toby S. Jenkins

Education for Liberal Democracy: Using Classroom Discussion to Build Knowledge and Voice
Walter C. Parker

Critical Race Theory and Its Critics: Implications for Research and Teaching
Francesca López & Christine E. Sleeter

Anti-Blackness at School: Creating Affirming Educational Spaces for African American Students
Joi A. Spencer & Kerri Ullucci

Sustaining Disabled Youth: Centering Disability in Asset Pedagogies
Federico R. Waitoller & Kathleen A. King Thorius, Eds.

The Civil Rights Road to Deeper Learning: Five Essentials for Equity
Kia Darling-Hammond & Linda Darling-Hammond

Reckoning With Racism in Family–School Partnerships: Centering Black Parents' School Engagement
Jennifer L. McCarthy Foubert

Teaching Anti-Fascism: A Critical Multicultural Pedagogy for Civic Engagement
Michael Vavrus

Unsettling Settler-Colonial Education: The Transformational Indigenous Praxis Model
Cornel Pewewardy, Anna Lees, & Robin Zape-tah-hol-ah Minthorn, Eds.

Culturally and Socially Responsible Assessment: Theory, Research, and Practice
Catherine S. Taylor, with Susan B. Nolen

LGBTQ Youth and Education: Policies and Practices, 2nd Ed.
Cris Mayo

Transforming Multicultural Education Policy and Practice: Expanding Educational Opportunity
James A. Banks, Ed.

Critical Race Theory in Education: A Scholar's Journey
Gloria Ladson-Billings

Civic Education in the Age of Mass Migration: Implications for Theory and Practice
Angela M. Banks

Creating a Home in Schools: Sustaining Identities for Black, Indigenous, and Teachers of Color
Francisco Rios & A Longoria

Generation Mixed Goes to School: Radically Listening to Multiracial Kids
Ralina L. Joseph & Allison Briscoe-Smith

Indian Education for All: Decolonizing Indigenous Education in Public Schools
John P. Hopkins

For a complete list of series titles, please visit www.tcpress.com/MCE

(continued)

MULTICULTURAL EDUCATION SERIES, continued

Racial Microaggressions
DANIEL G. SOLÓRZANO & LINDSAY PÉREZ HUBER

City Schools and the American Dream 2
PEDRO A. NOGUERA & ESA SYEED

Measuring Race
ROBERT T. TERANISHI ET AL.

Transformative Ethnic Studies in Schools
CHRISTINE E. SLEETER & MIGUEL ZAVALA

Why Race and Culture Matter in Schools, 2nd Ed.
TYRONE C. HOWARD

Just Schools
ANN M. ISHIMARU

"We Dare Say Love"
NA'ILAH SUAD NASIR ET AL., EDS.

Teaching What *Really* Happened, 2nd Ed.
JAMES W. LOEWEN

Culturally Responsive Teaching, 3rd Ed.
GENEVA GAY

Music, Education, and Diversity
PATRICIA SHEHAN CAMPBELL

Reaching and Teaching Students in Poverty, 2nd Ed.
PAUL C. GORSKI

Deconstructing Race
JABARI MAHIRI

Is Everyone Really Equal? 2nd Ed.
ÖZLEM SENSOY & ROBIN DIANGELO

Transforming Educational Pathways for Chicana/o Students
DOLORES DELGADO BERNAL & ENRIQUE ALEMÁN JR.

Un-Standardizing Curriculum, 2nd Ed.
CHRISTINE E. SLEETER & JUDITH FLORES CARMONA

Global Migration, Diversity, and Civic Education
JAMES A. BANKS ET AL., EDS.

Reclaiming the Multicultural Roots of U.S. Curriculum
WAYNE AU ET AL.

We Can't Teach What We Don't Know, 3rd Ed.
GARY R. HOWARD

Diversity and Education
MICHAEL VAVRUS

Mathematics for Equity
NA'ILAH SUAD NASIR ET AL., EDS.

Race, Empire, and English Language Teaching
SUHANTHIE MOTHA

Black Male(d)
TYRONE C. HOWARD

Race Frameworks
ZEUS LEONARDO

Class Rules
PETER W. COOKSON JR.

Achieving Equity for Latino Students
FRANCES CONTRERAS

Literacy Achievement and Diversity
KATHRYN H. AU

Understanding English Language Variation in U.S. Schools
ANNE H. CHARITY HUDLEY & CHRISTINE MALLINSON

Latino Children Learning English
GUADALUPE VALDÉS ET AL.

Asians in the Ivory Tower
ROBERT T. TERANISHI

Diversity and Equity in Science Education
OKHEE LEE & CORY A. BUXTON

Forbidden Language
PATRICIA GÁNDARA & MEGAN HOPKINS, EDS.

The Light in Their Eyes, 10th Anniversary Ed.
SONIA NIETO

The Flat World and Education
LINDA DARLING-HAMMOND

Educating Citizens in a Multicultural Society, 2nd Ed.
JAMES A. BANKS

Culture, Literacy, and Learning
CAROL D. LEE

Facing Accountability in Education
CHRISTINE E. SLEETER, ED.

Talkin Black Talk
H. SAMY ALIM & JOHN BAUGH, EDS.

Improving Access to Mathematics
NA'ILAH SUAD NASIR & PAUL COBB, EDS.

Beyond the Big House
GLORIA LADSON-BILLINGS

Improving Multicultural Education
CHERRY A. MCGEE BANKS

Transforming the Multicultural Education of Teachers
MICHAEL VAVRUS

Learning to Teach for Social Justice
LINDA DARLING-HAMMOND ET AL., EDS.

Learning and Not Learning English
GUADALUPE VALDÉS

Multicultural Education, Transformative Knowledge, and Action
JAMES A. BANKS, ED.

Let's Talk About DEI

Productive Disagreements About America's Most Polarizing Topics

Shaun Harper

Series Foreword by James A. Banks

Teachers College, Columbia University

In loving memory of Brother Ira L. Flowers, an amazingly generous mentor who taught me to courageously speak and reasonably listen

Published by Teachers College Press,® 1234 Amsterdam Avenue, New York, NY 10027

Copyright © 2025 by Teachers College, Columbia University

All rights reserved. No part of this publication may be reproduced or transmitted in any form or by any means, electronic or mechanical, including photocopy, or any information storage and retrieval system, without permission from the publisher. For reprint permission and other subsidiary rights requests, please contact Teachers College Press, Rights Dept.: tcpressrights@tc.columbia.edu

Library of Congress Cataloging-in-Publication Data is available at loc.gov

ISBN 978-0-8077-8746-5 (paper)
ISBN 978-0-8077-8747-2 (hardcover)
ISBN 978-0-8077-8328-3 (ebook)

Printed on acid-free paper
Manufactured in the United States of America

Contents

Series Foreword *James A. Banks*	xv
Preface	xxi
An Inspiring, Adaptable Model	xxiii
The Educational Benefits of Being in Touch	xxiv
A Vision for This Book	xxv
Productive Engagement Beyond Academia	xxv
Acknowledgments	xxvii

PART I: PRODUCTIVE DISAGREEMENTS ABOUT EDUCATION

1. Actions Educational Leaders Must Take When Kids Do Racist Things at School	3
Nico's Productive Disagreement	5
Productive Response From Nico's Professor	6
2. Why Politicized Attacks on DEI in Schools Are Occurring, and How They're Bad for America	8
Grace's Productive Disagreement	10
Productive Response From Grace's Professor	11
3. Supreme Court Ends Affirmative Action in College Admissions—Here's What Will Happen on Campuses	12
Will's Productive Disagreement	15
Productive Response From Will's Professor	16

4. **Eliminating Standardized Tests to Achieve Racial Equity in Post-Affirmative Action College Admissions**   17
    Alvin's Productive Disagreement   19
    Productive Response From Alvin's Professor   20

5. **Legacy Admissions at Harvard and Other Elite Institutions Advantage White Applicants**   21
    Isis's Productive Disagreement   22
    Productive Response From Isis's Professor   23

6. **Harvard University's Next President Is a Black Woman**   25
    Deonté's Productive Disagreement   27
    Productive Response From Deonté's Professor   28

7. **What It Means That a Black Woman Survived Only Six Months as Harvard's President**   29
    David's Productive Disagreement   31
    Productive Response From David's Professor   32

8. **What Deion Sanders's Departure From Jackson State Could Mean for the Business of HBCU Athletics**   33
    Timi's Productive Disagreement   35
    Productive Response From Timi's Professor   36

PART II: PRODUCTIVE DISAGREEMENTS ABOUT BUSINESS AND CORPORATE LEADERSHIP

9. **Why Business Leaders Are Pulling the Plug on DEI**   39
    Malavika's Productive Disagreement   41
    Productive Response From Malavika's Professor   43

10. **Elon Musk Articulates What Many DEI Opponents Think, but Are Too Afraid to Publicly Say**   44
    Christopher's Productive Disagreement   45
    Productive Response From Christopher's Professor   46

Contents   ix

11. **Your Company's DEI Training Isn't Critical Race Theory, No Need to Ban It**   48

    Yamile's Productive Disagreement   50

    Productive Response From Yamile's Professor   51

12. **Ways CEOs and Companies Fail Chief Diversity Officers**   52

    Juhwan's Productive Disagreement   55

    Productive Response From Juhwan's Professor   57

13. **Discrimination Against White Job Applicants and Employees, or Is It Racial Equity?**   58

    Kelsey's Productive Disagreement   60

    Productive Response From Kelsey's Professor   62

14. **Repeated Snubbing of Black Kids at Amusement Parks Shows Need for More Complex Bias Trainings**   63

    Linh's Productive Disagreement   65

    Productive Response from Linh's Professor   66

15. **Elon Musk Says He's Hiring a New Twitter CEO—Women Beware of the Glass Cliff**   67

    Samantha's Productive Disagreement   69

    Productive Response From Samantha's Professor   70

16. **New Bank of America Loan Could Further Push Black and Latino Families Out of Communities**   71

    Henry's Productive Disagreement   73

    Productive Response From Henry's Professor   74

17. **Adidas Gets Transphobic Backlash for "Woke" Pride Month Swimsuit Marketing**   75

    Sloane's Productive Disagreement   76

    Productive Response From Sloane's Professor   77

18. **Target Fumbles Black History Month, Pulls Offensive Item From Stores**   79

    Samantha's Productive Disagreement   81

    Productive Response From Samantha's Professor   82

19. **Why a "Lay Low" DEI Strategy Is Especially Bad Right Now**   83

    Meron's Productive Disagreement   85

    Productive Response From Meron's Professor   86

PART III: PRODUCTIVE DISAGREEMENTS ABOUT AMERICAN POLITICS AND ELECTED OFFICIALS

20. **They're Saying He's Too Old: Ageism in Media Discourse About Joe Biden's Reelection**   89

    Delaney's Productive Disagreement   90

    Productive Response From Delaney's Professor   92

21. **Who Told Nikki Haley and Ron DeSantis That America Has Never Been Racist?**   93

    Rachael's Productive Disagreement   95

    Productive Response From Rachael's Professor   95

22. **Kevin McCarthy's Failed Bids for House Speaker Expose the Ironies of Ideological Diversity and Homogeneity in the GOP**   97

    Mariessa's Productive Disagreement   99

    Productive Response From Mariessa's Professor   100

23. **If George Santos Were Black, There'd Be Harsher Consequences for the Congressman's Lies**   101

    Mathew's Productive Disagreement   103

    Productive Response From Mathew's Professor   104

24. **How Karen Bass Beat a Billionaire to Become First Woman and Second Black L.A. Mayor**   106

    Nicolette's Productive Disagreement   107

    Productive Response From Nicolette's Professor   108

Contents xi

25. Brittney Griner, Paul Whelan, or Nothing? Why the Biden Administration Chose the Black Woman ... 110

    Todd's Productive Disagreement ... 112

    Productive Response From Todd's Professor ... 113

PART IV: PRODUCTIVE DISAGREEMENTS ABOUT ENTERTAINMENT AND SPORTS

26. Beyoncé Wins the Most Grammy Awards, Becomes the Actual GOAT ... 117

    Sydney's Productive Disagreement ... 119

    Productive Response From Sydney's Professor ... 120

27. Megan Thee Stallion Supporters Call Out Misogynoir in Hip-Hop Industry—What It Is and Where Else It Exists ... 121

    Wayne's Productive Disagreement ... 124

    Productive Response From Wayne's Professor ... 125

28. Kanye West Could Lose Everything If Someone Doesn't Help Him ... 126

    Elena's Productive Disagreement ... 128

    Productive Response From Elena's Professor ... 129

29. *The Color Purple* Cinematic Remix Expands Cultural Contribution and Financial Impact ... 130

    Bill's Productive Disagreement ... 132

    Productive Response From Bill's Professor ... 133

30. Viola Davis Makes Compelling Case for Darker Skin Black Women in *The Woman King* ... 134

    Allison Joyce's Productive Disagreement ... 136

    Productive Response From Allison Joyce's Professor ... 137

31. What the Porn Industry Teaches Teens, Especially Guys, About Sex ... 138

    Max's Productive Disagreement ... 140

    Productive Response From Max's Professor ... 141

32. NCAA Basketball Champ Angel Reese Was Called "Classless" Because She's Black — 143

Destiny's Productive Disagreement — 145

Productive Response From Destiny's Professor — 145

33. What to Do When Drunk Fans Say Inexcusably Offensive Things at Sporting Events — 147

Paxton's Productive Disagreement — 149

Productive Response From Paxton's Professor — 150

PART V: OTHER PRODUCTIVE DEI DISAGREEMENTS

34. White Guy Says He'll Bring Fried Chicken to the Black Cookout—How to Recover From Racial Microaggressions — 153

Sean's Productive Disagreement — 155

Productive Response From Sean's Professor — 156

35. Remote Work Can Boost Diversity Yet Undermine Equity for Employees of Color — 157

Liz's Productive Disagreement — 159

Productive Response From Liz's Professor — 160

36. Black Cops Upheld Institutional and Cultural Racism in Fatal Attack of Tyre Nichols — 161

Obianeze's Productive Disagreement — 163

Productive Response From Obianeze's Professor — 164

37. What Executives Should Say to Employees When Police Officers Kill Unarmed Black People — 165

Shivani's Productive Disagreement — 167

Productive Response From Shivani's Professor — 168

38. ChatGPT Threatens Authenticity of DEI Communications From Leaders — 169

Shehab's Productive Disagreement — 171

Productive Response From Shehab's Professor — 172

39. Rite Aid Facial Recognition Lawsuit Shows AI Risks of Shopping While Black — 173

Pawan's Productive Disagreement — 175

Productive Response From Pawan's Professor — 176

40. Ways Philanthropic Foundations Can Respond to Costly Attacks on DEI — 177

Devon's Productive Disagreement — 179

Productive Response From Devon's Professor — 180

Endnotes — 181

Credits — 202

Index — 204

About the Author — 212

Series Foreword

As Shaun Harper points out in this visionary, informative, and practical book, the attacks on diversity, equity, and inclusion (DEI) are a "well-coordinated, intentionally orchestrated, and highly funded political movement that's succeeding. Lies, misinformation, and exaggeration fuel that movement" (p. 10). The attacks on DEI include banning books from schools and public libraries. Some of the most targeted books were written by authors of color or deal with LGBTQ+ issues (Harris & Alter, 2022). The *1619 Project* (Hannah-Jones et al., 2021), which resulted from an initiative sponsored by *The New York Times*, is one of the most frequently banned books. The opponents of DEI also falsely claim that critical race theory is being taught in the schools (Mervosh, 2022) and assert that mainstream white students should be protected and not be made uncomfortable by teaching historically accurate information about institutionalized racism in the United States. Christopher F. Rufo, a conservative activist at the Manhattan Institute and a failed candidate for the Seattle City Council, is a leader of the movement, which inaccurately claims that schools are teaching critical race theory. This assertion is being used to mobilize parents against teaching about race in the schools (Fortin, 2021; Ray, 2022; Wallace-Wells, 2021).

Harper acknowledges that there are undoubtedly professors who support DEI as well as those who oppose it who do not permit or encourage students to express diverse perspectives and beliefs in their classrooms. However, he argues compellingly that although he is strongly committed to DEI, he structures a democratic classroom that not only allows but encourages students to express different opinions and points of view. Pedagogical approaches that can be used to create democratic classrooms where divergent views are respected and students are encouraged and empowered to express points of view that differ from those of the professor and other students are the raison d'être of this book. Harper describes how he achieves this goal by creating space in his classroom where students can practice democratic values. By freely expressing their sentiments, beliefs, and perspectives, students can develop the skills, attitudes, behaviors, and habits of the heart needed to embrace the principles of democracy in a multicultural society.

Harper published 92 articles in *Forbes* magazine between July 2022 and July 2024. He required graduate students in his courses at the Rossier School of Education and the Marshall School of Business, both at the University of Southern California, to write 500- to 550-word responses to one of his *Forbes* articles. He asked them to "thoughtfully, respectfully, and courageously critique [his] ideas and stances; offer a more nuanced or entirely different viewpoint; present an alternative set of facts; and/or offer recommendations that are better than [his]" (p. xxiii). Harper wrote a brief response to each student's comments on his articles. The students' comments on Harper's *Forbes* articles and his rejoinders exemplify an excellent and powerful way to give voice, recognition, efficacy, and civic equality to students (Gutmann, 2024).

The students' responses helped them to develop essential skills for becoming effective and participating citizens in a democracy, which requires them to "master the ability to talk across political and ideological differences . . . to weigh evidence, consider competing views, form an opinion, articulate that opinion, and respond to those who disagree" (Hess & McAvoy, 2015, p. 5). Harper's rejoinders to each of the student's responses are incisive, compassionate, and respectful. Most significantly, they illustrate the importance of informed, respectful dialogue.

The description and illustration of a pedagogy that creates a democratic classroom that gives students voice, recognition, and efficacy make this book a significant and timely contribution to the Multicultural Education Series. The major purpose of the series is to provide preservice educators, practicing educators, graduate students, scholars, and policymakers with an interrelated and comprehensive set of books that summarizes and analyzes important research, theory, and practice related to the education of ethnic, racial, cultural, and linguistic groups in the United States and the education of mainstream students about diversity. The dimensions of multicultural education, developed by Banks (2004) and described in the *Handbook of Research on Multicultural Education, The Routledge International Companion to Multicultural Education* (Banks, 2009), and the *Encyclopedia of Diversity in Education* (Banks, 2012), provide the conceptual framework for the development of the publications in the series. The dimensions are *content integration, the knowledge construction process, prejudice reduction, equity pedagogy,* and an *empowering institutional culture and social structure.*

The books in the Multicultural Education Series provide research, theoretical, and practical knowledge about the behaviors and learning characteristics of students of color (Conchas & Vigil, 2012; Darling-Hammond & Darling-Hammond, 2022; Lee, 2007), language minority students (Gándara & Hopkins 2010; Valdés, 2001; Valdés et al., 2011), low-income students (Cookson, 2013; Gorski, 2018), and other minoritized population groups, such as students who speak different varieties of English (Charity Hudley & Mallinson, 2011), LGBTQ+ youth (Mayo, 2022), and students with disabilities (Waitoller & Thorius, 2022).

An important goal of this book's pedagogy is to provide a forum in which students can deepen their knowledge about race and institutional racism by freely examining and expressing diverse views about it. A number of books in the Multicultural Education Series examine institutional racism in educational institutions. These include Ozlem Sensoy and Robin DiAngelo (2017), *Is Everyone Really Equal? An Introduction to Key Concepts in Social Justice Education;*

Gary Howard (2016), *We Can't Teach What We Don't Know: White Teachers, Multiracial Schools*; Jabari Mahiri (2017), *Deconstructing Race: Multicultural Education Beyond the Color-Bind;* Zeus Leonardo (2013), *Race Frameworks: A Multidimensional Theory of Racism and Education*; Daniel Solórzano and Lindsay Pérez Huber (2020), *Racial Microaggressions: Using Critical Race Theory in Education to Recognize and Respond to Everyday Racism*; and Robin DiAngelo (2023), *Seeing Whiteness: The Essential Essays of Robin DiAngelo*.

The pedagogically sound and reflective way in which Harper teaches about DEI is especially appropriate and wise in these troubled and challenging times for DEI initiatives and multicultural teaching. There is a rough road ahead for DEI and diversity efforts for at least the next 4 years. President-Elect Donald Trump stated that he would end DEI efforts at the federal level after he was inaugurated (Terry, 2025). Trump followed through on his promise. On January 20, 2025, he issued this Executive Order, "Ending Racial and Wasteful Government DEI Programs and Preferencing" (Executive Order, 2025). In 2023, more than 20 states considered or passed laws that targeted DEI initiatives for reduction or exclusion (Goldberg, 2024). A number of major companies, reflecting the national political sentiments they perceive have emerged about DEI, such as Amazon, McDonald's, Walmart, Boeing, and Lowe's, are reducing or eliminating their DEI initiatives (Adamczeski, 2025; Goldberg, 2024). Other companies are reconceptualizing DEI programs to make them less vulnerable to legal challenges (Goldberg, 2024).

A recent poll reported in *The New York Times* indicates that about half of the U.S. population supports diversity and equity programs in schools and government (48%) and about half do not (47%). In the poll, approximately 22% of African Americans and 40% of Hispanic Americans supported ending diversity programs in schools and government (Peters & Igielnik, 2025). Because of the lack of strong support for diversity programs by the public and the current toxic political environment for DEI, it is educationally sound as well as astute and pragmatic for professors and teachers of DEI courses and programs to assure that students with different political, cultural, gender, and social-class characteristics can freely express their sentiments, beliefs, and perspectives in their courses. This pedagogy will lay the foundation for students to deepen their knowledge and understanding about DEI and about the racial, political, and social conditions in U.S. society. Harper exemplifies these characteristics in his teaching as evidenced in this book.

Shaun Harper shows that he is a master scholar and teacher in this book. He has constructed a pedagogy that enables students to acquire knowledge about divisive and controversial issues and policies while having an opportunity to express multiple perspectives on these issues and to acquire efficacy and recognition. Henry Adams famously said, "A teacher affects eternity; he can never tell where his influence stops" (Bartlett, 1992, p. 535). The influence of Harper's powerful and visionary teaching is boundless. I hope it will have the vast influence on other college and university teachers that it richly deserves.

—James A. Banks

REFERENCES

Adamczeski, T. R. R. (2025). These 15 major companies caved to the far right and stopped DEI programs. *Advocate*. https://www.advocate.com/news/companies-abandoning-dei

Banks, J. A. (2004). Multicultural education: Historical development, dimensions, and practice. In J. A. Banks & C. A. M. Banks (Eds.), *Handbook of research on multicultural education* (2nd ed., pp. 3–29). Jossey-Bass.

Banks, J. A. (Ed.). (2009). *The Routledge international companion to multicultural education*. Routledge.

Banks, J. A. (2012). Multicultural education: Dimensions of. In J. A. Banks (Ed.), *Encyclopedia of diversity in education* (vol. 3, pp. 1538–1547). Sage.

Bartlett, J. (1992). *Familiar quotations* (16th ed.). Little Brown.

Charity Hudley, A. H., & Mallinson, C. (2011). *Understanding language variation in U. S. schools*. Teachers College Press.

Conchas, G. Q., & Vigil, J. D. (2012). *Streetsmart schoolsmart: Urban poverty and the education of adolescent boys*. Teachers College Press.

Cookson, P. W., Jr. (2013). *Class rules: Exposing inequality in American high schools*. Teachers College Press.

Darling-Hammond, K., & Darling-Hammond, L. (2022). *The civil rights road to deeper learning: Five essentials for equity*. Teachers College Press.

DiAngelo, R. (2023). *Seeing whiteness: The essential essays of Robin DiAngelo*. Teachers College Press.

Executive Order. Ending radical and wasteful government DEI programs and preferencing (January 20, 2025). https://www.whitehouse.gov/presidential-actions/2025/01/ending-radical-and-wasteful-government-dei-programs-and-preferencing/

Fortin, J. (2021, November 8). Critical race theory: A brief history. *The New York Times*. https://www.nytimes.com/article/what-is-critical-race-theory.html

Gándara, P., & Hopkins, M. (Eds.). (2010). *Forbidden language: English learners and restrictive language policies*. Teachers College Press.

Goldberg, E. (2024). Facing backlash, some corporate leaders go "under the radar" with D.E.I. *The New York Times*. https://www.nytimes.com/2024/01/22/business/diversity-backlash-fortune-500-companies.html

Gorski, P. C. (2018). *Reaching and teaching students in poverty: Strategies for erasing the opportunity gap* (2nd ed.). Teachers College Press.

Gutmann, A. (2024). Unity and diversity in democratic multicultural education: Creative and destructive tensions. In J. A. Banks (Ed.), *Diversity and citizenship education: Global perspectives* (pp. 71–96). Jossey-Bass.

Hannah-Jones, N. (2021). *The 1619 project: A new origin story*. One World.

Harris, E. A., & Alter, A. (2022, January 30). Book ban efforts spread across the U.S. *The New York Times*. https://www.nytimes.com/2022/01/30/books/book-ban-us-schools.html

Hess, D. E., & McAvoy, P. (2015). *The political classroom: Evidence and ethics in democratic education*. Routledge.

Howard, G. (2016). *We can't teach what we don't know: White teachers, multiracial schools* (3rd ed.). Teachers College Press.

Lee, C. D. (2007). *Culture, literacy, and learning: Taking bloom in the midst of the whirlwind*. Teachers College Press.

Leonardo, Z. (2013). *Race frameworks: A multidimensional theory of racism and education*. Teachers College Press.
Mahiri, J. (2017). *Deconstructing race: Multicultural education beyond the color-bind*. Teachers College Press.
Mayo, C. (2022). *LGBTQ youth and education: Policies and practices* (2nd ed.). Teachers College Press.
Mervosh, S. (2022, August 27). Back to school in DeSantis's Florida, as teachers look over their shoulders. *The New York Times*. https://www.nytimes.com/2022/08/27/us/desantis-schools-dont-say-gay.html
Peters, J. W., & Igielnik, R. (2025, January 18). Support for Trump's policies exceed support for Trump. *The New York Times*. https://www.nytimes.com/2025/01/18/us/politics/trump-policies-immigration-tariffs-economy.html
Ray, V. (2022). *On critical race theory: Why it matters & why you should care*. Random House.
Sensoy, O., & DiAngelo, R. (2017). *Is everyone really equal? An introduction to key concepts in social justice education* (2nd ed.). Teachers College Press.
Solórzano, D., & Huber, L. P. (2020). *Racial microaggressions: Using critical race theory to respond to everyday racism*. Teachers College Press.
Terry, E. (2025, January 6). Trump says he'll end DEI at federal level, as report shows $1 billion in spending since 2021. *Deseret News*. https://www.deseret.com/politics/2025/01/06/federal-gov-spends-one-billion-in-dei-since-2021/
Valdés, G. (2001). *Learning and not learning English: Latino Students in American schools*. Teachers College Press.
Valdés, G., Capitelli, S., & Alvarez, L. (2011). *Latino children learning English: Steps in the journey*. Teachers College Press.
Waitoller, F. R., & Thorius, K. A. K. (2022). *Sustaining disabled youth: Centering disability in asset pedagogies*. Teachers College Press.
Wallace-Wells, B. (2021). How a conservative activist invented the conflict over critical race theory. *The New Yorker*. https://www.newyorker.com/news/annals-of-inquiry/how-a-conservative-activist-invented-the-conflict-over-critical-race-theory

Preface

The unwillingness of too many Americans to consider other citizens' viewpoints is one of the biggest, most consequential challenges facing our democracy. Polarization exists along identity, cultural, religious, socioeconomic, geographic, and ideological lines. Stubborn loyalties to partisan politics exacerbate this divisiveness. Social and digital media algorithms create homogeneous cyber corners in which users hear mostly from people who share their same opinions. Also, many cable news channels lopsidedly and narrowly misshape how viewers think about education, politics, the economy, and current events in the United States and across the globe.

Despite being a Democrat, I watch Fox News Channel several hours each week. I do so because I am interested in hearing what people who think and experience the world differently than me have to say—even though their analyses and sensemaking are almost always incongruent with mine. I also have friends who are considerably more conservative than me. I try hard to listen to what they have to say and respectfully articulate my stances. We rarely completely agree but instead meet somewhere in the middle or peacefully agree to remain in disagreement. I desperately want more, not less of this for our democracy. I am able to control my own openness and engagement, as well as deliberately engineer conditions in my classrooms that require students to do so.

Many conservatives critique American institutions of higher education for being too liberal. Professors like me are accused of being the culprits. I know two things to be simultaneously true: (1) Some students and employees who are Republicans feel an insufficient sense of belonging on college campuses and are uncomfortable sharing their conservative viewpoints in particular environments; and (2) many people who make campuses diverse often deem classroom and workplace cultures unresponsive to their cultural histories, identities, and interests. The latter has consistently emerged in campus racial climate studies I have conducted in every geographic region across the United States over the past 2 decades. I have gathered insights into the former from conversations with my conservative friends and the hundreds of hours I have spent watching Fox News. Without fully disregarding their perspectives, I usually ask and wonder how much time conservative critics have spent in actual classrooms; who the instructors were; what was in the curriculum; whether they found perceivably "too woke" content in all or most courses, or in just a few; and what the races, ethnicities, genders, and sexual orientations were of the students and employees with whom they spoke.

Turning Point USA publishes an online watchlist that aims to "expose and document college professors who discriminate against conservative students and advance leftist propaganda in the classroom."[1] A few friends of mine who are on it say it is a badge of honor for them. I somehow ended up on the list. I am not honored. In fact, it disappoints and disturbs me because I am the only person who has been to every single class session I have taught over the past 24 years. Conservative students have never told me to my face or anonymously in course evaluations that they felt unsupported, shut down, or unfairly graded in any course I have taught. Because of what I study and the topics on which I write, there apparently is an unfounded presumption that I discriminate against students whose views are different from mine. My approach is the exact opposite, in fact. I have long been uninterested in creating classroom echo chambers in which learners only consider one-sided views and all think, feel, and interpret topics in the exact same ways. I do not deny the existence of some liberal professors who do what Turning Point USA alleges. They do not comprise the majority, though. And I most certainly am not one of them.

American colleges and universities are supposed to be sites for the productive contestation of ideas and debates that ultimately deepen learning. I have always been committed to these ideals. My sense is that most educators (including colleagues who teach in K–12 schools) are both open to and interested in this, but often lack the skills necessary to manufacture such a challenging brand of teaching and learning. Few were taught how to do so when they themselves were students in teacher preparation and graduate-level programs. Hence, they fear that conversations will become explosive and irreparable harm will be done to classroom cultures. Furthermore, many educators are not intentional about making their own ideas vulnerable to students' critiques. Even if they are not deliberately silencing learners, it is important for teachers and professors to understand how our power to determine students' grades can have a silencing effect on classroom discussions. The field needs more models and examples of how to foster and successfully manage educational spaces in which respectful disagreements thrive, hence the purpose of this book.

Numerous topics engender widespread disagreement and polarization among Americans. But in recent years, none have been as misunderstood as matters pertaining to diversity, equity, and inclusion (DEI). Too many citizens have been duped into believing that all DEI programs and policies are divisive, anti-white, anti-male, anti-American, overfunded, and ineffective. This explains, at least in part, why DEI-focused books have been banned, spending on professional development for educators has been outlawed, culture centers have been closed, chief diversity officers and other DEI practitioners have been fired, and truths about our country's racial past have been scrubbed from the curriculum in more than 20 states. In response to misinformation and disinformation, corporations are walking back their DEI commitments. And then there is the Dismantle DEI Act that

Ohio Senator and then-Republican vice presidential candidate J. D. Vance introduced in June 2024.[2] If passed, the law would eliminate all federal DEI programs and discontinue DEI-related funding for agencies, contractors, organizations, and educational accreditation agencies that receive federal funding. It is clear to me that more dialogue about every dimension of DEI is urgently needed during these dangerously polarized times. Common ground about DEI would strengthen our democracy.

AN INSPIRING, ADAPTABLE MODEL

In 2021, Teachers College Press published *A Search for Common Ground: Conversations About the Toughest Questions in K-12 Education*.[3] My friends Rick Hess (who is politically conservative) and Pedro Noguera (who is politically progressive) cowrote this remarkable book that brilliantly models what respectful engagement could and should look like among Americans with vastly different political ideologies and life experiences. I read their book and found it impressive. I was therefore unsurprised when the Association of American Publishers presented the authors its 2022 PROSE Award in Education. Each chapter follows the same format: Hess wrote a letter to Noguera (or vice versa); the letter recipient wrote a response; and the original letter author wrote a short reply to the response. Noguera and Hess respectfully engaged and pushed each other's thinking on a range of politically polarizing topics. *Let's Talk About DEI* adapts this innovative format.

I published 92 *Forbes* articles between July 2022 and July 2024. Collectively, they have been read by nearly 1.4 million people. Over three semesters, I required graduate students in the Rossier School of Education and the Marshall School of Business, both at the University of Southern California, to complete this assignment:

> Choose one of my Forbes articles and write a 500-550-word response in which you thoughtfully, respectfully, and courageously critique my ideas and stances; offer a more nuanced or entirely different viewpoint; present an alternative set of facts; and/or offer recommendations that are better than mine.

Over 150 students who took my DEI courses in both schools completed this "Respectful Disagreements" assignment. To strengthen their confidence in critiquing my ideas, I awarded the maximum number of points to all students who completed this assignment (which was everyone), regardless of how harsh their appraisals and responses were. I also promised them that I would not become defensive, feel insulted or personally attacked, or find some way to later retaliate against them. I was genuinely impressed by how they meaningfully critiqued my ideas and deepened my thinking. This book includes 40 articles from my *Forbes* catalog, one student's 500–550-word critique of each piece, and my response to what each student wrote. Some topics pertain specifically to K–12 and higher education institutions, while others focus expansively on recent DEI issues in business, politics, sports, entertainment, policing, and technology.

THE EDUCATIONAL BENEFITS OF BEING IN TOUCH

Writing articles about Beyoncé, Megan Thee Stallion, Rihanna, Usher, Elon Musk, Brittney Griner, Drake, Kendrick Lamar, Deion Sanders, Charlamagne tha God, and Kanye West deepened my pop culture credibility with students and afforded us opportunities to talk about DEI issues in ways that resonated with them. We also connected these topics to education or business. I have designed and delivered numerous professional learning experiences and engaged in strategy advising, crisis recovery, and DEI executive coaching with leaders across more than 400 educational institutions, corporations, nonprofit and government agencies, military branches, and other organizations. A point of pride for me is that students in my afternoon courses often benefit from work I did with actual practitioners and leaders earlier that same day. This, combined with dozens of *Forbes* articles that focus squarely on real-time problems of practice, protects me from being perceived as an out-of-touch ivory tower academician who does not know what is *really* happening in schools and corporate contexts. Because I am a faculty member in three professional schools here at USC, being in touch with the realities of what is occurring in practice is important to me.

My *Forbes* catalog also includes pieces on Joe Biden, Donald Trump, former GOP presidential candidates Nikki Haley and Ron DeSantis, House Speaker Hakeem Jeffries, former House Speaker Kevin McCarthy, ousted Congressman George Santos, Los Angeles Mayor Karen Bass, and other elected officials. The "Respectful Disagreements" assignment gave students permission to engage with politics in our class discussions. These conversations were never one-sided; they did not become volatile or otherwise unproductive. Week after week, I walked away feeling like my students were very much in touch with what was happening in political contexts, industries, and our broader society.

Noteworthy is that the "Respectful Disagreements" paper is typically due the 5th week of the semester. A marvelously palpable cultural shift occurs from that moment on. Students who did not talk so much in the first few weeks noticeably have more to say. Subsequently, more of them challenge my ideas and do so in a respectful way. In course evaluations, one-on-one conversations, and end-of-semester debriefings with the full class, many students say this assignment gave them both the permission and the confidence to put a different viewpoint on the table. They say they would have been considerably less comfortable doing so absent the low-stakes rehearsal opportunity offered through the "Respectful Disagreements" paper. I think a powerful lesson here for other educators, as well as for leaders across industries, is that DEI does not have to be unidimensional, divisive, explosive, or avoided in learning and workplace settings.

A VISION FOR THIS BOOK

Foremost, I want *Let's Talk About DEI* to be a fresh, timely resource that offers multisided viewpoints on seemingly divisive, politically polarizing topics. I also want to model for other educators at least one effective way to create learning experiences in which students feel safe and empowered enough to challenge ideas with which they disagree. This entails humbling ourselves to learn from students' critiques of our ideas. This is not a new philosophical stance for me. I have long respected students enough to recognize and appreciate that they learn from me, I learn from them, and we all learn from each other in the educational spaces we co-occupy and collaboratively construct. This book is an example of how educators can embrace the mutually beneficial possibility of professor–student learning opportunities. One additional goal is to reach organizations beyond K–12 and postsecondary institutions—to model for professionals across industries how to engage in respectful disagreements about and critiques of DEI.

PRODUCTIVE ENGAGEMENT BEYOND ACADEMIA

As previously noted, I have done rigorous, high-quality DEI work with hundreds of educational institutions and organizations. The U.S. Air Force, Nike, Google, Microsoft, T-Mobile, Mattel, Anheuser-Busch, NBCUniversal, Hulu, Zoom, Major League Baseball, and the National Football League are just a few examples of organizations I have worked with outside of education. Like at many K–12 schools, colleges, and universities, professionals and leaders in workplaces outside of education avoid talking about DEI broadly and about race specifically. There are five common explanations for this. First, discussing these issues is countercultural—meaning, avoidance was a cultural norm long before contemporary employees entered the workplace. Second, white professionals do not want to say the wrong thing and be perceived as racist. Third, professionals of color are often tired of always having to be the people who bring up racial topics. Many of them also fear retaliation and other negative reactions from colleagues as a consequence of raising race questions. Fourth, white people and people of color alike do not want conflict with their colleagues. Avoidance is easier and politically safer. And fifth, American workers lack access to models of productive disagreements. Hopefully this book shows them what is possible.

Shaun Harper
Los Angeles, California

Acknowledgments

I applaud and appreciate the 152 education and business graduate students who engaged with and critiqued my ideas. Their feedback confirmed two things for me. First, that professors can indeed learn much from students. And second, that academic echo chambers can be intentionally disrupted via innovative assignments that invite productive disagreements between learners and teachers. I will be forever indebted to all these USC Trojans, not just the 40 whose responses appear in this book. My sincerest gratitude also belongs to A. J. Mada and Jacob Roberson, two phenomenal teaching assistants who helped make my Marshall MBA course a smashing success. Many thanks to Pedro Noguera and Rick Hess for gifting our field with their groundbreaking text and inspiring me to adapt its deliciously novel approach. I also honor the legendary James Banks, my generously supportive longtime role model, for inviting me to publish this book in his Teachers College Press series.

Feedback from my *Forbes* editors Jeffrey Marcus, Jair Hilburn, and Corinne Lestch often made my work better. I appreciate them for an amazingly fulfilling opportunity to publish 92 articles that reached nearly 1.4 million readers over 2 years. I am grateful to Shawn Hill, my wonderful husband, for giving me space on our vacations and at other times to write so many *Forbes* articles and academic papers, prepare to teach my classes with excellence, and pursue an absurdly high number of my wildest professional dreams. The support I receive at the University of Southern California, especially from our president Carol Folt and my USC Race and Equity Center colleagues, significantly strengthens my work. Lastly, I salute educators and citizens everywhere who commit themselves to advancing our democracy through an openness to others' viewpoints, ideas, and lived experiences. Our democracy needs more, not fewer Americans who are willing and able to productively disagree and then find common ground.

Part I

PRODUCTIVE DISAGREEMENTS ABOUT EDUCATION

CHAPTER 1

Actions Educational Leaders Must Take When Kids Do Racist Things at School

In February 2023, students at a Southern California elementary school chose to celebrate Valentine's Day and Black History Month in alarmingly racist ways. One greeting card was addressed to "my favorite cotton picker," and it said "you're my favorite monkey." It also included a crayon drawing of a monkey and a person hanging from a tree. The card was made specifically for Black students at Pepper Tree Elementary School in Upland, California. When situations like this occur, Black students, their parents and family members, and Black educators often deem school leaders' responses inadequate.

Christopher Newman, the parent of two Black boys who attend the school, told me that leaders were made aware of the racist valentine two weeks before any action was taken. It was drawn in his son's 6th-grade classroom. "Meanwhile, my son had to sit with this student in his class for that entire time," Newman noted. "The student who made the card called him a monkey, a slave, and a cotton picker for weeks prior to the valentine's card being sent out. Other Black kids at the school were told they would be hung from a tree." Accordingly, schoolmates also made monkey sounds when Newman's son and other Black children walked by.

In a KTLA television interview,[1] Maylana and Rome Douglas, an interracial couple who have three children attending Pepper Tree, described other ways students there were celebrating Black History Month. Accordingly, one of their daughters was told she was going to receive a card saying "you're my favorite slave, and they were going to show her as a slave hanging from a tree." Also, classmates were reportedly giving back rubs to Black kids because February is their month. Rome said their daughter was told she'd receive massages just half the month because she's only half Black.

Newman, a professor of education at a local university, contended these aren't isolated occurrences. A year prior to the Valentine's Day incident, he said Black students were taunted with monkey sounds. Their parents demanded the school take action. Leaders promised training for teachers and staff, Newman recalled, but contended it was too late in the school year to initiate new professional learning workshops about racism. As far as he knows, those workshops never occurred. Unsurprisingly, then, there were subsequent racial incidents. For instance, one Black student was called a "nigger" while playing soccer on the school's playground the previous September.

Upland is an ethnically diverse community located 38 miles east of Los Angeles. According to data from the California Department of Education,[2] Pepper Tree Elementary School is 3.1% Black, 13.1% Asian American, 38.6% Latino, and 35.6% white. Give or take a few percentage points, the school's racial composition largely reflects Upland's demographics. Regardless of how many or how few of them attend a school or live in a community, no Black child anywhere deserves what those at Pepper Tree have been experiencing. It's noteworthy, though, that these racist incidents didn't occur in some rural town that's 90% white—it happened in what's effectively a suburb of our nation's second-largest city.

In our 2019 *Education Week* article,[3] my former PhD advisee James Bridgeforth and I explained why we weren't shocked by a recently released photo of four elementary schoolteachers posing with a noose at a school located in Los Angeles County. Admittedly, we were surprised that the principal was the photographer. Bridgeforth and I also highlighted in the article other racist incidents that had recently occurred at K–12 schools in Alabama, Ohio, Iowa, Idaho, and elsewhere in California.

Bridgeforth has since systematically catalogued more than 500 racist incidents that took place in K–12 schools across every geographic region in the United States between 2014 and 2019. In addition, his recent research study published in the *Journal of School Leadership*[4] is based on a rigorous analysis of 140 press releases, emails, letters, and social media posts that educational leaders released in the aftermath of racist incidents that occurred in their schools. Then-principal Becki Modereger sent a one-page letter to the Pepper Tree School community.[5] Beyond writing statements, what should educational leaders do when students behave in racist ways at school?

There are four reasons why I'm not inclined to recommend suspension and expulsion as the only disciplinary options. First, every situation is different. Some, but not all, warrant kicking a kid out of school. Second, decades of research—including my and Edward Smith's study of 3,022 public school districts across 13 states[6]—shows that Black students are suspended and expelled more often for the exact same or less egregious behaviors than are their white classmates. I therefore worry that Black children will be disciplined more frequently and more harshly than their white peers for saying or doing something racially offensive. Third, suspending students punishes them but doesn't guarantee that they or their schoolmates will understand why something was deemed racist. And fourth, individual suspensions ultimately absolve the school of its culpability in maintaining an educational environment that allowed such incidents to occur.

Here are five actions educational leaders must take when kids do racist things at school:

1. **Reject the "Kids Are Just Being Kids" Explanation**—Adults too frequently excuse incidents like those that occurred at Pepper Tree by arguing that kids aren't racist and that immature jokesters didn't

really mean to cause harm. School leaders have a responsibility to help members of their school communities understand that it's neither normal nor acceptable for anyone to behave in racist ways, including students.

2. **Communicate Authentically**—Even though she likely wrote it herself, Principal Modereger's letter to her school community sounds no different from an emotionless racism response message crafted via ChatGPT. Situations like those that occurred at Pepper Tree ought to outrage leaders and everyone else who works at the school. Sanitized notes that neglect to specify what happened make leaders sound like they don't really care about the students and families whom the racism harmed.

3. **Don't Swiftly Move On**—When racist incidents occur, leaders typically feel a desperate urge to move on as quickly as possible. I advise against this. Instead, leaders should move on when the students and families who were harmed agree it's time to do so. Also, to minimize the risk of recurrence, leaders should use these situations as case examples in professional learning workshops for teachers and school staff in future years.

4. **Prioritize in Proper Sequence**—Above all, leaders ought to prioritize the students and families whom racist incidents most negatively affected—listen to them, express and demonstrate genuine care for their wellness, and seek their input on what would make the situation right. Second, leaders should focus on ensuring that students who behaved in racist ways don't feel ashamed but understand why what they did was wrong.

5. **Don't Wait Weeks**—Black parents say Pepper Tree's principal knew about the racist valentine for weeks before taking action. Due process is important. Some situations require leaders to conduct a thorough investigation before taking action. While that's occurring, though, something has to be communicated to the school community. Absent this, students and families who were targets of racism are left feeling neglected.

Instead of waiting until a crisis erupts, it's better for educational leaders to get ahead of situations like those that occurred at Pepper Tree. They shouldn't assume that students know better or that teachers know what to do when racist things happen in their classrooms. This is one of many reasons why educational leaders must unite with others to resist politicized campaigns that aim to ban the teaching of racial topics to students in K–12 classrooms and to educators who participate in professional development activities.

NICO'S PRODUCTIVE DISAGREEMENT

In reading your article that offers educators and school leaders five steps to take when racist acts take place in their schools, I felt that a much-needed perspective was missing: that of someone oriented about human lifespan development as the conduit for understanding the root cause of racist harm, and for repairing it.

When I read your first recommendation, "Reject the 'kids are just being kids' explanation," I felt that an important truth was forgotten: Children can lack the knowledge that certain things are wrong to say or do. In other words, the entire onus of what took place should not be placed on the children who say or do these things. As numerous cognitive and social lifespan developmental theorists like Jean Piaget and Erik Erikson would put it, children may very well lack the integrated view of the world that would help them realize that some things are wrong. As you stated in your writing, this does not mean that perpetrators of racist harm should be excused for what they've done. However, we must be cautious when labeling these children as racist simply because they lack the understanding of what is and what is not racist.

To bolster what you have already written, I might offer another recommendation for school leaders and educators to take on to help hold accountable the systems that perpetuate racist harm among students and other stakeholders in schools. All the steps you suggested to administrators and teachers are reactive in nature. What if we instituted proactive, educational teach-in engagements for schools to prevent racial violence from taking place? Bringing back the developmentalist perspective, each module can be designed to best meet the needs of each role within the school. These forums would best be held in-person, to ensure that dialogue across difference (like intersecting identities) can take place. They should be facilitated by people both internal and external to the school, as a visiting professional will not know the nuances of the school's social, political, economic, and cultural demographics as well as someone who works there.

These sessions should also be recurring rather than sporadic; they should be frequent gatherings to promote sustained racial equity. Weekly faculty and staff meetings could be transformed into meaningful incubators of developmentally appropriate and significant racial justice activities within the school, preventing racist incidents from taking place in the future.

With platforms like PragerU and groups like the Patriot Front and Turning Point USA becoming more fervent in their outreach to young people, proactive approaches to combatting their hateful agendas are the most effective means of preventing racist incidents in the future. Of course, you did mention at the end of your article that "it's better for educational leaders to get ahead of situations like those that occurred at Pepper Tree," though the piece lacked substantive ways to "get ahead." It is my hope that what I offered can be helpful in supplementing what you have already written.

PRODUCTIVE RESPONSE FROM NICO'S PROFESSOR

Being on the receiving end of racism is dehumanizing. Elementary school children don't have as much experience with it as do adults. Kids haven't had enough time to develop protective coping and response strategies. Their dehumanization was top of mind for me as I wrote about what occurred at Pepper

Tree. Notwithstanding, I appreciate Nico's empathetic emphasis on humanizing all young people, including those who do and say racist things. We agree that children are not born racist and that the onus really should be on adults to eliminate conditions that allow racist situations to occur in schools. The developmental perspective that Nico amplifies here is quite reasonable and substantiated by decades of theories and research. It seems important to acknowledge, though, that experiencing racism at an early age poses significant threats to the healthy development of children of color. Therefore, one additional thing for teachers and leaders to consider when racism occurs at school is a balancing of developmental understandings and developmental harms.

CHAPTER 2

Why Politicized Attacks on DEI in Schools Are Occurring, and How They're Bad for America

Books that include LGBTQ+ persons and families have been banned[1] in many school districts across the country. Toni Morrison classics have been pulled from library shelves,[2] as have other texts written by influential authors of color. Educators have been forced to discard lessons on various diversity, equity, and inclusion (DEI) topics from the curriculum. Despite far too little evidence that critical race theory is being taught to schoolchildren, *Education Week* reports that 44 states have introduced bills since January 2021 to ban CRT or otherwise suppress teaching about race.[3] Anti-DEI laws have been passed in 18 of those states. Even conservative school districts in progressive states like California have implemented policies to ban books and lessons pertaining to influential LGBTQ+ Americans, racism, and other dimensions of diversity.[4]

Many states have placed restrictions on the expenditure of public funds on DEI-focused professional development experiences for employees of K–12 schools and higher education institutions. Former presidential candidate and present governor Ron DeSantis (R-FL) has banned public spending on DEI initiatives at colleges and universities in his state.[5] More recently, both chambers of the Texas legislature passed a bill that bans DEI offices and programs at public colleges and universities.[6] All these DEI suppression activities are going to have devastating effects on our democracy and American businesses.

It's important to understand why these politicized attacks are occurring. DEI initiatives in educational institutions have always been met with internal and external resistance. In other words, the backlash we're seeing at this time isn't new. But the opposition has been especially and dangerously intense since Barack Obama left the White House in 2016. Many Americans erroneously convinced themselves that by electing a Black man to the U.S. presidency, our nation was instantly done with racism. There was the myth of a post-racial America.[7] The Obama administration did much to affirm DEI. Then entered Trump.

On election night in 2016, CNN political commentator Van Jones emotionally explained that Trump's victory was a "whitelash against a changing country, a whitelash against a Black president."[8] During the 2016 campaign, Trump made numerous offensive remarks about Muslims, immigrants, Black Americans, Mexicans, Asians, and many other people who make our nation diverse. According to Pew Research Center data, 54% of white voters cast their ballots for Trump—compared to 6% of Black and 28% of Latino voters, respectively.[9] That nearly 63 million Americans, the overwhelming majority of whom were white, voted for Trump to become president was a strong rejection of diversity and inclusion.

Once he assumed office, Trump continued making offensive comments about diverse populations without penalty or apology. In September 2020, he signed an executive order banning DEI trainings in federal workplaces, including our nation's military.[10] *The New York Times* reported just a few weeks later that Trump's Executive Order on Combating Race and Sex Stereotyping had a "quick and chilling effect" on diversity trainings in government agencies.[11] Those effects also extended to public K–12 schools and higher education institutions, as leaders worried that the continuation of DEI efforts would jeopardize their federal funding. Even though Joe Biden reversed Trump's executive order on his first day in office,[12] efforts to dismantle DEI in schools had already snowballed into a large-scale political movement.

It's noteworthy that Trump's ban on DEI trainings was issued less than 4 months after Minneapolis police officer Derek Chauvin murdered an unarmed Black man.[13] Uprisings ensued across America and around the world as teenager Darnella Frazier's video of Chauvin pressing his knee on George Floyd's neck for 10 minutes, 9 seconds emerged and went viral.[14] That moment forced long-overdue national conversations about systemic racism.

That grappling was suddenly happening among family members at kitchen tables, between neighbors, in places of religious worship, on social media, in workplaces, and in schools. In most contexts, the reckoning lasted less than 6 weeks. But its endurance in schools persisted. Not everyone was in favor of that. Some parents didn't want their children being taught the truth about America's racial past and present because it was inconsistent with lies they'd been taught in their own schooling experiences. A few years later, that continues to be the case.

Another notable explanation for the attacks on DEI is the spread of misinformation via social media. Unsubstantiated claims are made every day about what's occurring in K–12 classrooms and on college campuses. DEI opponents often post one example of one book or one lesson or one drag queen reading to schoolchildren or one Pride Month celebration occurring in a single school under the exaggerated guise that those things are happening everywhere. They aren't.

There's absolutely no evidence, for example, that children are being taught that all white people are racist in any widespread fashion at schools across the country. In social media posts, DEI obstructionists are lifting up M. L. Webb's book *The GayBCs* as an example of what's being taught to kids in schools.[15] There's no evidence that Webb's book is on shelves in even 0.005% of classrooms and school libraries. Yet outrage on social media would have people thinking this text and other LGBTQ+-inclusive books are being assigned in just about every school. They aren't.

While there are dozens of other explanations for the current politicized attacks on DEI in schools, here's just one more: There's an actual well-coordinated, intentionally orchestrated, and highly funded political movement that's succeeding. Lies, misinformation, and exaggeration fuel that movement. White supremacy, systemic racism, xenophobia, homophobia, transphobia, sexism, and Islamophobia undergird the movement. Parents and families are being manipulated by the movement. It is succeeding in largest part because not enough people are fighting to stop it.

Today's students will become adults. If they're denied opportunities now to learn about racism and other dimensions of DEI, they'll enter professions in which they make discriminatory decisions and consequential missteps, unintentionally offend and exclude people, reproduce and exacerbate inequities, and erode the global competitiveness of America's businesses and military (research makes irrefutably clear that diverse and inclusive organizations are higher performing). Also, conflicts and violence between racial groups will increase because citizens didn't learn enough about other racial groups or about our nation's racial history when they were in school. Democracy will suffer. There's too much at stake to allow anti-DEI efforts and related misinformation campaigns to continue. A well-coordinated, intentionally orchestrated, and highly funded countermovement is urgently needed to defend our democracy.

GRACE'S PRODUCTIVE DISAGREEMENT

On its face, Dr. Harper's analysis is straightforward and familiar to anyone paying attention to U.S. politics. To further his analysis, this response adds nuance by calling out oversimplification and presenting additional framing.

Harper describes "whitelash" (i.e., the Trump presidency as a reaction to the Obama presidency) when 63 million people voting for Trump represented "a strong rejection of diversity and inclusion." It is unfair to attribute all votes for Trump as anti-DEI votes and to paint all voters for Trump as monolithic in their decision-making, values, and motivations. A vote for Trump is not necessarily a rejection of DEI. There are a range of possible drivers of voting behavior, including religion, patriotism, economics, family or cultural traditions. Some voters back the party and the platform regardless of the candidate.

Harper posits a false dilemma by suggesting that there are only two options: conservatives against DEI sowing lies and harming democracy and the economy, or liberals supporting DEI spreading truth and righting wrongs. This oversimplification ignores potential middle grounds or alternative perspectives. Voting behavior and politicized attacks on DEI are also complicated by fear and ignorance about liberal doctrine, academic freedom, and free speech. The article portrays and perpetuates an "us versus them" mentality. Harper's message may plant more seeds of understanding by disentangling some of these concepts for scholarly scrutiny.

The article misses a few opportunities to present counterarguments and counterevidence in response to these attacks on DEI. Missing is mention of DEI historically, before we called it "DEI." DEI are fundamental American values on which this country was founded, not a progressive, new radical fad. Attacks on DEI are attacks on American values. The "whitelash" is not new, and successful bipartisan and Republican-led DEI legislation is also not new (e.g., GI Bill or Servicemen's Readjustment Act of 1944, Individuals with Disabilities Education Act of 1975, and Title IX, to name a few).

Harper portends "devastating effects on our democracy and American businesses" but neglects to detail the relationship between DEI in schools and our democracy. There is a missed opportunity to pinpoint how learning about race and racism can strengthen and sustain democracy. DEI is a means of expanding democracy, not subverting it. Understanding the historic and current impacts of racism promotes informed citizenship, encourages civic engagement, and strengthens democratic institutions by increasing accountability for fairness and integrity. Finally, in focusing on all the types of programming that are being scapegoated, misrepresented, and imagined, it misses the opportunity to describe DEI initiatives that will help our students, faculty, and staff feel seen, heard, understood, and equipped. By providing a more nuanced stance and additional evidence of historic and current impacts of DEI, Harper's argument would be even more compelling and may even reach a broader, less "woke" audience.

PRODUCTIVE RESPONSE FROM GRACE'S PROFESSOR

I start where Grace ended—reaching a "less woke audience" is indeed an everyday aim of mine. I embrace it as a necessary feature of my commitment to educating the public, including Americans who voted for Donald Trump in the 2016, 2020, and 2024 presidential elections. Grace is right: Many factors compelled citizens to cast their votes in support of Trump; some of those voters are family members of mine. My challenge is that DEI becomes destructively entangled with politics in ways that undo decades of progress toward equity and social justice. I am fine with Americans maintaining fidelity to their principles and values—I just don't want misinformation, disinformation, and misunderstandings to misshape those stances and inform curriculum, policies, and programs that were created to right past and present wrongs. I don't want the United States to keep taking three steps forward and two steps back on DEI issues. I agree with Grace that an "us vs. them" ethos will maintain divisiveness. For this reason, I try instead to take a "fact vs. fiction" approach to raising our nation's consciousness about what DEI is and does.

CHAPTER 3

Supreme Court Ends Affirmative Action in College Admissions—Here's What Will Happen on Campuses

After decades of legal opposition, affirmative action in college admissions is dead. The U.S. Supreme Court Justices ruled race-conscious admissions unconstitutional in the Students for Fair Admissions (SFFA) cases against Harvard University and the University of North Carolina. While this policy change will affect every college and university in the country, it will be most devastating to our nation's highly selective public and private higher education institutions. In the *Grutter v. Bollinger* case involving law school admissions at the University of Michigan, Supreme Court Justice Sandra Day O'Connor noted, "We expect that 25 years from now, the use of racial preferences will no longer be necessary to further the interest approved today." That case was decided in June 2003. The current Court actualized O'Connor's prediction five years early. Whether in 2023 or in 2028, the discontinuation of race-consciousness in college and graduate school admissions has long felt inevitable.

It's been 47 years since the *Regents of the University of California v. Bakke* Supreme Court case upheld the consideration of race as a factor in the applicant evaluation process. In 1996, California voters struck down race-conscious admissions via Proposition 209. Since that time, affirmative action bans have been enacted in nine other states: Arizona, Florida, Idaho, Michigan, Nebraska, New Hampshire, Oklahoma, Texas, and Washington. Twenty-four years after a predecessor banned affirmative action in his state, Governor Jay Inslee (D-WA) rescinded Directive 98–01, which prevented government agencies and public institutions from considering race or sex when making hiring decisions. The Texas ban was also overturned.[1]

Justice O'Connor's prediction has become national law. Based on trends and outcomes across the 10 states that previously passed affirmative action bans, here are some predictions of what will occur in response to the June 2023 Supreme Court ruling:

> **Black Student Enrollments Will Decline at Many Predominantly White Institutions**—While the discontinuation of race-conscious admissions

policies and practices will negatively affect students of color across a range of racial and ethnic groups at predominantly white institutions (PWIs), Black applicants will be most devastated. This has long been the consequence of Prop 209 on the University of California, my state's most highly selective public higher education system. Exactly 1 decade after California voters struck down affirmative action, UCLA had only 96 Black students in its incoming class of 4,852 freshmen, *The Los Angeles Times* reported.[2] A large share of them were athletes.

Enrollments Will Increase at Historically Black Colleges and Universities—Since the mid-1800s, HBCUs have continuously and reliably provided college access to incredibly bright Black Americans whom PWIs systematically deny. *The Washington Post* analyses show that applications to and enrollments at HBCUs increased after the 2020 summer of racial reckoning, the protest movement in response to the murder of George Floyd.[3] Much of this was attributed to HBCUs offering Black students psychologically safer, culturally affirming educational alternatives to PWIs. As has always been the case, HBCUs will continue to recruit and admit talented Black students without discriminating against applicants from other racial groups.

Schools With Big-Time Sports Programs Will Miraculously Find Admissible Black Athletes—In a 2018 research report, I noted that Black men were 2.4% of undergraduates enrolled at universities across the five most profitable NCAA Division I sports conferences but comprised 55% of football teams and 56% of men's basketball teams (the two sports that generate the most revenue).[4] In our nation's post–affirmative action era, Black student representation at most PWIs will decline everywhere except in revenue-generating sports. Coaches will continue traveling far and wide to find extraordinarily gifted Black student-athletes, including Black women who comprise significant shares of basketball and track teams.

Interpretive Overreach Will Lead to Decreases in Race-Focused Campus Initiatives—Even though the Supreme Court ruling makes unlawful the use of race as a factor in admissions, many employees at higher education institutions will convince themselves that it extends to just about everything else pertaining to race. They will argue that establishing college readiness programs in Latino communities, or that funding predominantly Black student organizations, or that creating African American studies departments, or that constructing new culture centers for Indigenous or Asian American students all are constitutional violations. None of those activities are suddenly unlawful. The SCOTUS ruling will be misused as an excuse to abandon race-conscious activities that resisters never actually wanted.

Numbers of Faculty and Administrators of Color Will Decline—Inevitably, affirmative action in admissions will extend to affirmative action in employment practices at higher education institutions. Race won't be considered as a factor when hiring a faculty member, even in academic departments that have no or too few professors of color. Cluster hires and other faculty diversification strategies will be outlawed. Despite being underrepresented among full-time faculty and in leadership roles, I noted in my 2020 testimony to the U.S. House of Representatives (which was subsequently adapted for publication in the *American Journal of Education*) that employees of color comprise 46% of professionals in low-level service roles (e.g., groundskeepers, maintenance workers, food service staff, and custodians) on campuses.[5] The representation of diverse employees in those specific positions at most PWIs won't decline much, if at all.

People of Color Will Be Further Marginalized at PWIs—It remains the case in 2023 that a student could be the only Black woman in an academic major (and therefore in every class she takes) or that a professional could be the only Latino person in the campus unit where she works. Underrepresentation results in marginalization for many students and employees of color at PWIs. Decreases in the numbers of Asian American, Black, Indigenous, Latinx, multiracial, and Pacific Islander persons on campuses will exacerbate feelings of isolation, erasure, and unimportance. Encounters with microaggressions and overt demonstrations of racism will worsen these feelings. Consequently, more students of color will drop out of PWIs and turnover rates among employees of color will increase.

White Students Will Learn Too Little and Enter Professions Even Less Prepared—Meaningful engagement with persons from a diversity of racial groups typically leads to stereotype reduction and opportunities for the cultivation of healthy interracial relationships. A decline in the number of people of color on campuses will deny white students powerful opportunities to unlearn prejudices, biases, and racist perspectives. They will carry this inexperience with them into workplaces after college. They won't know how to lead racially and ethnically diverse teams. Many will unintentionally say and do racist things to coworkers of color because they interacted with so few people like them in prior residential and educational contexts.

Justice O'Connor's predicted timing was off, but what she imagined would happen to race-conscious admissions in this decade was right. I actually want to be wrong about my predictions (well, except for the second prediction, given that I'm an HBCU alumnus). Based on what we've seen in California and the nine other states that banned affirmative action in previous years, I'm sadly confident in each of my projections. My seven-point forecast doesn't fully capture all the ways that the June 2023 SCOTUS ruling will negatively impact our democracy, people of color, white Americans, higher education institutions, and workplaces. But it does offer a horrifying glimpse of what's ahead.

WILL'S PRODUCTIVE DISAGREEMENT

You argue that the recent Supreme Court ruling against race-conscious admissions in college and graduate school admissions will negatively impact students of color and diversity efforts in higher education. While the article presents a compelling narrative, there are several points that I would like to further examine.

First, the article's stance implies that race-conscious admissions are necessary for achieving diversity and equity in higher education. However, some may argue that affirmative action policies can be seen as discriminatory and may overlook other forms of diversity such as socioeconomic background, personal achievements, and the unique talents that prospective students bring to the table. A more nuanced approach to admissions could consider a wider range of factors beyond race to achieve a diverse and well-rounded student body. These factors could include cultural experiences, educational adversity factors, or any of the other factors mentioned above. For example, one way to address diversity in admissions is to give preference to applicants with low-income and educationally adverse environments. A history of structural racism has left American families of color with less wealth than white families. Considering class-based admissions would increase racial diversity on college campuses without directly considering race.

Second, the article predicts a decline in Black student enrollments at predominantly white institutions (PWIs) and an increase in enrollments at historically Black colleges and universities (HBCUs). One trend I think that we will also begin to see is more and more partnerships between HBCUs and elite universities. For example, Tougaloo College, an HBCU, and Brown University have had a longstanding partnership that includes high school, undergraduate, graduate, and faculty programs.[6]

Additionally, the article suggests that the discontinuation of race-conscious admissions will lead to a decline in race-focused campus initiatives and a decrease in faculty and administrators of color. While it's important to promote diversity in faculty and leadership positions, relying solely on affirmative action for hiring practices may not address underlying issues of systemic bias and lack of representation. Institutions can explore proactive strategies to attract and keep diverse faculty and staff through professional development opportunities, targeted recruitment efforts, and inclusive workplace policies.

The article also predicts that white students will be negatively impacted by a lack of exposure to racial diversity on campuses. I completely agree with this point of view. Education plays a powerful role in fostering empathy, critical thinking, and understanding of diverse perspectives. However, developing cultural competence without a racially diverse environment will present challenges surrounding preparedness leading diverse teams in the workplace. To combat any potential reduction in diversity due to the Supreme Court's decision, colleges and universities should make DEI education and awareness a core part of the curriculum and university initiatives. This education will hopefully lessen the impact of potentially fewer diverse voices present on campus.

In conclusion, while the article raises valid concerns about the potential consequences of the Supreme Court ruling, it is important to consider alternative viewpoints and approaches to promoting diversity and equity in higher education. A more holistic approach that considers a range of factors in addition to race in admissions and embraces inclusive practices in hiring and campus initiatives could contribute to a more diverse and equitable educational environment.

PRODUCTIVE RESPONSE FROM WILL'S PROFESSOR

The first paper I wrote in my master's degree program in 1998 was on affirmative action. I never believed it was the cure-all to the underrepresentation of people of color in higher education. Yet I always worried about what would occur in the aftermath of its discontinuation. Truth is, affirmative action failed to reach its full potential for students and employees of color at PWIs. Decades of data make irrefutably clear that white women were its biggest beneficiaries. Will calls for a more comprehensive cocktail of approaches to achieve and sustain racial diversity. I agree that more methods and an expansive range of legally allowable activities are far better than is sole reliance on affirmative action. The problem, though, is that the variety that Will advocates is being undermined by overinterpretation of the June 2023 SCOTUS ruling and broader politicized attacks on DEI. It's worth noting that Will and I have different stances on income-based remedies to racism. He accurately acknowledges the ways in which socioeconomic status and race comingle in the United States to systematically disadvantage low-income citizens of color. But I know that class-based, raceless solutions to racial inequities won't fix racial inequities.

CHAPTER 4

Eliminating Standardized Tests to Achieve Racial Equity in Post-Affirmative Action College Admissions

College and university leaders say they're committed to finding legally defensible ways to maintain racial diversity in the aftermath of the U.S. Supreme Court's decisions in a pair of lawsuits against Harvard and the University of North Carolina that ended race-conscious admissions practices.[1] Some institutions have taken one specific action in recent years that's worthy of widespread replication and will help ensure that talented students of color have access to highly selective undergraduate, graduate, and professional degree programs: They eliminated standardized entrance exam requirements.

Eight weeks before the consideration of race as a factor in admissions became unlawful, presidents of highly selective liberal arts colleges wrote a statement in which they vowed to sustain their institutions' racial equity efforts, regardless of the then-impending affirmative action lawsuits.[2] Immediately after the SCOTUS ruling was released, dozens of colleges and universities posted diversity-affirming statements to their websites and social media accounts. But they didn't say how they'd achieve and sustain their unspecified racial equity goals. Because new evidence shows that legacy admissions overwhelmingly advantage white applicants,[3] discontinuing those policies and practices is one clear way. Suspending or permanently abandoning use of the SAT, ACT, GMAT, GRE, LSAT, and other entrance exams is another lever institutions have pulled.

The University of California, our nation's most selective public higher education system, stopped requiring the SAT and ACT for admission to its nine undergraduate campuses in 2021.[4] The consequences: More highly qualified students of color are being selected; Berkeley and UCLA are still tied for the #1 spot among public universities in the annual *U.S. News & World Report* rankings; and the UC System maintains its stellar reputation, its desirability and accessibility to white applicants, and its research prowess and funding. In other words, the negative effects of scrapping the standardized testing requirement, if there are any, are neither well documented nor pervasive in the system that received 884,655 applications in the 2022 undergraduate admissions cycle, a significant increase over prior years.

UCLA professor Sylvia Hurtado, an Association for the Study of Higher Education past president whose research has been extensively cited in U.S. Supreme Court affirmative action cases over the past 2 decades, says that eliminating the standardized testing requirement helped the UC System get a better sense of public demand for higher education: "All racial and ethnic groups benefited with increases in admissions. Not only were more eligible students identified, campuses also became more selective by using a wide range of criteria to identify talent in holistic review processes."

Hurtado also notes that over many years, students who've transferred to UC campuses from community colleges performed well academically and graduated at impressively high rates. UCLA, Berkeley, and the other undergraduate campuses don't require transfer applicants to submit test scores—the institutions instead place heavy emphasis on those students' grades in their community college courses, among other factors.

"Research shows that standardized tests are far from objective measures of academic merit, potential, or talent, and are instead better proxies of family wealth and resources," adds Liliana Garces, a University of Texas at Austin professor who holds appointments in education, law, and the Center for Mexican American Studies. "By discontinuing them, colleges and universities can have a fairer system for admitting qualified and talented students, particularly in the aftermath of the U.S. Supreme Court's decision, which severely restricts institutions' abilities to admit racially and ethnically diverse student bodies and meet their educational missions."

Generational wealth, parents' educational attainment levels, zip codes, household income, socioeconomic profiles of K–12 schools attended, and the ability to afford private coaching and high-cost test prep courses are among the most powerful predictors of student performance on exams that institutions use for admission to undergraduate, graduate, and professional degree programs. They aren't IQ tests. The SAT and ACT have been shown to be highly correlated with undergraduate students' freshmen year grade point averages. Yet there are so many other, far more compelling factors that also reliably determine 1st-year academic performance, grades in subsequent years, and bachelor's degree completion rates.

On its website, ETS, makers of the GRE, advocates for holistic reviews of applications and advises against the use of minimum scores.[5] "GRE scores help you compare applicants, but if you use a cut score as a criterion, you could miss an applicant who would be a great asset to your program," the company warns. Whether operationalized formally through admissions policy (which is rare at this point) or informally (which is far more common), cut scores are mostly used as a convenient way to "review" large quantities of applications. This makes it easier for undergraduate admission officers to conveniently sort thousands of applicants into high, maybe, and no possibility piles.

Similar behaviors occur within faculty review panels of graduate school applicants. University of Southern California professor Julie Posselt's book *Inside Graduate Admissions: Merit, Diversity, and Faculty Gatekeeping*,[6] is based on observations of admissions committees and interviews with faculty members in

10 top-ranked PhD programs. Posselt found that GRE scores and college GPAs, as well as the prestige of the undergraduate institutions applicants attended, were overwhelmingly used to make first cuts in admissions processes.

"Holistic review" supposedly means that admissions officers and committees consider everything in candidates' files. But truthfully, standardized test scores often overpower other factors. Sometimes, files aren't even read if the test scores are perceivably too low. Too many talented students of color know this and are therefore discouraged from applying to institutions that put too much stock on test scores—it produces a racialized brand of test trauma for some. Removing test scores entirely from the admissions process would not only ensure that all applicants are given equal consideration, but it would also be a responsible way to redress longstanding socioeconomic disadvantages that disproportionately account for below-average scores among applicants of color from lower-income and working-class families.

In addition, colleges and universities become less susceptible to legal challenges, specifically accusations of racial preferences, when they remove standardized test scores as a variable in the admissions process. It becomes harder for white applicants to claim that they were discriminated against just because their scores were higher than the average among students of color who were offered admission. Some institutions have stopped using standardized entrance exams. Others that are interested in maintaining racial and socioeconomic diversity in this post–affirmative action era should do the same.

ALVIN'S PRODUCTIVE DISAGREEMENT

While I do agree with Dr. Harper that standardized tests are more representative of family affluence and access to resources than they are of academic ability and potential, I believe that standardized tests still have a role in the world of college admissions.

Due to the nature of the tests being standardized, scores are one factor that can balance relatively less consistent measures also used in college admissions, such as grade point averages. With some academic institutions practicing academic inflation, this provides a less representative metric for determining academic proficiency than a standardized test score. Additionally, with the curriculum covered on said tests being standardized, the educational system can ensure that all students vying for an undergraduate degree have a similar foundation of knowledge in language and mathematics, which are foundational for a significant portion of degrees that aspiring students wish to pursue.

While I agree that Dr. Harper is correct in asserting that "generational wealth, parents' educational attainment levels, zip codes, household income, socioeconomic profiles of K–12 schools attended, and the ability to afford private coaching and high-cost test prep courses are among the most powerful predictors of student performance" on standardized testing, I believe that the current system can be reworked to serve as a more indicative and useful metric for assessing student aptitude. On a macro level, the state or federal government could allocate financial incentives to test preparation services to operate affordably in low-income areas, thus providing more equitable access to the resources that others use to succeed. Additionally, local universities could provide something similar by allowing college hopefuls to get access to a tutor, either a student or faculty member; this program could be funded by a work–study program for students or additional income for faculty members.

Given that standardized testing performance is often dictated by access to resources, standardized testing organizations could also implement a region-specific percentile ranking system. Financial and academic demographics, two important factors to predicting testing success, vary by zip code. To provide better insight into relative performance, I believe that ranking student scores relative to those of their peers in a certain area (e.g., zip code or school) would prove to be a beneficial solution. In doing so, the scores would be contextualized by holding external factors constant. Students in lower-income areas would be compared with others that faced similar sets of circumstances. While it is not a perfect metric that may be exploited, this system would serve as a good step toward making standardized testing more impactful.

In a radically changing world where the conversations around race and equity become more important day by day, it is no surprise that these sentiments are being reflected in the college admissions space. College admissions is a systemically inequitable space. In the pursuit of greater equity for underrepresented groups, some institutions believe that the right thing to do is eliminate standardized testing altogether. When utilized properly, however, standardized testing could become a helpful tool in both ensuring baseline competence and measuring students against their similarly advantaged peers.

PRODUCTIVE RESPONSE FROM ALVIN'S PROFESSOR

Alvin's proposal to interpret test scores within the context of one's high school and/or socioeconomic context fascinates me. Notwithstanding, I am certain that racial segregation in residential neighborhoods and in K–12 schools would make implementation of this strategy just as susceptible to legal pushback as was race-based affirmative action. Rich white applicants and their families would surely contend that the process unfairly disadvantaged them, as Abigail Fisher (a white woman) alleged in her legal complaint against the University of Texas at Austin's Top 10% plan.[7] Alvin also suggested that state and federal governments could provide more test prep resources. Doing so would not address the larger, most systemic forces that cyclically manufacture score inequities. It also won't address the issue of geniuses who are absolutely prepared for success in higher education but simply aren't strong performers on high-stakes standardized entrance exams. On a personal note, my GRE scores would've erroneously suggested that I was unqualified to someday become Alvin's professor. Thankfully, Indiana University didn't care about my low scores—3.91 and 3.87 cumulative GPAs in my master's and PhD programs, respectively, confirmed my deservingness.

CHAPTER 5

Legacy Admissions at Harvard and Other Elite Institutions Advantage White Applicants

Three Black and Latino groups filed a racial discrimination lawsuit against Harvard University. Chica Project, African Community Economic Development of New England (ACEDONE), and Greater Boston Latino Network (GBLN) submitted a 31-page complaint to the U.S. Department of Education alleging the Ivy League school systematically violates the Civil Rights Act of 1964 by privileging the children of donors and wealthy alumni in its annual student selection process.[1] Legacy admissions, a practice that Harvard and other elite institutions have long maintained, is inescapably racialized.

According to the lawsuit, between 2014 and 2019, donor-related applicants to Harvard were nearly seven times more likely to be accepted than were other admission seekers. Similarly, students whose parents and family members were alumni of the institution were nearly six times more likely to be admitted. In 2022, Harvard's overall acceptance rate was 3.2%. The average admit rate was approximately 42% for donor-related applicants and 34% for legacies, the court document states.

The trio of complainants found disparities not only in who gets admitted but also in who is extended opportunities to impress the most powerful gatekeepers in Harvard's admissions process. Accordingly, legacy and donor applicants are nearly 20 times more likely than others to be interviewed by Harvard admissions office employees.

In a pair of cases that the conservative group Students for Fair Admissions brought forth against Harvard and the University of North Carolina, the U.S. Supreme Court deemed the consideration of race in college admissions unconstitutional.[2] But Chica Project, ACEDONE, and GBLN point out one major problem with this ruling: Nearly 70% of donor-related and legacy admits to Harvard are white. While it could be argued that the preferential treatment of these applicants doesn't fit the Supreme Court's definition of race-consciousness, it most certainly isn't color-blind. Whether or not they intend to, people who work in admissions offices play a major role in systematically privileging white applicants through their continued use of legacy policies and practices.

According to an April 2023 report from the College and University Professional Association for Human Resources,[3] nearly 70% of admissions coordinators and counselors are white. Among chiefs, directors, and heads of admission, 78% are white. The racial demographics of professionals who work in Harvard's admissions office aren't available on the university's website. But if the composition there is similar to the college admissions profession overall, it's an overwhelmingly white team of leaders and staff that maintains a system that cyclically advantages mostly white applicants with familial or financial ties to the institution.

In admissions offices that give preferential treatment to legacies, there's a chance that many white employees (and perhaps even some professionals of color, too) haven't really thought much about the race of applicants whom this practice disproportionately benefits or the snowballing racial inequity that it produces year after year. Not being fully conscious of this doesn't make the practice itself or the outcome color-blind. As evidence furnished in the racial discrimination lawsuit against Harvard reveals, legacy policies and practices uphold a system that irrefutably benefits one racial group at the expense of others.

In recent years, the University of Georgia, Amherst College, Johns Hopkins University, Texas A&M University, the entire University of California system, and every public higher education institution in Colorado have discontinued the use of legacy preferences in admissions practices.[4] Congressman Jamaal Bowman (D-NY) and Senator Jeff Merkley (D-OR) introduced the Fair College Admissions for Students Act in 2022.[5] If passed, the federal legislation would ban legacy admissions at all U.S. higher education institutions.

In response to the June 2023 SCOTUS affirmative action ruling, Harvard and other institutions posted statements to their websites and social media platforms expressing serious dedication to pursuing diversity within our nation's new legal parameters. Eliminating a practice that unfairly benefits applicants (the overwhelming majority of whom are white) just because their parents are alumni and donors is one of many actions that will help these institutions enact their espoused commitments.

ISIS'S PRODUCTIVE DISAGREEMENT

The article raises many valid and incredibly concerning points about how the legacy program at institutions such as Harvard University vastly benefits wealthy white applicants. While I agree with the irrefutable data presented in the article that states that legacy admissions policies disproportionately favor white applicants, in reading the article, I could not help but wonder what happens to the children of staff, faculty, or alumni who are not white but who could benefit from such a policy.

According to *The New York Times*, a 2018 study looking at legacy admissions policies found that "42 percent of private universities—including most of the nation's elite institutions—and 6 percent of public colleges used the strategy."[6]

Using USC, my own undergraduate institution, as an example to examine this policy, legacy students accounted for 14% of admitted students in its 22–23 application cycle.[7] While the racial/ethnic breakdown of this 14% has not been made public, if we are to assume that USC's legacy admissions trends are similar to Harvard's, then the legacy policy at USC is also disproportionately benefiting white applicants.

When I applied to USC in 2017 as the child of an employee, although I was rejected from the university, I was offered the Trojan Transfer Plan, which allowed me to get a strong preference in admission after completing a year at community college. As a first-generation, low-income Latina, I was incredibly grateful for being able to benefit from such a program. Although I recognize that people with backgrounds like mine who benefit from legacy admissions policies are the exception and not the rule, I still cannot help but feel that completely eliminating legacy admissions could harm historically marginalized students in at least some capacity.

In the 2022–23 academic year, USC employed 4,624 faculty and 17,216 staff.[8] Although it is unclear how many employees at the university come from the local community or the racial/ethnic backgrounds of employees, I think it is safe to assume that at least some of its employees are from the community or neighborhoods surrounding the campus; similarly, one can assume that if this is the case, many of these employees are members of historically underrepresented communities. Based on this, I feel that legacy could theoretically work to help first-generation, low-income students of color get admitted to the university.

The history of institutions of higher education in America, especially private universities, is one that has historically worked to benefit and serve white, wealthy males. Currently, the way in which legacy admissions has been implemented at most universities largely helps to expand on this history of exclusion. In spite of this, rather than eliminating legacy as a whole, I wonder if perhaps universities could instead find a way to balance their policies so that the legacy strategy could become a tool used to empower a university's BIPOC alumni and employees. If restructured to become more equitable, legacy could be a tool for BIPOC families to accrue generational wealth and status, as well as a way for an institution to support members of the local community.

PRODUCTIVE RESPONSE FROM ISIS'S PROFESSOR

Isis is the beneficiary of an employee benefit that I strongly support. Wealthy private universities with huge endowments should make tuition free or as affordable as possible for the children of faculty and staff who devote a reasonable number of years to the institution. As I understand it, though, those applicants are not given special privileges in the actual admission process—it is more of a financial aid incentive *if* they get into those universities. Programs like these make USC economically possible for first-generation, low-income students of color like Isis.

These aren't the same as legacy admissions practices that deliver concierge-level privileges to students who arguably need them the least. At most institutions that offer this incentive, it is unlikely (though not entirely impossible) that the average admit rate for employees' children is 42%. But even if it were that high, that number should be disaggregated by race, role type, and compensation level. Are the children of professionals who work in food service, custodial, groundskeeping, and maintenance positions (jobs disproportionately performed by employees of color) admitted at the same rates as the kids of tenured faculty members (positions overwhelmingly held by middle-class white Americans)? Probably not.

CHAPTER 6

Harvard University's Next President Is a Black Woman

The oldest institution of higher education in the United States announced in December 2022 that Claudine Gay had been selected as its 30th president.[1] When her term began the following July, Gay was the first Black person to serve in Harvard's top leadership role since its founding in 1636. Each president before her had been white. With the exception of Drew Faust, who led the university from 2007 to 2018, all of them had been men.

"This is a historic appointment considering how few Black presidents have led American universities," said UCLA professor Eddie R. Cole, a historian and expert on presidential leadership in higher education. "At a time when Harvard's own race questions—affirmative action, campus climate, and its profits from slavery—have captured the nation's attention, this will be one of the most significant presidential hires for years to come."

Because it's one of the wealthiest and most prestigious educational institutions in the world, because she's a woman, and because she's Black, some will undoubtedly ask if Gay was merely an affirmative action hire. Definitely not. Was she qualified? Incontestably. Gay is an extraordinarily accomplished scholar and experienced leader who's deeply familiar with the institution. She earned her PhD from Harvard in 1998. She then spent several years on the faculty at Stanford University, her undergraduate alma mater, where she earned tenure. Gay returned to Harvard in 2006 as a tenured professor in the Department of Government. Two years later, she also joined the Harvard Department of African and African American Studies.

In 2015, Gay was awarded the distinguished Wilbur A. Cowett endowed professorship and began a 3-year tenure as dean of social science. She was then promoted to the Edgerley Family Dean of Harvard's Faculty of Arts and Sciences, a position she held between 2018 and 2023. She is founding chair of Harvard's Inequality in America Initiative, which its website characterizes as "a multidisciplinary effort to elevate and energize teaching and research on social and economic inequality and to use what we learn to inform the public debate and public response to these challenges." In addition to campus leadership roles, Gay serves on the boards of the Pew Research Center, the American Academy of Political and Social Science, and Phillips Exeter Academy.

Jarvis R. Givens, a professor in the Harvard Graduate School of Education and a faculty affiliate in the African and African American Studies Department, has had opportunities to witness Gay's leadership. "She's a brilliant scholar, a visionary leader, and an ethical person," he observed. "I've also been consistently impressed by her timely and critical responses to a significant number of challenging situations at the University, from the pandemic to matters related to gender equity. Our university is lucky to have Claudine Gay steering the ship."

Gay's research and teaching have primarily focused on race and politics in the United States. She has written about inequities in housing mobility, tensions between Black and Latino Americans, the effects of Black congressional representation on political participation, environmental determinants of racial attitudes and political behaviors, and race relations in Brazil. Just months prior to being selected as Harvard's new president, she was elected to the prestigious American Academy of Arts and Sciences.

While Gay was the first person of color to serve as Harvard's president, she wasn't the first to lead an Ivy League university. Ruth Simmons, a Black woman, served as Brown University's 18th president from 2001 to 2012. Prior to that, she was president of Smith College for six years. Simmons earned her PhD from Harvard.

UCLA professor Lori Patton Davis, the nation's top expert on Black women in higher education, dubbed Gay a "possibility model" who will surely inspire other Black women to pursue leadership roles at colleges and universities. "It's taken more than 20 years following Ruth Simmons' presidential appointment at Brown for another Ivy League campus to experience the greatness of a Black woman president," Patton Davis noted. "My hope is that Gay's presidency reveals not only the possibility, but also the promise of higher education when Black women lead."

Because there have been so few presidents of color at U.S. higher education institutions (most especially research universities like Harvard), Gay's selection is monumental and praiseworthy. But ensuring the conditions are right for a Black presidential first to ultimately succeed at a place where whites comprise the single-largest racial group among students, faculty, staff, alumni, and donors is more important.

My research on campus racial climate at colleges and universities consistently shows that executives and senior leaders of color often experience racialized political resistance to their appointments. Trustees, faculty members, and sometimes even members of their own cabinets undermine their leadership in various ways that are attributable to race—and for women of color, attributable to the intersectionality of race and gender. "History demonstrates that any president, but especially a Black leader at a predominantly white campus, needs the autonomy to truly lead," Cole asserted.

In addition, leaders of color often tell my research team members and me that they have to balance larger institutional priorities with addressing long overdue diversity, equity, and inclusion problems. Many reflect on the ridiculous presumption that simply hiring a first-ever president of color will magically, instantly fix decades (in Harvard's case, centuries) of racism, racial harm, and institutional neglect. That expectation often places unfair pressure on those leaders and results in unearned critiques and disappointments.

Additionally, a Latina president, for example, usually has to worry about how the campus community will react if her leadership team becomes perceivably "too Latino" (based on the addition of one to three people), or if none of her new hires are white. They get accused of reverse discrimination, despite the irrefutable evidence that confirms the overrepresentation of white colleagues among tenured faculty members, department chairs and deans, and mid-level and senior administrators. Also, leaders of color too frequently receive racist emails, encounter racial microaggressions and stereotypes, and are caricatured in racist cartoons and other ways online.

Unfortunately, Gay's stellar academic credentials and impressive administrative resumé won't exempt her from some of these experiences. Navigating these challenges and realities probably won't be new to her, though as Harvard's president she'll likely experience them more often and with greater intensity. Hopefully not. "While I'm excited about her leadership, I'll also be observing how President Gay is treated and the expectations placed upon her," Patton Davis said. "Being a trailblazer is groundbreaking, but it also comes with a specific set of experiences, particularly for women of color."

DEONTÉ'S PRODUCTIVE DISAGREEMENT

While I was elated to hear about Claudine Gay's appointment as the next president of Harvard University, we should not continue to praise institutions that elect or appoint their "first Black" anything. Celebrating institutions for doing so is akin to the practice of handing out participation trophies to every player on a neighborhood little league team. Gay deserves praise and recognition for ascending the ranks of what is arguably the most prestigious university in the world. However, Harvard shouldn't receive any of that praise as an institution that predates the country by over 100 years. So many prominent Black leaders, scholars, and trailblazers have passed through Harvard's halls; why did it take so long for such an appointment to happen? I see Gay's appointment as an opportunity for those in academia and beyond to reflect on the glaring disconnect between representation and an institution's capability to actually support, nurture, and empower people of color.

Is Harvard's community adequately equipped to bolster a prominent Black woman? Past events say otherwise. Lorgia García Peña, a professor of romance languages and literature and a groundbreaking scholar, was denied tenure at Harvard in 2019.[2] Like Gay, García Peña was unequivocally qualified for the position. What has Harvard done since her move to Princeton to ensure that talented women of color don't continue to be overlooked? In the article, professor

Lori Patton Davis refers to Gay as a "possibility model" that will motivate other Black women to ascend the ranks of their respective institutions. However, I think this misrepresents the issue. As one of the most educated demographics in America, Black women generally aren't lacking ambition or motivation to become the next "first." What most Black women do lack is a workplace culture that enables them to succeed while being their full selves.

This begs another important question: Was Gay's appointment easier for the Harvard Corporation to swallow because she attended Harvard herself? Does her elite education make her a more palatable Black woman? I'm willing to go out on a limb and say the answer to both questions is a resounding yes. Again, there is no doubt in my mind that Gay is qualified and has the ability to significantly impact the institution and by extension, the world. However, every Harvard president (except for Drew Faust, who attended the University of Pennsylvania) attended the school. However, Harvard's peers have had presidents that attended HBCUs and flagship state universities. Why has Harvard remained so insular and seemingly reluctant to accept presidents from a wide range of educational backgrounds?

While I fully understand the desire and need to celebrate other Black people for breaking barriers and becoming pioneers, doing so just because they're Black isn't the healthiest thing to do. This knee-jerk reaction prevents us from answering an imperative question: Will they leave the door open for other Black people, or will they slam the door shut behind them? As the saying goes, "Not all skin folk are kinfolk." For now, I'll withhold my excitement until I see how or if Gay will create a more inclusive, equitable Harvard for Black people.

PRODUCTIVE RESPONSE FROM DEONTÉ'S PROFESSOR

At some point, there must be a first. Barack Obama was the first Black U.S. president. Kamala Harris was the first woman of color to be elected vice president and to secure the presidential nomination of either major political party. People of color (and many white people, too) celebrate these barrier-breaking moments because they are so long overdue. I understand and appreciate that this is one key aspect of the argument Deonté is making. He's right: There shouldn't be "firsts" at this juncture in our nation's history. It's inexcusable that there are still so many educational institutions and corporations that have had no Black CEOs, so many states that have never elected a Black governor or senator, and so many other leadership seats that have never been held by talented Black professionals (e.g., deanships, association presidencies, and boards of directors). I also agree with Deonté that it can't be just about hiring the first Black person—commitments must be made to ensure their success. As noted in the next chapter, that wasn't Claudine Gay's ultimate experience as Harvard's president.

CHAPTER 7

What It Means That a Black Woman Survived Only Six Months as Harvard's President

Just moments after she was named president of Harvard University, I proudly and excitedly wrote my first Claudine Gay article for *Forbes*.[1] I intentionally noted her race and gender in the title. The intersectionality of the two was just as significant then as it is now. Facing unthinkable volumes of pressure, racial epithets, and death threats, Gay resigned from her executive leadership role after only 6 months, the shortest presidential tenure in the University's 387-year history. In a *New York Times* essay published the day after her resignation, Gay explains that what happened to her at Harvard is emblematic of larger problems in our democracy.[2] That this was done to such a brilliant, highly accomplished Black woman has numerous implications.

Women have long been underrepresented in the higher education CEO role. In 1986, they comprised just 9.5% of college and university presidents, according to a recent American Council on Education report.[3] In 2022, women made up just under one-third (32.8%) of presidents. They're even more underrepresented at doctoral-granting research universities like the Ivies. Gender inequity in the presidency is chronically and especially pronounced for women of color. Harvard inaugurated Drew Gilpin Faust, its first woman president, 371 years after the institution's founding. Gay was its first Black woman president. It would seem that an appointment so historic would've deserved the university's full force of protection from politicized, mostly external attacks on Gay. It didn't.

Also facing pressures following a congressional hearing about rising and inexcusable levels of anti-Semitism on campuses, Liz Magill resigned from the University of Pennsylvania presidency.[4] Because they both are women, some may argue that race played no role in Gay's departure from Harvard's top spot. Here's one noteworthy difference: Magill was the third white woman to serve as Penn's president. Some in the campus community there were undoubtedly excited that a third consecutive woman was selected—that enthusiasm, though, would've been about Magill's gender, not her race. In other words, she was not the first white woman in the role, which made her appointment comparatively less historic than was Gay's.

Immediately following the hearing on Capitol Hill, there were calls for the three presidents who spoke that day—Gay, Magill, and MIT president Sally Kornbluth—to resign. Seventy-four members of Congress signed a joint letter calling for their removal and demanding greater protections for Jewish and Israeli students.[5] Kornbluth, who is Jewish, is the second woman to serve as MIT's president. She and Magill surely received lots of hate mail that said all sorts of awful things, but it's highly unlikely that any of it included use of the N-word. Gay says in her *Times* article that she's been called the N-word more times in recent weeks than she cares to even count. Her resignation letter,[6] as well as the Harvard Corporation's written response to it,[7] notes that "racial animus" and "racist vitriol" had been hurled at her, presumably with increased intensity after the congressional hearing.

Ruth Simmons was the first Black president of an Ivy League institution. She led Brown University from 2001 to 2012. That's 11 years, not 6 months. So, what accounts for the difference in the length of their tenures given that both she and Gay are Black women? The Simmons presidency occurred during a different political and technological time. I would be surprised if she received no letters or emails calling her the N-word during her years in office (I may be wrong about this, but probably not given the horror stories I've long heard from presidents of color elsewhere). Even if Simmons were indeed on the receiving end of such racism and hate, social and digital media weren't the accelerants then that they are now, which helped intensify the attacks on Gay.

Elise Stefanik (R-NY) was among the congresspersons who grilled the Harvard, Penn, and MIT presidents during the anti-Semitism hearing. Following Magill's resignation, Stefanik wrote in a statement, "One down. Two to go."[8] Higher education is at a dangerous moment when congresspersons and other politicians are claiming victory for taking down presidents of perceivably "too woke" institutions. Their obvious motive is to score points with voters. Re-election is the strategic aim. If the goal were, in fact, to make campuses free of hate and violence for all students and employees, why, then, haven't congresspersons fiercely interrogated, investigated, and held accountable presidents who've failed to protect Black people from well-documented, longstanding, and at times fatal encounters with anti-Black racist hate on campuses?

"This university doesn't care about Black people" is what many Black students have been consistently telling me in my campus racial climate studies over the past 2 decades. Black employees in higher education and corporate workplaces often say versions of this same thing to my research team members and me. Across contexts, it's Black women who express this most often and with the highest degree of certainty. That she survived only 6 months strongly conveys that Harvard didn't *really* care about its first Black woman president. She wasn't worth the investment of its financial, reputational, and political influence. This is how lots of Black people within and outside the university have been making sense of it on social media and elsewhere since the announcement of her resignation. Harvard failed Gay, not the other way around, is what many Black Americans are insisting.

Tufts University professor Daniel Drezner wrote a *Chronicle of Higher Education* essay titled "You Could Not Pay Me Enough to Be a College President."[9] I bet it resonated with many talented professionals across campuses who'd make excellent presidents. For many Black women, Gay's example probably raises the following question: "If a Black woman who'd held an endowed chair and been an academic dean at Harvard couldn't thrive in a presidency, then how can I?" When a white president fails, the impact on white presidential hopefuls isn't as devastating. Why? Because the overwhelming majority of college and university presidents, historically and contemporarily, have been white. Gay represented a powerful possibility model for Black women and other leaders of color. The tragic demise of her presidency will likely make not only securing but ultimately succeeding in top leadership roles at elite institutions seemingly less possible for them.

And then there's the climate for Black women students and employees at Harvard. How is Gay's transition affecting them? Do they feel as seen, valued, and affirmed as they did when Gay began her presidency in July 2023? Sadly, they probably don't. Do they have confidence that the Harvard Corporation, campus leaders, or anyone else there would go to reasonable lengths to protect them from the intersectionality of racism and sexism? Or from the intersectionality of racism, sexism, and anti-Semitism experienced by Black Jewish women? Or from the intersectionality of racism, sexism, and Islamophobia experienced by Black Muslim women? Besides Black women themselves and other Black people on the Harvard campus, who there even cares?

DAVID'S PRODUCTIVE DISAGREEMENT

As someone deeply impacted by the October 7th terrorist attack and the subsequent rise of anti-Semitism on college campuses, I closely followed the congressional hearings in which Claudine Gay took part and became familiar with her case and the controversy surrounding her eventual resignation.

To begin, I would first like to address the points in your article with which I agree, as there is a lot of merit in the concerns and questions you raise. For example, you are right about the issues you addressed in regard to the mistreatment of Black people in universities, as well as the lack of representation of Black people (and women, especially women of color) in positions of leadership, especially the position of president that Gay was able to attain. Since the beginning of her tenure, Gay faced unnecessary criticism and backlash purely due to the fact that she is a Black woman. In addition, during the peak of this controversy, her skin color and gender definitely led her to facing a higher volume and more extreme backlash, threats, etc., which is abhorrent.

Would Gay have been treated better throughout this whole controversy if she was a white man? Absolutely. However, with her severe mistakes and clear lack of leadership, would Gay still have lost her position as president if she were a white man? I wholeheartedly believe she would have.

This is where I disagree with your article. There seems to be a disregard for major facts of the case and actually addressing what Gay did, not just who she is. I am of the opinion that Gay did deserve to lose/resign from her position and she should not be exempt from punishment just because she is a Black woman.

Gay made two severe mistakes in her position as president. First, her response to the October 7th attacks was nowhere near satisfactory, and she never did enough to rectify this. This is clear by her testimony to Congress in which she says that calling for the genocide of Jews only qualifies as harassment "depending on the context," implying that there is some context in which that is acceptable. No individual who says that deserves to lead an academic institution. Her testimony was widely critiqued by both sides of the political spectrum.

That is the main reason why Gay was right to feel the pressure to resign. The second reason is that she was not only accused of plagiarism, but plagiarism in her work has actually been discovered. Of course, people can debate the severity of her plagiarism—was it a mistake, was it on purpose? The fact of the matter is that no president of Harvard should even have those types of questions surrounding them. Many people in lower positions than her would be at risk of losing their jobs over the same thing. Overall, though, I understand your side and the general principles you laid out, but in this specific case of Claudine Gay, I tend to disagree with your final conclusion that she was unfairly ousted from her position.

PRODUCTIVE RESPONSE FROM DAVID'S PROFESSOR

Anti-Semitism is abhorrent. There ought not be any excuses for it—or for Islamophobia, racism, sexism, and other forms of harassment, discrimination, hate, and violence. I have been repeatedly told that Gay's "it depends on the context" responses were in the talking points that university attorneys prepared for McGill, Kornbluth, and her. Reportedly, in their prehearing prep, the trio of presidents were strongly advised to stick to the script. I have not sought confirmation of this. But even if it is indeed true, Gay, as president, could have refused to articulate that specific talking point. David raises a really valuable question: In what context is violence against Jewish people okay? I agree with him—there isn't one. David highlights the citation issues in Gay's work that were used to intensify pressure to remove her from the Harvard presidency. For some reason, when people are outraged by something a white president says or does, rarely are their dissertations and other academic papers scrutinized the way that Gay's were. For many Black people (myself included), the project seemed clear: Do whatever it takes to remove this Black woman from one of America's most coveted presidencies. I still maintain that Harvard did too little to protect her.

CHAPTER 8

What Deion Sanders's Departure From Jackson State Could Mean for the Business of HBCU Athletics

Pro Football Hall of Fame member Deion Sanders left his high-profile job as head football coach at Jackson State, a public historically Black university in Mississippi. He accepted the head coaching role at the University of Colorado, the school announced in December 2022.[1] Sanders was offered more than $5 million per year as head coach of the Buffaloes, according to CBS Sports.[2]

Sanders's departure is a big deal because attracting someone of his caliber to the head coaching position 3 years prior was colossal for Jackson State. It was also a huge grab for sports at HBCUs, an important set of institutions that have long been disadvantaged by systemic resource inequities. These colleges and universities usually cannot afford to attract and pay high-profile head coaches. Because it introduced a replicable shift in the recruitment of talented head coaches to HBCUs, persuading Sanders to bring his talents to JSU in 2020 was arguably more significant than his most recent move.

In his three seasons, "Coach Prime," as Sanders is affectionately known, helped the JSU Tigers win back-to-back conference championships. They also achieved the university's first-ever undefeated football season in 2022.[3] That year, his 27–5 record was one of the best winning percentages in Division I football, the NCAA's highest and most competitive level. He's leaving for the PAC-12, a Power 5 conference.

Jackson State and its SWAC conference opponents appeared more on ESPN and garnered tremendously more press during his coaching tenure than had been the case in prior eras. JSU wasn't the only beneficiary of the hype that Coach Prime stimulated. HBCU sports collectively benefited. Now that he's left for a predominantly white university, will HBCUs return to a long, unfortunate history of underappreciation in the landscape of mainstream college football? They don't have to.

In 2020, ESPN reported that Sanders signed a deal with Jackson State worth $300,000 per year.[4] He also agreed to donate half of his first-year salary to complete the university's football facility. According to *Sports Illustrated*, Sanders's contract obligated him to pay JSU a $300,000 buyout if he left before 2024.[5]

In a 2018 USC Race and Equity Center research report, I noted that Black men were only 2.4% of undergraduate students enrolled at universities in the five most competitive athletic conferences (ACC, Big 10, Big 12, SEC, and PAC-12), yet they comprised, on average, 55% of football teams across those campuses.[6] Additionally, in a February 2022 *Washington Post* article, I highlighted the fact that nearly 70% of players in the NFL are Black, but the League had just one Black head coach at the time.[7] These numbers strongly suggest there are Black men with significant player experience who, like Sanders, could easily become high-performing head coaches.

Sanders hadn't been a college head coach before JSU hired him. But he was a college football All-American who'd enjoyed a successful career in the NFL. Good for Jackson State for having the confidence to believe they could hire such a decorated football expert to lead its program. They didn't talk themselves out of trying. Other HBCUs should follow JSU's promising model.

There are hundreds, perhaps thousands of Black men who amassed tremendous football expertise during their collegiate and professional careers. Like Sanders, some of them might be open to bringing their talents to HBCUs as head coaches. There's a chance that HBCUs can afford to hire them.

It's worth acknowledging that being an exceptional player doesn't guarantee that someone will be an effective college coach. Jackson State surely understood this when its leaders put their faith in Sanders. Predominantly white universities, as well as NFL teams, often hire young white guys to lead programs despite having little or no head coaching experience.

Sanders's willingness to accept a head coaching job for $300,000 per year is what I call possibility confirmation. There are quite possibly other Black men who made millions in the NFL to whom being paid an enormous coaching salary is unimportant. "It's not about a bag, but it is about an opportunity," Sanders said to his JSU players as he broke the news of his departure to them.[8] For some others, being afforded the opportunity to coach young men, most of whom are Black, would be a sufficiently rewarding opportunity, even if the pay is drastically lower than what Power 5 coaches earn.

According to the NCAA Demographics Database, only 8% of head football coaches across all NCAA divisions (excluding HBCUs) are Black.[9] Student-Athletes across all racial groups (including white football players) deserve exposure to a more diverse cadre of head coaches. Just 2% of undergraduates are Black at the University of Colorado. Black men comprised nearly 45% of the football team there in 2021, according to NCAA data. Comparatively, all but three scholarship recipients on Jackson State's 2021–22 football team were Black.

Both college and professional football programs need greater demographic alignment—meaning, having the representation of Black head coaches more closely mirror the representation of Black men who play on those teams. This alignment already occurs at HBCUs. It's longstanding. Maybe, just maybe some other Black Hall of Famers would be more interested in coaching at places where such demographic alignment (and what I call "demographic integrity") exists.

As the Sanders example shows, recruiting former Black football stars to serve as head coaches may be much less expensive than HBCU leaders presume. Attempting to replicate JSU's successful approach is certainly worth a try. "What's the point if they're going to leave after three seasons," some might ask. The average tenure of a Division I head football coach is 3.8 years (it's around 4 years in the NFL), thus Coach Prime's 3-year stint at Jackson State isn't at all unusual. Surely, the publicity and exposure that high-profile yet surprisingly affordable coaches like Sanders would bring will benefit HBCU athletics far beyond the 3–4 years (or whatever length of time) they spend there.

TIMI'S PRODUCTIVE DISAGREEMENT

Professor Harper argues that college and professional football programs need greater demographic alignment. Although Black athletes are significantly represented in most football programs, Black head coaches are rarely employed to lead Black men. Therefore, HBCUs are strategically positioned to take advantage of this unequal alignment. HBCU leaders should further push to employ high-profile Black head coaches (e.g., former Black football stars or influential young Black coaches) to replicate Jackson State's success and bring further exposure and investment into these programs.

Harper is absolutely correct in identifying the need for football program leaders to reflect the demographics of football players. However, I would like to respectfully challenge his argument that "recruiting former Black football stars to serve as head coaches may be much less expensive than HBCU executives presume." Harper highlights that Jackson State was able to hire Deion Sanders for $300,000 per year, where 50% of Sanders' 1st-year salary went toward improving Jackson State's football facilities. He uses this example to show that many Black coaches may be willing to chase an opportunity rather than a "bag," which should assist HBCU leaders in recruiting these former Black football stars.

However, Sanders's recruitment is likely more of an anomaly than an indicator of a future HBCU recruitment strategy. Unlike many potential Black coaches and even former Black football stars, Sanders had already earned nearly $45M from his playing career in the NFL and MLB. This earnings total does not include earnings from brand sponsorships, which included Nike, American Express, and Pizza Hut, or his 10-year career as a media personality. Additionally, Sanders's recruitment to Jackson State included the recruitment of his son Shedeur Sanders, former Jackson State quarterback. Deion Sanders was in a financial and personal branding position where opportunities and JSU exposure were significantly more lucrative than financial compensation.

It is unlikely that other Black football stars will be as uniquely positioned to join an HBCU without significant financial incentives. For example, the average NFL assistant coach position pays around $400,000 per year, which eclipses the average HBCU head coach yearly salary of around $75,000. Additionally, many former Black football stars who are seeking coaching employment may believe that an NFL assistant coach position will provide better opportunities through national exposure, the NFL's coaching tree, or even the poorly implemented Rooney Rule. It is imperative for HBCUs to hire more acclaimed coaching prospects; however, it is unlikely to be inexpensive.

Ultimately, HBCUs should also look toward alternative recruitment strategies to develop their programs. With the implementation of NIL policies, HBCUs should lean on their extensive celebrity alumni such as Jerry Rice, Shannon Sharpe, and Chris Latimer to link potential top recruits to lucrative sponsorship opportunities. Through obtaining top recruits, HBCUs will intrinsically create environments that entice better coaching and alumni donations. This should then create a more permanent structure to uphold the HBCU system.

PRODUCTIVE RESPONSE FROM TIMI'S PROFESSOR

Confession: I hadn't considered the great points Timi made about the wealth that enabled Deion Sanders to accept Jackson State's salary offer. He is right that not everyone will be able to afford to take a head coaching job at an HBCU—or at a lower-profile Division I school, community college, or Division II or III institution. The December 2024 head coaching appointments of former NFL stars Michael Vick at Norfolk State and DeSean Jackson at Delaware State, two public HBCUs, are additional examples of a potentially replicable model. My larger hope for intercollegiate athletics is that more former Black players are given opportunities to bring their expertise on their respective sports to coaching roles at HBCUs and predominantly white institutions. It is inexplicable to me that sports like football, women's and men's basketball, and track and field have so much Black representation among players, but so few of them benefit from pathways into coaching. I'm ultimately glad that JSU was able to attract Coach Prime, which was ultimately great for the institution, for him, and for HBCU athletics. Thankfully, he was wealthy enough to accept that opportunity.

Part II

PRODUCTIVE DISAGREEMENTS ABOUT BUSINESS AND CORPORATE LEADERSHIP

CHAPTER 9

Why Business Leaders Are Pulling the Plug on DEI

A shaky, uncertain economy isn't the real reason. Nevertheless, it's being used as the excuse for getting rid of chief diversity officers; significantly reducing DEI budgets and staffs; and pivoting to raceless, all-lives-matter-style workplace culture initiatives. It's happening across industries, most intensively in larger corporations. But why? And why now, just 5 years after business leaders made such bold declarations of their commitments to DEI and anti-racism following the murder of George Floyd?

Here are 10 explanations:

> **The Commitment Wasn't Real**—Black employees were rightfully skeptical of what leaders were saying in June 2020 about their organizations' newfound commitments to DEI.[1] Prior experiences in those workplace contexts made them and other employees of color doubtful of the switch that had been flipped overnight. It felt performative, like the company had merely jumped on a bandwagon to not appear racist. Those leaders weren't actually committed, at least not for the long haul.
>
> **George Floyd Corporate DEI Response Efforts Were Haphazard**—Many companies pledged millions of dollars (more than $200 billion altogether)[2] without a clear plan of how they'd invest the funds. Too many others hired their first-ever chief diversity officers with unclear visions of what they wanted those professionals to do. Others created DEI councils comprised of employees whose hearts were in the right place, but they lacked subject-matter expertise and most certainly weren't qualified to develop sustainable DEI strategy.
>
> **Too Much Anti-Racism at Once**—Before Derek Chauvin's murder of George Floyd forced a national conversation about systemic racism, employees and leaders deliberately avoided discussing race in most workplaces. Moving abruptly from race evasiveness to conversations about uncomfortable racial realities overwhelmed organizations that had maintained longstanding cultures of avoidance. Making all-employee DEI workshops mandatory frustrated people who didn't want to talk or learn about these topics. Many have been eager to return to pre-2020 workplace norms.

Anti-Blackness—Because the 2020 summer of racial reckoning was in response to a white police officer murdering an unarmed Black man, antiracism was the emphasis of many DEI activities at that time. It's important to note, however, that gender, accessibility, and LGBTQ+ programming continued, plus attention was devoted to the important Stop Asian Hate movement and efforts to eradicate anti-Semitism. Even so, DEI agendas became perceivably too Black. Deemphasizing racism and decentering Black employees are what's happening now. Getting rid of the Black CDO and the largest possible numbers of the Black professionals that person hired is just one example of how anti-Blackness is playing out in many companies.

Whitelash—In his *New York Times* best-selling book *American Whitelash*, Pulitzer Prize-winning journalist Wesley Lowery compellingly chronicles how white Americans have reacted historically and contemporarily to racial progress that produced gains for people of color.[3] Their resistance yields a seemingly never-ending three steps forward, two steps back outcome for our nation. In most large companies, boards of directors and C-suites, as well as senior- and mid-level leadership ranks, are overwhelmingly (in some instances, entirely) comprised of white people. What they view as too much emphasis on race compels many white leaders to behave in defensive and at times staunchly oppositional ways. Collectively, they're having an allergic reaction to DEI progress.

Transphobia—Few professionals can accurately disentangle sex and gender, or articulate differences between transgender persons, genderqueer people, and drag queens—nor do they care to learn. Trans and genderqueer employees have always been present in workplaces, yet colleagues failed to acknowledge, include, and make companies safe for them. Being expected in recent years to include pronouns in email signatures, attend gender inclusion workshops that conflict with what they learned in their families and churches, and mindfully avoid misgendering coworkers has been disorienting for a lot of employees.

Replacement Theory Fears—There's tremendous fear that the diversification of the American workforce will put numerous white men out of work and lock them out of leadership opportunities. Even though there's so little evidence to confirm it's actually occurring, the mere possibility of a zero-sum game is scary to those who've always benefited most. Many also worry that the white, masculine, heterosexist, ableist cultures that were created long ago in companies will no longer exist and the persons who created those cultures will no longer have a place.

Misinformation and Disinformation—One example of a single DEI facilitator telling white workshop attendees they're racist gets widely circulated on social media and mischaracterized as what's happening in all companies. It isn't. One-off examples are used to strategically manufacture stories of widespread DEI ridiculousness and extremism.

People therefore become opposed to something they've heard about but never observed firsthand. For instance, how many congresspersons who recently voted to pass a bill that will ban DEI efforts in the military[4] have actually experienced one of those trainings or reviewed the curriculum?

Culture Wars Have Come to Work—DEI is under attack in K–12 schools, at colleges and universities, in our nation's military, and in communities across the country. Corporations and other workplace organizations aren't exempt from this highly organized, well-funded political movement. Governor Ron DeSantis (R-FL), who recently ran for president of the United States, has declared a "war on wokeness."[5] Other Republicans are copying and pasting DeSantis's blueprint, and it's spreading like wildfire from public educational institutions and state agencies to other organizations, including private companies.

Executives Lack Courage to Fight Back—As politicized attacks on DEI rapidly make their way into workplaces, executives are running scared. Too few are standing up against misinformation and disinformation, defending their DEI initiatives, and refusing to surrender to anti-woke critics who know far too little about what's really occurring in businesses. The scary letter that 13 Republican attorneys general recently sent the *Fortune* 100 CEOs about racial discrimination in hiring will surely have a chilling effect on corporate DEI efforts more broadly—that was its intent.[6] Executives are afraid of lawsuits and becoming the next target on conservative news outlets and social media. Watering down or altogether abandoning DEI efforts is easier, more comfortable, and perceivably less risky for those execs.

This list of explanations isn't exhaustive, but everything on it is pervasive. As companies continue to walk back the DEI commitments they previously made, these and other rationales will become more deeply understood. Leaders don't have to continue these trends. Indeed, they could devote themselves and expect all their employees to advance and sustain DEI initiatives. There are enough of them, and they collectively have enough power to wage counterattacks on politically motivated efforts to make American businesses less diverse, equitable, and inclusive. Which leaders will have enough integrity and courage to actually do it? We'll see. Those who do so with authenticity, bravery, and strategy will play a significant role in saving our democracy.

MALAVIKA'S PRODUCTIVE DISAGREEMENT

Dr. Harper's article has some excellent points on an organization's commitment to DEI. However, the commitment to DEI in corporate settings comes from alternative explanations that influence this shift. The article's argument that the commitment was not real and that Black employees were skeptical of the organization's commitment to DEI cannot be an accurate statement to make. Many leaders recognized the need for change by addressing the longstanding issues of inequality and discrimination in their workplaces. While skepticism is valid, it's essential to recognize the potential for genuine introspection and growth within corporate leadership, even if the initial actions are perceived as hurried or incomplete.

Harper points out that many companies have invested more than $200 billion in DEI without a clear plan and that many have hired chief diversity officers without clear visions. Characterizing corporate DEI response efforts as haphazard overlooks the complexity of organizational changes. While some companies may have struggled with implementing and clarifying their DEI initiatives, many others undertook deliberate and strategic actions to address systemic inequities within their workplaces. Also, allocating financial resources and hiring diversity officers (although they need a clear vision) is a step forward to fostering an inclusive environment in the workplace.

While it is true that the discussion of race was avoided until the events surrounding George Floyd's murder, talking about the issues first gives not only uncomfortable realities but also a meaning for progress. Transitioning from avoidance to open dialogue about racial realities is necessary to foster understanding and empathy and, ultimately, to create more inclusive workplaces. Harper stated that "Even so, DEI agendas became perceivably too Black." This shows the removal of Black chief diversity officers or professionals hired to address systemic racism should not be automatically equated with anti-Blackness. Another viewpoint to consider is that sometimes, changes in staffing or leadership roles are made for various reasons, not necessarily related to discrimination or bias. For example, restructuring or budget constraints may lead to shifts in personnel. It's essential to assess each situation individually and consider the broader context before jumping to conclusions about motives or intentions.

Many big companies are run mainly by white leaders, but saying that opposition to diversity initiatives is just because of race isn't the whole picture. Some leaders might resist these changes because they're scared it'll shake things up or they'll worry about how it will affect their power. In addition, professionals may struggle to understand and navigate concepts related to gender identity and expression; it's important not to generalize this to all individuals. Many people are open and willing to learn about diverse gender identities and create inclusive environments. Expecting employees to include pronouns in email signatures and attend gender inclusion workshops isn't about conflicting with personal beliefs but rather about fostering respect and inclusivity for all colleagues. Creating a safe and inclusive workplace for transgender and genderqueer employees is essential for promoting diversity and equality.

Harper's article sheds light on essential considerations regarding organizations' commitment to DEI; it's crucial to approach the topic with nuance and consider alternative viewpoints. By considering a range of perspectives and engaging in constructive dialogue, organizations can continue to advance their DEI efforts and create environments where everyone feels valued and supported.

PRODUCTIVE RESPONSE FROM MALAVIKA'S PROFESSOR

Malavika helped me recognize that I did something in this article that I consistently advise against in my teaching: I made generalizations about what's happening in companies and other organizations in which DEI efforts are being scaled back or eliminated. She is right that there may be other factors beyond those I identified. Malavika did another thing that I often insist that students in my classrooms do: She gave business leaders and professionals the benefit of the doubt, and didn't presume a universality of negligence or carelessness. It's entirely possible that some executives are doing the very best they can to uphold their personal and organizational commitments to DEI. It aggravates me when people make sweeping claims about DEI. Because of Malavika's critique, I will aim to be more mindful about not unfairly applying trends that I'm seeing in lots of organizations to every school, university, government agency, or corporation that—for one reason or another—is revising DEI programs and policies.

CHAPTER 10

Elon Musk Articulates What Many DEI Opponents Think, but Are Too Afraid to Publicly Say

"Diversity, equity and inclusion are propaganda words for racism, sexism, and other -isms" is what Elon Musk posted to X, the social media platform formerly known as Twitter.[1] "This is just as morally wrong as any other racism and sexism. Changing the target class doesn't make it right!" The Tesla and SpaceX CEO's understanding and characterization of DEI are wrong. But at least he's brave enough to communicate his stance.

Many Americans share Musk's views on DEI. Like him, some are corporate executives and billionaires. Others are everyday Americans who are frustrated by policies and programs that aim to make workplaces more reflective of our nation's demographics, fairer, and more inclusive. Too many are persuaded by one-sided critiques they hear on conservative cable news channels and the disinformation they read on social media. And then there are those who've either chosen or been conditioned to have discriminatory and hateful beliefs.

America's wealthiest person paid $44 billion for Twitter in 2022.[2] Because he owns the platform, Musk can use it to proclaim whatever he wants. But more importantly, freedom of speech affords him the right to critique DEI initiatives and everything else. The question is, though, on what is Musk's disdain based? In how many DEI programs has he participated in recent years? What were the topics? Who were the presenters? Were they all racist, sexist, and otherwise divisive? Even if this were the case in his companies, how can Musk be so absolutely sure this is happening in every other organization across all other industries?

People should avoid criticizing a book they haven't read or a movie they have yet to watch. Similarly, making sweeping generalizations about DEI efforts in which one hasn't participated or even taken the time to carefully review is dishonest. It's especially reckless for someone who has as much influence as Musk. His anti-DEI tweet has been viewed more than 4 million times and has garnered hundreds of comments. Some respondents challenged his universal assumptions about DEI, but far too many others affirmed his perspective. Regarding the latter, did all or even most of the people who commented have negative firsthand experiences with DEI initiatives in their workplaces, schools, or other settings? Probably not.

Noteworthy is that not all DEI activities are high quality, evidence based, or good for organizations. There's no shortage of self-anointed DEI consultants who market weak, unvetted services on LinkedIn and elsewhere. Some have irresponsibly designed and facilitated workshops that caused harm and division within organizations. Notwithstanding that, there's no evidence whatsoever that this is characteristic of the overwhelming majority of DEI programs, practices, and policies. It's highly unlikely that Musk has such evidence. Even if he does, the answer isn't to abandon those efforts altogether and declare them unanimously bad for companies—instead, it is to distinguish not-so-great DEI services from those that actually help organizations enact their espoused values. Plenty of the latter exists.

Again, Musk has the right to say whatever he wants. At least he's willing to convey a perspective—albeit a dangerous, likely uninformed one—that lots of business professionals and other Americans share. Perhaps it could be helpful if resistant leaders courageously articulated their true feelings about DEI instead of faking support, contradicting themselves, doing the bare minimum, or blaming DEI budget reductions on enterprise-wide financial woes. At least saying it, as Musk has, lets employees, customers, and partners know where those executives stand. Some may choose to challenge those leaders' standpoints by furnishing evidence on what is and isn't occurring in the name of DEI. Some others may choose to take their talents or spend their money elsewhere.

Attacking or eliminating DEI efforts won't magically eradicate racism, sexism, ableism, sizeism, homophobia, heterosexism, transphobia, anti-Semitism, Islamophobia, and other forms of harassment and discrimination in companies. Plenty of existing evidence confirms that these are persistent and pervasive workplace problems. High-quality educational programs that teach professionals how to address these challenges, policies that hold employees across all levels accountable, and practices that help leaders foster environments that include everyone are what's needed.

Baseless, overgeneralized social media posts are harmful to our democracy and its organizations. Tearing down DEI, which seems to be Musk's proposal, will no doubt make companies worse. At the very least, he and other opponents really ought to sit through a defensible sampling of DEI programs and actually read what related policies say before continuing to destructively misrepresent all of them as "morally wrong."

CHRISTOPHER'S PRODUCTIVE DISAGREEMENT

The intent of Shaun Harper's article is understandable in trying to encourage DEI opponents to be more honest and transparent in their viewpoints. However, there were several striking perspectives in the article, as well as omissions, that raised concerns when reading it.

The target audience for Harper's article seems to be conservative-minded leaders who do not wish to face backlash for their, perhaps privately held, anti-DEI opinions and already committed actions, that undermine DEI progress. Using "courageously" is confusing because the term typically implies a positive action, unlike Elon Musk's public statements. When Elon is the example of a courageous actor, there is an unintended implication that expressing a poorly informed opinion is acceptable. This connotation is even more concerning when the viewpoint is coming from Elon, a person who has shown resistance to listening to opposing perspectives.

As a lead spokesperson for the anti-DEI movement, Elon Musk should face the same strength of criticism as bad actors like Elise Stefanik and Christopher Rufo, who mask their harmful actions with "good faith" messages that serve to delegitimize years of impactful DEI progress.[3] To strengthen this article's argument for the value of exposing and addressing anti-DEI viewpoints, high-quality counterpoints could have been outlined for each of Elon Musk's opinions he has proclaimed on X and in interviews. This approach could have better exemplified the importance of more transparent DEI conversations in businesses through applying fact-based and statistically significant evidence.

A major challenge when it comes to delivering high-quality DEI activities is that there is not a gold-standard resource for appropriate practices on DEI education. If business leaders had better access and guidance toward resources that describe what a truly impactful DEI program entails, they may not question their efforts so much when they can ensure the quality of DEI programs. Because of the lack of such public resources, there is a higher chance that they are making a false equivalence between DEI quality and reality.[4]

Instead of primarily reflecting on Elon Musk's actions, perhaps this article could have served better as an opportunity to highlight courageous champions of DEI, particularly given an internationally recognized platform like *Forbes*. Especially when voices like Elon's are so loud as spokespeople for the anti-DEI movement, this article could have served as a more powerful vehicle for change if it highlighted underrecognized leaders that others should be following and listening to instead of him.[5] Refocusing the DEI narrative on more constructive voices could provide better ammunition for changing resisters over the long term to promoters of the DEI movement.

With the continued politicized attacks on DEI, now more than ever it is critical to take careful and measured steps toward developing and promoting healthy DEI conversations that increase awareness and education. This article, while well intentioned, may be limited in its impact to drive the messages that it is espousing to DEI opponents and doubters. Follow-up articles may serve to address the weaknesses or limitations of this article's scope.

PRODUCTIVE RESPONSE FROM CHRISTOPHER'S PROFESSOR

"Both/And" is my response to Christopher's critique. Yes, highlighting and amplifying the voices of underrecognized DEI leaders is essential. Others and I have not leveraged our platforms enough to do this. I also think it's important, though, to engage with opponents like Elon Musk and call attention to what they are saying, how they are saying it, and how their words are further fueling the anti-DEI movement. To be sure, I wasn't praising Musk for what he said. It's just that I know there are too many others who hold similar beliefs yet won't say so out loud or on social media. Christopher's recommendation to deconstruct point by point all the DEI falsehoods that Musk and others are spreading is good and worthwhile. Perhaps that would've been a better use of the 737 words I invested into this particular *Forbes* article. I want Americans to be inspired and persuaded by truths about DEI, not further emboldened by mascots like Musk who dangerously spread misinformation and disinformation.

CHAPTER 11

Your Company's DEI Training Isn't Critical Race Theory, No Need to Ban It

Critical race theory (CRT) has been popularized and destructively misunderstood over the past 4 years. But first, what is it? CRT is an academically credible set of analytic tools legal scholars created more than 4 decades ago to help judges, attorneys, expert witnesses, law students, and others in the courts understand the role of race in the determination of judicial outcomes. Scholars and legal practitioners who use CRT acknowledge the persistence and pervasiveness of racism in America; challenge claims of objectivity, color-blindness, and universal meritocracy; insist on full, accurate teachings of historical facts pertaining to race; and situate people of color as experts on our own experiences with racial injustice.

Kimberlé Crenshaw, an acclaimed law professor at both UCLA and Columbia University, made a significant contribution to CRT in the late 1980s by introducing "intersectionality" as a prism through which to understand how the convergence of racism, sexism, poverty, religious discrimination, homophobia, transphobia, and other social forces place Black women at particular vulnerability for the miscarriage of justice in the law. I will explain later why I specifically called out intersectionality from among the many tenets, propositions, and theses that comprise CRT.

The major takeaway is that CRT was created by legal scholars—mostly academicians of color—for the legal profession. It has since been imported into the social sciences and other academic fields. Noteworthy is that few of our nation's law schools offer CRT courses. In fact, most students will complete 3 years of law school without reading anything about CRT. I have taught a graduate-level CRT course at the University of Pennsylvania and the University of Southern California annually over the past 15 years. My students, like most who are introduced to CRT at higher education institutions, are master's and doctoral degree seekers, not undergraduates—and certainly not third-graders.

CRT became a political grenade in the 2021 Virginia governor's race, as Republican Glenn Youngkin ran fear-mongering television commercials warning voters that Governor Terry McAuliffe, the Democrat incumbent, wanted to teach their children CRT in schools.[1] Despite being untrue, it worked. Many uninformed voters said it was the most important issue in the race, yet few of those opponents could articulate a definition of CRT.[2] The ridiculousness didn't end in the Commonwealth of Virginia. *Education Week* reports that 42 states have pending or fully enacted bans on the teaching of CRT in K–12 schools.[3] The biggest problem with this is that there's practically no evidence that CRT is being taught to our nation's schoolchildren. I have publicly and repeatedly called for someone, anyone to produce a confirmable list of 50 educators who are teaching CRT in elementary, middle, or high schools across America. No one has furnished any such list. Why? Because there aren't 50.

So, why then has a thing that's not happening been banned in such a rapid, widespread fashion? There are so many absurd explanations. I'll offer just three here. The murders of George Floyd, Breonna Taylor, and Ahmaud Arbery and the corresponding social unrest that ensued in summer 2020 forced a long overdue national conversation about structural and systemic racism. That racial reckoning occurred not only on the streets of America and in workplaces but also in schools. There was a call to finally teach the full truth about our nation's racial past and present. A lot of miseducated people who had only been taught a one-sided, sanitized version of U.S. history had a violent reaction to this that they took out on CRT.

That opponents outlawed something they hadn't read is a second explanation for the CRT bans. "Tell me specifically which CRT writers you have read, and which articles of theirs informed your oppositional stance," is a pair of questions I have posed to critics. They almost always fumble and ultimately fail to name specific scholars and pieces they've read. Or they name papers that have little to no CRT in them. Policymakers banning something they haven't read is indisputably reckless. A third explanation is the one that extends from education into business. CRT opponents typically conflate anything and everything pertaining to diversity, equity, and inclusion (DEI) with CRT. They're not the same.

Bans on the teaching of something not being taught in schools followed a September 2020 memo from the Trump administration that instructed every federal agency "to identify all contracts or other agency spending related to any training on critical race theory, white privilege or any other training or propaganda effort that teaches or suggests either (1) that the United States is an inherently racist or evil country or (2) that any race or ethnicity is inherently racist or evil."[4] The White House memo noted that "according to press reports," these ideals were being taught to government employees—neither specific media sources nor any other evidence that this was happening in any widespread fashion were furnished. Notwithstanding that, federal agencies as well as public schools and universities across the country swiftly halted trainings on race specifically, and in some instances, DEI more broadly.

In 2020, businesses created or expanded DEI education for employees. Much of it was broadly focused on topics like implicit bias, ableism, gender discrimination, and heterosexism, to name a few. Many of those workshops focused specifically on race, racism, and racial equity. An emphasis on race doesn't automatically make trainings about CRT. For instance, in many companies, teaching about intersectionality is on trend to help employees better understand how queer women of color or employees of color with disabilities, for example, uniquely experience their workplace settings because of the convergence of their multiple marginalized identities. While developed by a CRT expert, the manner in which intersectionality is taught in corporate trainings is a far departure from the complexity and criticality that Professor Crenshaw intended. Most intersectionality sessions are "CRT lite" at best, but really not even.

Chief diversity officers, HR professionals, consultants, and others who design and deliver DEI learning experiences to business professionals aren't teaching complex academic concepts that legal scholars developed in the 1970s. Surely, employees would find such trainings too inaccessibly academic and insufficiently focused on solving practical business problems. It isn't happening. Leaders really need not worry at all about CRT making its way into their companies, government agencies, and other workplace settings. As is the case in K–12 schools, there won't be anywhere near 50 people teaching CRT to American workers. DEI or racial equity trainings based explicitly on critical race theory are too rare to warrant senseless corporate bans.

YAMILE'S PRODUCTIVE DISAGREEMENT

Although I fundamentally agree that companies and K–12 systems should not be banning education around the topic of diversity, equity, and inclusion, I do think that these conversations are inherently steeped, on some level, in CRT—and I don't think that's a bad thing.

As you highlight in your article, CRT is largely an academic tool and relates primarily to the inequalities baked into the judicial system in the United States. While this is true, I, like Professor Crenshaw notes in a *New York Times* article, view CRT as "more of a verb than a noun,"[5] one that asks us to look critically at the systems of racism inherent in our country's legal system, yes, but that by its nature requires us to address and account for the ways and reasons those systems were created in the first place. For this reason, I believe that conversations around DEI truly can't exist without some degree of CRT; if we want to be able to discuss the inequality of marginalized peoples fully, we have to acknowledge the system we live in and the experiences of adversity marginalized groups face that are perpetuated by a legal system that is, in itself, comprised of racism and inequality. I feel it's hard to truly have a conversation around inclusion without acknowledging this lack of inclusive legislation.

That said, I do believe it's worth noting that CRT is often relegated to graduate and doctoral-level scholars, and is often not adequately distilled down for a corporate workshop in the same way that DEI has been in recent years. CRT is still a hard subject for many to tackle because they don't have the tools or the language to use to understand how to discuss historical and institutionalized racial systems without feeling as though they're simply saying that "all white people—and therefore they themselves—are racist." More emphasis should be placed on academic scholars to work with professionals and institutions building strong DEI trainings to find a better way to have the hard conversations around CRT and not assume DEI training is enough.

While I agree with you that DEI and CRT are not the same thing, I do believe that they are intrinsically linked, and it does ourselves and our younger generations an injustice to try to separate them. Until we, as a society, are able to look our history in the face and acknowledge the injustices that were created as the result of a racist mentality, we won't be able to find complete solutions for enabling lasting change. Removing CRT from conversations around DEI is asking us to have only half of the conversation we should be having. I worry that, for the sake of digestibility we are taking CRT out of the conversation and leaving it to the academic world when it should, in fact, be had more broadly. Senseless corporate bans of CRT are not necessary, no, but I feel more can be done to address our nation's ugly history, and talking about CRT more is part of that.

PRODUCTIVE RESPONSE FROM YAMILE'S PROFESSOR

While I'm impressed by the structural and systemic emphases of Yamile's response, I'm maintaining my stance on what is and isn't CRT. Having studied, taught, and contributed to literature on CRT, I'm a stubborn purist. For decades now, Derrick Bell's work has inspired me. I think it's offensive to confuse race-lite corporate trainings with the depth of Bell's genius analyses and theses. Nearly 30 years ago, Kimberlé Crenshaw and a trio of colleagues published *Critical Race Theory: The Key Writings That Formed the Movement*, a 528-page anthology.[6] Taken together, the 27 chapters in that book would help readers truly understand what CRT is, where it came from, and ultimately how it differs from broader considerations of DEI. That foundational textbook and CRT-focused law review articles are not typically assigned readings in corporate training, and most certainly not in K–12 schools. As Yamile knows, I'm not usually so inflexible and unpersuadable. But I've insisted to students in my actual CRT courses over the years that it is a very particular set of analytic tools created by expert academicians and legal scholars that ought not be watered down. Here's where I'm willing to meet Yamile in the middle: Even though CRT and contemporary notions of DEI aren't exactly the same, Bell and other CRT architects deeply embedded the ideals of diversity, equity, inclusion, and justice into its original scholarly foundation.

CHAPTER 12

Ways CEOs and Companies Fail Chief Diversity Officers

Chief diversity officers (CDOs) are set up to fail in many companies. These talented DEI professionals often experience tremendous disappointment and depart with really negative feelings. An alarming number of corporate CDOs stay less than 2 years. Given how essential DEI is to the success of today's businesses, CEOs really need CDOs to stay and succeed.

I've worked extensively with CDOs over the past 2 decades; many have expressed their frustrations to me. I've also been able to make my own determinations about why they weren't achieving the DEI results their organizations were pursuing. Additionally, between 2021 and 2023, I learned a lot in semi-structured forums with corporate CDOs spanning just about every industry—including panels and conversations about their leadership challenges. These leaders worked in public and private sectors, and in organizations of all sizes that are mostly headquartered in the United States. I also interviewed more than two dozen CDOs specifically for this article.

Here are 12 ways CDOs consistently say CEOs and companies fail them:

CDOs Are Chiefs and Vice Presidents in Name Only—CDOs rarely have seats at the table with other C-suite executives. In many ways, one of these VPs isn't like the others. They don't have the same decision-making authority. Compared to other VPs, CDOs say their budgets and staffs are much smaller. Also, their compensation packages are reportedly much lower than counterparts within the company who have similar titles. Everyday reminders of these inequities are paradoxical and understandably frustrating to the person whose job it is to be the company's top equity officer.

CEOs Rarely Talk to CDOs—In recruitment conversations, CEOs often tell prospective CDOs how much they personally value DEI, yet they don't get to spend much time with CDOs after they accept the positions. The CDO doesn't have the same access to the CEO as do other VPs. One told me he'd talked with the CEO a total of 30 minutes over a 2-year period; 20 of those minutes were during their one-on-one when he was interviewing for the job.

CDOs Don't Report to the CEO—Despite the position supposedly being responsible for the integration of DEI into every aspect of the business, the CDO's boss in many places is the chief human resources officer (CHRO). It's worse in some instances: Despite having chief and VP titles themselves, CDOs report to someone who reports to the CHRO. This makes them two layers removed from the CEO. Some were told they'd be reporting dually to the CEO and HR chief—they say it's a terrible arrangement because substantive engagement with the CEO is relatively lower, oftentimes nonexistent.

CDOs Are Hired Into Haphazardly Conceived Jobs—In too many businesses, CEOs jumped on the "everybody else is doing it" bandwagon and created CDO positions without being entirely clear about what the role was really supposed to be and do. In the weeks after George Floyd's murder, lots of businesses abruptly created CDO positions. Many DEI professionals who took those jobs less than 3 years ago have already left. To be sure, executives were hastily creating these positions long before summer 2020, sometimes under intense pressure from their diverse employees to do something in response to specific internal DEI crises.

CDO Roles Are Lopsidedly HR Focused—Like financial operations, communications, human resources, marketing, and legal affairs, DEI should be a cross-business function. In many places it's isolated to one area of the company: HR. Some DEI professionals ascend to the CDO job through diversity recruiting roles, but this isn't the case for all. Regardless of their paths to the CDO position, many understand the job they accepted to be multidimensional, all-encompassing. They recognize that their company's DEI needs, challenges, vulnerabilities, and possibilities include, but expand far beyond, HR-related responsibilities. "They pay people to do HR; I should be partnering with them, not doing the HR team's diversity work entirely for them," a former tech industry CDO told me.

Execs Attempt to Solve DEI Problems Without CDOs—Weirdly, when there's a crisis that involves racial or gender discrimination, the CDO is too often left out of the conversation. Instead, legal and communications teams work on making the crisis go away as quickly, quietly, and inexpensively as possible. They too often mishandle these situations in ways that disappoint women and employees of color in the company, as well as invite criticism from diverse customers and others on social media. CDOs say certain missteps could've been avoided had their cultural intelligence and expertise on diverse communities been invited to the crisis response table. It isn't just about being invited—they also want their expertise to be as valued as the expertise colleagues from legal and communications bring.

What CDOs Say About Racial Problems Gets Discredited—The CDO tells the CEO the company has a serious racial problem. It's based on what they've experienced firsthand or observed, or it's credibly informed by what employees of color have reported to them. The CEO ignores this, tells the CDO all the reasons why they're wrong, lists a few things the company has recently done for people of color (thereby arguably making it incapable of racism), seeks out a handful of other execs (sometimes, but not always people of color) who say there isn't a problem, and then ultimately rejects the CDO's advice on what the company should do. Versions of this occur far too often, mostly to CDOs of color and most especially to women of color.

DEI Work Isn't Deeply Connected to the Business Strategy—It's painfully apparent to many CDOs that the work they lead isn't nearly as connected as it should be to other parts of the business. With the exception of demographic representation numbers, the CEO and executive leadership team usually don't have the same expectations for key performance indicators (KPIs); the same shared, enterprise-wide accountability standards; and the same strategic concern for DEI as they do other things. Most CDOs strongly believe that good business strategy has DEI deeply, measurably, and sustainably embedded into its every dimension.

What CDOs Do Isn't Viewed as High Stakes—Many CDOs pursued and accepted their jobs because they care deeply about DEI. They want to help companies enact espoused organizational values and improve on longstanding failures. The work feels urgent to them but oftentimes not to other executives at their level and above. CDOs report that something else is almost always seemingly more urgent than DEI, despite the looming threat of one massive discrimination or harassment lawsuit potentially costing the company millions of dollars and tarnishing its brand.

CDOs' Professional Reputations Are Put at Risk—When the company fails to address workplace homophobia, a gay or lesbian CDO can lose credibility with queer colleagues. Similarly, when businesses are in the news for racial discrimination, CDOs of color could be viewed as incompetent, which might disqualify them from future leadership roles elsewhere. "To be fair, this is the occupational hazard that any executive takes on when they accept a position on the executive leadership team," a CDO in the financial sector told me. "The problem is that we aren't really executives, we aren't on those leadership teams where people get paid enough money to assume this level of what can easily become long-term damage to our professional reputations."

Nothing (or Very Little) Is Done to Retain CDOs—As previously noted, too many talented professionals transition in and out of CDO roles within 2 years. Many say the executives to whom they were reporting did very little (in some instances, nothing) to retain them. Usually, no offer is made to fix the cultural, structural, and systemic issues that compel frustrated CDOs to leave. Some executives convince themselves that the CDO is simply moving on to an opportunity that's a better fit. "They wouldn't let a great CFO leave after 18 months without trying to negotiate a different set of arrangements that satisfy that person's expectations," one health care CDO said in an interview. "But there's no negotiating with us; they're unwilling to bend on fixing a structure that we keep telling them is fucked up."

Nothing Changes From One CDO to the Next—A CDO leaves and execs swiftly hire someone else without doing an autopsy of what went wrong. They don't make significant structural revisions to the role. The new CDO is therefore set up to fail.

A company's DEI effectiveness depends greatly on its CDO being positioned for success. Having a seat at the table alongside other C-suite executives is essential. Making them report to someone other than the CEO strongly and offensively conveys to these DEI leaders that they aren't real executives. Also, CEOs have to pay CDOs like they pay other executives (the same level salaries, bonuses, stock options, and all), empower them with the same level of authority and autonomy, and give them budgets and staffing structures that are appropriate for an enterprise-wide function.

Moreover, CDOs have to be treated like the experts they are. CEOs ought to rely on them heavily for advice, avoid attempting to resolve DEI crises without their significant input, and believe them when they say the company has a serious DEI problem that places it at reputational and financial risk. What the CDO does has to be treated as consequentially as what the CTO (chief technology officer) does (like if the business was expected to function without email for a month, for example). Situating the CDO's work entirely or even primarily in HR denies a company the infrastructure that's required to fully execute a comprehensive, integrated DEI business strategy.

CDOs need CEOs and other C-suite peers to partner with them on creating and sustaining cultures, structures, and systems that hold every employee (including themselves) accountable for actualizing the company's DEI commitments. Lastly, CEOs really must stop letting extremely talented CDOs walk out the door without investing considerably more effort into retaining them.

JUHWAN'S PRODUCTIVE DISAGREEMENT

The structural challenges that Professor Harper outlines resound profoundly with me, particularly through the lens of my military experiences. The underrepresentation of Latin members in leadership within the military starkly illuminated systemic inequities, driving home the need for a transformation in how leadership and inclusion are approached. This backdrop informs my critique of Harper's analysis, pushing for a foundational reimagining of DEI initiatives within organizational frameworks.

Harper adeptly highlights the myriad hurdles CDOs encounter, from constrained authority to scant CEO interaction. While insightful, his exploration prompts me to advocate for a more radical rethink on integrating DEI into corporate structures. Drawing from my military tenure, where championing inclusive leadership and fairness was pivotal in overcoming systemic barriers, I see an analogous imperative in the corporate sphere to fundamentally embed DEI into the fabric of organizational culture and operations.

Proposing an alternative, I envision a departure from conventional corporate hierarchies toward a model that embraces a more integrated DEI framework. This approach disperses DEI responsibilities across all organizational levels, akin to the military's ethos of shared leadership responsibility, thus addressing the isolation and resource limitations CDOs often face. Organizations like Patagonia and Ben & Jerry's exemplify the success of embedding DEI into their operational core, underscoring my critique of Harper's propositions. These cases demonstrate the viability and advantages of prioritizing DEI as an essential aspect of a company's strategy and identity, challenging the assumption that DEI must adapt to fit existing corporate molds and suggesting a significant shift toward making DEI a core component of corporate identity is required.

In building on this critique, I suggest several strategies to refine Harper's recommendations. Implementing a distributed DEI responsibility model resonates with my military experience, where collective accountability fostered a culture of inclusivity. This model ensures DEI is a shared objective, deeply integrated into every department and team's goals. Additionally, establishing a DEI Integration Task Force, inclusive of diverse organizational levels and the CDO, would play a critical role in continuously weaving DEI principles throughout the business. This task force mirrors the inclusive leadership advocated in the military, ensuring DEI's seamless integration into the company's ongoing evolution. A dynamic, continuous DEI education program for all employees would further cultivate an in-depth, practical comprehension of DEI principles, necessitating adaptability to societal changes and feedback from across the organization, mirroring the military's commitment to perpetual learning and adaptation. Lastly, a commitment to transparent DEI metrics and reporting would bolster accountability and foster open discussions around DEI initiatives, essential for building trust and engagement, reflecting the military's focus on transparency and integrity.

I respect Harper's viewpoints and appreciate his articles. His work provides a crucial foundation for understanding the challenges faced by CDOs. However, my military experience suggests that there is a need for a deeper reevaluation of organizational structures, with DEI at their core, to create truly inclusive, equitable, and successful workplaces. I would welcome the opportunity to effectively integrate my ideas with his in the future.

PRODUCTIVE RESPONSE FROM JUHWAN'S PROFESSOR

The distributed approach to DEI that Juhwan calls for is most ideal. It would be great if, in fact, every employee at all levels in an organization assumed leadership for ensuring that women received equal pay for equal work, that professionals of color had equitable opportunities for advancement to leadership, that queer employees were safe from bullying and discrimination, and so on. Great, strong DEI programs and policies aim to equip professionals with the knowledge, tools, and skills to meaningfully contribute in these and other ways. But there are at least two noteworthy problems that impede the actualization of the distributed approach that Juhwan recommends. First, when no one is ultimately in charge, the people who aspire to be helpful or more useful have no one to lead them. Hierarchy is one longstanding feature of military organizations like the one in which Juhwan served. A second challenge is that without CDOs and other DEI leaders, there's no epicenter for the work—it could become too disjointed, diffuse, and unnecessarily duplicative. My main objective in the article was to help expose some ways CDOs are mistreated and offer guidance on ways to better support them in organizations that have created centralized units for their work.

CHAPTER 13

Discrimination Against White Job Applicants and Employees, or Is It Racial Equity?

In 2023, Republican attorneys general of 13 states sent a letter to *Fortune* 100 CEOs.[1] Highlighting the recent U.S. Supreme Court ruling that banned affirmative action in college admissions, the letter explicitly directs executives to avoid the use of racial preferences in corporate hiring practices. "Racial discrimination in employment and contracting is all too common among *Fortune* 100 companies and other large businesses," the conservative AGs contend. Given the examples cited throughout the letter, it's clear that they're advocating on behalf of one particular group of workers. As companies have implemented racial equity initiatives, white applicants and employees have increasingly sued for claims of racial discrimination.

"If your company previously resorted to racial preferences or naked quotas to offset its bigotry, that discriminatory path is now definitively closed," the letter states. "Your company must overcome its underlying bias and treat all employees, all applicants, and all contractors equally, without regard for race." The seven-page document concludes by warning execs that they'll be held accountable if they discriminate on the basis of skin color. Their determinations of what constitutes racial preferences and discrimination are ambiguous. Does this mean that companies must abandon all of their racial equity programs and race-conscious policies? A 10-page response letter signed by 21 Democratic attorneys general insists not.[2]

"We write to reassure you that corporate efforts to recruit diverse workforces and create inclusive work environments are legal and reduce corporate risk for claims of discrimination," the Democrats assert. "In fact, businesses should double-down on diversity-focused programs because there is still much more work to be done." They also argue that intimidation was the goal of the Republican AG letter and that examples furnished therein weren't sufficiently illustrative of DEI efforts that are common across companies. "The letter's attempts to equate these permissible diversity efforts with impermissible hiring quotas is a clear effort to block opportunities for women and people of color—especially Black people." It's noteworthy that considerably more AGs of color are among the Democratic signatories, not so much for the Republicans.

Racial Equity Is Not Discrimination Against White Applicants

White workers have been suing companies for claims of racial discrimination for years. For example, David Duvall, a former Novant Health senior vice president, won a $10 million lawsuit as he lost his job during a time the company was aiming to diversify its leadership ranks.[3] Novant executives said it was Duvall's "deficient performance," not his race or gender, that led to his firing. But being replaced by two women, one of whom is Black, was a factor cited in the case. "Novant Health is one of thousands of organizations to put in place robust diversity and inclusion programs, which we believe can coexist alongside strong nondiscriminatory policies that extend to all races and genders, including white men," the company's media relations spokesperson wrote in an email to CNN following the 2021 court ruling.[4]

AT&T, Google, Uber, YouTube, American Express, Infosys, Revolt TV, and PECO (Philadelphia's largest energy provider) are just some of many companies white workers have sued for racial discrimination in recent years. In June 2023, Shannon Phillips, a white woman and former Starbucks regional director, was awarded $25.6 million after a jury determined she was fired because of her race.[5] The Philadelphia Starbucks at which two Black men were wrongly arrested in 2018 was in Phillips's region.[6]

The June 2023 U.S. Supreme Court affirmative action ruling and the Republican attorneys general letter are guaranteed to spook many executives. Surely, both will also engender confusion about which racial equity activities can lawfully occur within companies. Frightened business leaders will roll back or altogether abandon existing anti-racism commitments. Additionally, they'll instruct their employees not to create new race-conscious initiatives that have any potential of inviting legal scrutiny. This doesn't have to be their response.

Below are four examples of racial equity actions I've either advocated or helped companies implement in recent years. In all four cases, at least one person asked me, "but isn't this reverse discrimination?" The answer is no.

> A CEO says in a speech that DEI is her highest priority, and she's going to hold everyone accountable for ensuring the business becomes more diverse at all levels over the next 3 years. Some employees erroneously hear her say that no additional white people will be hired or promoted. The CEO can make painstakingly clear that diversification doesn't have to be a zero-sum game. Additionally, she and other leaders can transparently show that as the number of people of color increases, white people remain very well represented.
>
> The executive leadership team has always been almost entirely white. In fact, it's never had a Latino member. There's a significant underrepresentation of senior-level Latino leaders beyond the company's C-suite. One white SVP retires. Instead of posting the position, the CEO decides to directly target an irrefutably qualified, highly accomplished Latino SVP who's achieving impressive results at another company. The CEO could hire this person without interviewing others.

More than 85% of the firm's managers and leaders are white; most employees of color are stuck in entry-level roles. To address this, the firm creates a yearlong leadership acceleration academy aimed at racially and ethnically diverse employees. Preparing a more diverse bench of prospective leaders for future roles is its goal. Employee resource groups (ERGs) are heavily engaged as partners for academy applicant recruitment, and promotional materials showcase people of color in ways that make clear which groups are the academy's primary targets. The firm can neither tell white workers they're ineligible to apply nor systematically discriminate against them in the academy selection process. Chances are, though, not many white employees will apply.

Because Black women are underrepresented throughout the company, the HR, communications, marketing, and DEI teams collaborate with the Black ERG and women's ERG on a print, digital, and social media campaign aimed at attracting more Black women applicants. They also ensure the company has a significant presence at the annual *Essence* Festival, which attracts thousands of Black women professionals; partners with alumnae chapters of the four historically black sororities, as well as with the alumnae associations of Spelman and Bennett Colleges (the two HBCUs for women); and designs job announcement ads that feature Black women. Nothing about this is unlawful. The materials just can't say, "we're only hiring Black women, whites need not apply."

These are just four examples of what can be done; there are many more. Truly committed leaders will find innovative, lawful ways to achieve, advance, and sustain racial equity within their workplaces. Equality entails doing the exact same thing for all employees. In most companies, white applicants and workers don't need race-conscious initiatives to engineer or sustain their representation. Equity requires targeted, customized approaches. It demands reparations for past wrongs and historical negligence. It's about ensuring that underrepresented groups and professionals who are often placed on the margins get afforded well-deserved opportunities to succeed.

Unfortunately, many white American workers will neither understand nor appreciate equity for others. They will convince themselves that gains for professionals of color are occurring at their expense. Many more of them will file lawsuits. Despite these threats, companies and the people who lead them should pursue racial equity with confidence, seriousness, and legally permissible race-conscious strategies.

KELSEY'S PRODUCTIVE DISAGREEMENT

To say that I have complex views on the issues raised in the "Discrimination Against White Job Applicants and Employees, or Is It Racial Equity" piece would be an understatement. In many, many ways, I exist as part of the majority—I am white. However, I also exist as part of the minority, at least when it comes to corporate America: I am a woman.

While getting hired or making the team was undoubtedly difficult, what came after is often even harder—integrating as "one of the guys" and earning respect as an equal peer in a culture where I sometimes doubted (or doubt) I belonged. For me, this includes my pre-MBA career in private equity and currently as a leader and active participant in the Los Angeles cycling community—both of which are largely comprised of white men.

With this lens, I have layered perspectives on the diversity issues raised in the article. I absolutely support equity efforts to remedy historical exclusion. However, some well-intentioned initiatives—such as targeted leadership programs—create unintended consequences.

More diversity in leadership is vital. However, I believe there is a risk that the optics of creating an "acceleration academy" assumes that all minority employees need special help, thus perpetuating stereotypes. And if programs seem to reserve advancement opportunities for certain groups, what message does that send to excluded groups? Employees that don't "qualify" for the academy may feel unfairly held back, which could lead to resentment.

I also have concerns around potential backlash if employees feel divided into "us vs. them." Progress requires bringing people together, not pitting groups against each other. Rather than focus on stark demographic metrics, I would argue that companies should prioritize inclusive cultures and developing all individuals on what it looks like to be part of an inclusive workplace. Hiring is certainly the first step, but I think the article discounts the importance of the post-hire experience. It is vital to examine how employees with diverse backgrounds are treated and supported once they've joined the team.

Leaders like Elon Musk who speak against DEI exemplify why culture matters so much when bringing in diverse talent. No employee, regardless of identity, can thrive in a toxic environment after they have been hired. In a perfect world, companies could set representation targets and use merit-based advancement focused on individual capabilities simultaneously and without bias. The world is far from perfect; however, developing transparent pathways (including company hiring policies and goals), mentorship, and sponsorship accessible to all are, in my opinion, key components in allowing merit to shine while also improving diversity.

It is vital for companies to establish a culture that avoids assumptions and listens to all perspectives, including concerns some white employees may have. With care, courage, and compassion, I am hopeful we can build workplaces where employees feel empowered to succeed on their own merits, and are supported to do so by upper management, colleagues, etc. The path forward is complex, but continuing to focus on shared humanity and individual value at the company level is essential in establishing and maintaining an equitable workplace where all employees can thrive.

PRODUCTIVE RESPONSE FROM KELSEY'S PROFESSOR

Like Kelsey, I want everyone to be included, valued, and supported in their workplaces. I also want every employee (including white people across all genders) to have equitable opportunities for advancement. As noted in Chapter 3 of this book, white women have been the biggest beneficiaries of affirmative action policies and programs for decades. I want white women to have opportunities to succeed and to receive equal pay for equal work—but I want the same for women of color, too. Affirmative action confirmed for us that a universal approach could still yield inequities. Hence, I call for a multitude of strategies, programs, and investments that address population-specific needs, trends, expectations, challenges, and realities. White women and Asian American women, for instance, could indeed benefit from meaningful professional advancement activities—so too could their same-race male colleagues. But the discrimination that white and Asian American women face isn't the same in most organizational contexts. And what both groups of women need to ensure their representation in positions of leadership often differs from the needs of male counterparts within and beyond their racial groups. Customized, targeted racial equity initiatives can exist alongside highly effective gender equity initiatives that benefit white women—it doesn't have to be either/or.

CHAPTER 14

Repeated Snubbing of Black Kids at Amusement Parks Shows Need for More Complex Bias Trainings

Two videos recently emerged of life-size *Sesame Street* character mascots disregarding Black children in parades at Sesame Place theme parks. Nathan Fleming posted a video to social media that shows a character apparently coming to greet his daughter Olivia but suddenly pivoting to shake another kid's hand.[1] Olivia is a 5-year-old Black girl. The race and age of the child standing next to her weren't confirmed. It seems clear, though, that the lucky recipient of the handshake isn't a Black girl.

In a CBS3 Philly News interview,[2] Fleming reported that following the incident, Olivia deemed the characters "mean," and she subsequently wanted nothing to do with them—not just during the remainder of the parade and elsewhere throughout the theme park, but she no longer wanted to see them on television. A few days after Fleming's post, Jodi Brown uploaded a video to Instagram of her daughter and niece reaching out to shake the hand of a Sesame Place character who visibly rejected them.[3] The character waved the two Black girls off in an irrefutably dismissive fashion just seconds after shaking hands and giving lots of high fives to white parade goers. "This disgusting person blatantly told our kids no, then proceeded to hug the little white girl next to us," Brown alleged on Instagram.

The Brown video outraged actress and Destiny's Child singer Kelly Rowland. "Had that been me, that whole parade would have been in flames," Rowland said in a video she posted in response to the incident.[4] The Fleming and Brown situations are likely to be misunderstood as a pair of unfortunate yet isolated occurrences. Several Black people have a different interpretation.

In addition to expressing support for Brown and Fleming, many Black Americans affirmed the two families' experiences by recalling similar firsthand encounters at theme parks, not just Sesame Place. Some remembered it happening directly to them when they were younger. Others described times when their Black kids were snubbed and white children were acknowledged and embraced. Additional videos similar to those Brown and Fleming posted have since been shared via social media.

It's unreasonable to expect every mascot to have the capacity to interact with every child along a theme park parade route or any other place where there are thousands, hundreds, or even dozens of kids who are excited to meet life-size versions of their favorite Muppets and cartoon characters. However, reasonableness becomes discrimination for Black families as they watch Black kids being passed over time and time again as white mascots obviously favor children who aren't Black. Does this mean theme park character mascots are racist?

Since Hillary Clinton mentioned implicit bias in a 2016 presidential debate,[5] the concept has garnered significant attention in businesses and communities across America. Several companies spanning industries have since made it a requirement for all employees to participate in one-time bias workshops. Implicit bias was the centerpiece of the 4-hour training Starbucks made all its employees attend during the one afternoon approximately 8,000 of its locations closed in 2018.[6] This was the company's biggest response to a racial profiling incident involving two Black men in a Philadelphia Starbucks. Bloomberg estimates the company forfeited $16.7 million in revenue during the afternoon of the nationwide training.[7]

While some had done it prior to Derek Chauvin's murder of George Floyd, many more police departments across the country engaged in mandatory implicit bias trainings for cops in the 2020 summer of racial reckoning.[8] Given its popularity, could it be that implicit bias training somehow skipped Sesame Place and its parent company, SeaWorld Parks & Entertainment? Maybe. I don't know for sure. But here's what I have learned in my work with companies over the past several years: One-time implicit bias trainings do very little to actually disrupt implicit (or unconscious) bias. Most companies start and stop with a single workshop on the topic.

The science of unconscious bias makes clear that we all have it, despite our best intentions and espoused personal commitments to diversity, inclusion, antiracism, and racial justice. Implicit racial bias comes from a lifetime of exposure to harmful messages that people receive about other races, ethnicities, and cultures via children's books, television shows and movies, social media, and messages from family members and others. In some instances, it emerges from observations or experiences that involve only one or a relatively small number of people from a racial group but get generalized to the entire group.

Whether the Sesame Place mascot is a 17-year-old white kid or a 39-year-old person of color, it's possible that person has been unknowingly conditioned to view white or lighter-skinned people as friendlier, more appealing, and more deserving of hugs and high fives. Sesame Workshop wrote this in its statement following the Brown incident: "We have been in contact with Sesame Place, our licensed park partner, and they have assured us that they will conduct bias training and a thorough review of the ways in which they engage with families and guests."[9]

The bias training that Sesame Workshop promises, as well as versions of it happening in other companies, ought not be a single occurrence. The training is especially susceptible to ineffectiveness if it is delivered in a generic "sit, passively watch, click, and quiz" asynchronous module offered only during new employee orientation. It has to be multidimensional and inclusive of concrete examples that are directly relevant to that particular business context. It's plausible that a well-designed bias workshop may raise theme park workers' consciousness about what implicit bias is and a few ways that it broadly shows up in human interactions. That's insufficient.

A better multisession professional learning series would make space for employees to identify and reflect on their own unconscious biases, discuss personal and shared discoveries with teammates, and determine ways to help hold each other accountable for recognizing and confronting those biases when they emerge in the workplace. Additionally, the series should make use of the Fleming and Brown videos to illustrate to trainers, managers, and workers who perform character mascots how implicit bias shows up along parade routes and elsewhere in theme parks. Seeing the actual videos and unpacking why and how racialized snubbing of kids occurs would be helpful.

Amusement park snub stories that Black people and families shared via social and digital media should also be included in the series. This will help employees more deeply understand the impact their implicit biases have on racially diverse customers. Research shows that knowing how people in an industry perpetrate bias increases the likelihood of its professionals being more mindful of those biases and making corrective actions in future situations.[10] Every industry needs its own unique curriculum for multisession implicit bias professional learning experiences. One-time, too-broad trainings will continue to result in unintended snubs, discrimination, and racial inequities.

LINH'S PRODUCTIVE DISAGREEMENT

Following the racist controversy at Sesame Place, Shaun Harper concluded that the situation was another example of why companies need to invest in better implicit bias training. One week later, Sesame Place announced it would impose comprehensive actions to advance DEI, including a racial equity assessment and substantive training education program.[11] Though Harper's call-to-action is an improved version of one-time bias training, it lacks scientific evidence to support his argument that complex bias training can sufficiently address racist behavior in the corporate world.

In his analysis, Harper recommends industry-specific "multisession implicit professional learning experiences" to prevent future prejudice. He argues this will help professionals be more mindful of their biases. His suggestion relies on an underlying assumption in his article that the knowledge of implicit and explicit bias will cause employees to hold themselves and others accountable after the training sessions.

No studies prove that understanding and identifying cognitive bias will definitively result in behavioral changes on the job. According to a research report by the Equality and Human Rights Commission, 18 investigations found that while unconscious bias training could increase awareness of implicit bias, no studies effectively measured desired changes in behavior, and trainings backfired in some cases.¹² For participants to adopt anti-discriminatory practices, the company needs to reform its current system, from recruiting to reporting. Additionally, any policy changes must be at least partially based on input from the employees themselves, not just executives or external consultants. This would help mitigate the potential negative reactions from participants who feel like they are being controlled, according to a study by Legault et al.¹³

A 2020 NYPD report on the impacts of implicit bias training states, "implicit bias training could not by itself eliminate disparities in policing, for the disparities stem from employment, education, housing, health care, etc."¹⁴ Similarly, implicit bias training, no matter how comprehensive, cannot independently rectify the racist practices embedded in the amusement park industry. Andrew Lawrence, senior features writer for *The Guardian*, explains the history of theme parks and how historically, African Americans were simultaneously excluded from and exploited for white people's entertainment.¹⁵ Even with the passing of the 14th Amendment, Black people still could not access parks and other recreational spaces because of the socioeconomic disparities that had compounded over time. Understanding this history would challenge businesses to be anti-discriminatory on the operational and strategic levels. For instance, theme parks could target new locations to provide access to underrepresented communities.

While I agree education about implicit bias is necessary, Harper's analysis of the racist incident at Sesame Place was a missed opportunity to educate readers of the discriminatory laws and systems that exist within the amusement park industry. His recommendation lacked adequate research and an explanation of what supporting policies needed to be implemented on company, industry, and system-wide levels.

PRODUCTIVE RESPONSE FROM LINH'S PROFESSOR

There's a chance that Linh and I are saying different versions of the same thing. Some implicit bias trainings are weak and ineffective. As I read some of the studies that Linh referenced and other research on the impact of corporate bias reduction activities, I'm often left wondering about duration, intensity, and repetition. If many of those workshops were one-time occurrences, decontextualized, short (say, under an hour), and not talked about among colleagues in subsequent team meetings, then I'm not at all surprised that researchers deemed them ineffective. That approach seems most popular in companies, unfortunately. Therefore, Linh is right in noting that my argument that complex bias trainings can address racist behaviors in workplaces lacks sufficient evidence. Because the scaffolded, repeated, curricular approach that I advocate occurs so infrequently in organizations, it hasn't been rigorously studied by other social scientists and me. I hope to someday be afforded opportunities to juxtapose one-time bias trainings with more complex alternatives to determine which has better, more durable effects on human behavior within workplace settings.

CHAPTER 15

Elon Musk Says He's Hiring a New Twitter CEO—Women Beware of the Glass Cliff

Elon Musk asked the public in a tweet if he should step down as CEO of Twitter.[1] He vowed to do what the majority of respondents recommended. More than 17.5 million people voted, 57.5% of whom felt he should step down. In response to the results, Musk tweeted this: "I will resign as CEO as soon as I find someone foolish enough to take the job! After that, I will just run the software & servers teams."[2]

Might Musk's foolish successor be a woman? Given that nearly 90% of tech company executives are men, selecting a highly qualified woman as CEO of one of the largest social media platforms would be a huge win for the industry. But would it be good for her career?

The answer depends, in part, on how much more damage is done while Musk remains at the helm. The amount of power and authority he relinquishes will also be a factor in whether she has any chance at ultimately succeeding. It's worth noting that Gwynne Shotwell, a woman, is president and COO of SpaceX, a company Musk founded. She didn't walk into the same pandemonium that exists at Twitter when she joined SpaceX 20 years ago.

Just 14 minutes after launching his public resignation poll, Musk tweeted, "The question is not finding a CEO, the question is finding a CEO who can keep Twitter alive."[3] Surely, many high-achieving, deeply experienced women leaders can keep the company alive. But will it be on life support by the time one of them is chosen to lead it?

The glass ceiling concept is fairly well known. It refers to irrefutably qualified women looking up at who's in the highest-paid, most significant leadership roles and seeing an overrepresentation of men who are often less qualified and less accomplished than themselves and other women. Comparatively speaking, the concept of the glass cliff has received less attention yet is nonetheless an important gendered reality in many businesses. Any woman who succeeds Musk ought to be worried about this.

The glass cliff represents the risk for a woman when she's selected to lead an organization that's in crisis. She's required to spend most of her time cleaning up the disaster her predecessor left behind; helping the business recover financially,

67

reputationally, and culturally; and restoring both internal and external confidence in the company's long-term survival. The stakes for her are unfairly high. Failing could do irreparable damage to her reputation and disqualify her from future CEO roles elsewhere.

Some might argue that a man who takes over a business in crisis faces the same challenges and vulnerabilities. At least three dimensions of the glass cliff explain the gender differences. First, women are too often denied opportunities to serve as CEOs of healthy, well-functioning businesses. They're more likely to be chosen in the aftermath of scandals and catastrophes.

Second, if a man fails to fix a crisis-inflamed organization, few people will attribute his failure to his gender. A woman, on the other hand, not only represents herself as an individual, she also represents other women who've been systematically locked out of top leadership opportunities. Unfortunately, her failure is likely to be explained by sexist and misogynistic claims that men are stronger leaders than are women. Furthermore, if she fails, it's unlikely that another woman will be chosen to serve as the next CEO.

The disparate effect on one's future career is a third noteworthy gendered aspect of the glass cliff. "He was placed in an impossible situation" is the benefit of the doubt afforded to men who are unsuccessful in rescuing failing businesses. For a woman, skepticism and distrust follow her as she attempts to transition to a healthier organization. It becomes a permanent part of her professional biography in ways that it doesn't for men. Unfair emphasis is placed on what she was unable to accomplish, not enough on the chaos she inherited from the man or generations of men who preceded her as CEO.

Since Musk took over Twitter in October 2022, nearly 3,700 employees have been laid off,[4] and several top executives have been fired.[5] These cuts disproportionately impacted women, according to a recent class-action lawsuit against the company.[6] Reportedly, women comprised 57% of employees who were let go between October and December 2022.

In addition, research shows that anti-Semitism, racism, and hate speech on the platform increased almost immediately after Musk came aboard as CEO.[7] Also, Musk disbanded the company's Trust and Safety Council,[8] the accountability group that helps moderate harmful content on the platform; reinstated the accounts of Donald Trump,[9] Kanye West (though he was subsequently kicked off again), and other controversial figures; and suspended the accounts of several journalists who've been critical of him.[10] And then there are the numerous celebrities and other high-profile people who've publicly fled Twitter in protest of its new leader.[11]

In sum, Musk has made a mess. Any woman who accepts his offer to be CEO would be doing so at tremendous risk of her reputation and professional future. She'll have one more thing to worry about: the richest man in America who bought Twitter for $44 billion lurking as an insider. According to Musk, he plans to remain in the company to lead its software and servers teams. His mere presence will undoubtedly undermine the next CEO's authority. Gender differences between them will surely intensify this.

SAMANTHA'S PRODUCTIVE DISAGREEMENT

Shaun Harper makes a compelling case for why bringing a woman CEO into a chaotic environment like Twitter does more to hurt her career and the reputation of other women in her industry than it does to advance it. According to Michelle Ryan and S. Alexander Haslam, the scholars behind the glass cliff concept, in instances of company turmoil, women's "leadership appointments are made in problematic organizational circumstances and hence are more precarious."[12] I argue that this original definition of the glass cliff does not equate with Harper's belief that women are set up to dissatisfy when positioned on a glass cliff. Instead, I believe that a precarious situation amidst a company in chaos may provide women with tremendous potential to succeed.

Anecdotally, some of the most respected women in business became CEOs under similarly challenging circumstances. Ursula Burns, for example, became the CEO of the Xerox Corporation in 2007. During her tenure as CEO, Burns reinvigorated Xerox from a floundering organization to a formidable competitor by leading the acquisition of ACS, raising their total market opportunity to $500 billion, and growing Xerox's employee base to 130,000.[13] Another excellent example of a woman entering a challenging workforce and transforming it is Indra Nooyi, the former CEO of PepsiCo. Nooyi famously recognized that the global conversation in food was steering toward nutrition and led the acquisition of Tropicana and Quaker Oats to navigate PepsiCo into more balanced alternatives for consumers.[14] Burns and Nooyi exemplify how many women atop the glass cliff can be successful despite their obstacles.

Hiring women as CEOs, even in times of company turmoil, is also a method of bringing in additional talented women to the workforce. Burns and Nooyi, for example, are recognized in their respective industries as outspoken advocates for hiring other women into leadership positions, and they are not exceptions. According to a study led by the Female Quotient, 37% of women said that the last person who promoted them was female, compared to 19% of men.[15] Therefore, female CEOs are an important catalyst for hiring and promoting other women in the industry both in stable and unstable times. Additionally, while Harper's description of the glass cliff positions women to be largely unsuccessful, in a recent study published in *Harvard Business Review*, women were rated as more effective leaders in times of crisis.[16] While women should not be promoted for this reason alone, it is an important consideration when looking at who may be more successful during times of turbulence.

While the glass cliff is a precarious position, I argue against Harper's opinion that women should not be atop it and believe that this position should be viewed as an opportunity. Women have a history of turning companies around, are more likely to hire other women leaders during their tenure, and are statistically more likely to handle an organizational challenge well compared to their male counterparts. Therefore, it is more important to promote women into CEO positions and allow them the chance to try than it is to remove them entirely from the running in case they may not succeed.

PRODUCTIVE RESPONSE FROM SAMANTHA'S PROFESSOR

For the reasons Samantha articulated as well as others, more women should be appointed to CEO roles. However, I want women to be just as desirable for top spots in healthy, stable, and financially profitable companies as they are for businesses that are in crisis. I agree with Samantha that women absolutely can lead effectively in the latter. But I also know that many, many more of them deserve opportunities to lead in environments that are not so toxic and disproportionately risky for their long-term careers. Although Twitter and corporate contexts are at the center of my and Samantha's exchange, it makes me think about our institution. University of Southern California endured scandal after scandal between 2017 and 2019. Our trustees wisely selected Carol Folt, an experienced college president, to come clean up the mess here. "I am relieved that we have hired a new president who has experience leading an institution in recovering from massive scandals" is what I told a *Washington Post* reporter shortly after news broke of her appointment.[17] "Hopefully President Folt will help us maintain all that makes USC such an excellent university, while holding all in our campus community accountable for acting with the highest levels of integrity." Our university's first woman permanent CEO exceeded my expectations. She was exactly the president we deserved during those embarrassingly and excruciatingly tumultuous times. But USC, corporations, and other organizations also deserve talented women CEOs like Folt during normal times.

CHAPTER 16

New Bank of America Loan Could Further Push Black and Latino Families Out of Communities

Bank of America introduced a new program in 2022 that's intended to expand home ownership in predominantly Black and Latino neighborhoods. According to a statement on its website, the Community Affordable Loan Solution aims to help eligible individuals and families obtain mortgages in Charlotte, Dallas, Detroit, Los Angeles, and Miami.[1] There could be a big problem with who's eligible. It appears the loans aren't necessarily restricted to Black and Latino Americans. Legally, they could be explicitly targeted to these racial groups through Special Purpose Credit Programs (SPCPs) that the federal Equal Credit Opportunity Act makes allowable.[2] It's therefore interesting that Black and Latino *neighborhoods* are specified in the new loan program announcement, but Black and Latino *people* aren't.

Instead of relying too heavily on credit scores, BofA plans to consider a blend of other factors such as demonstrated histories of paying rent, auto insurance, and other bills on time. And of course, income will be a factor. In its first iteration, the program will focus on particular low-income urban neighborhoods. This new solution builds on an existing program that has shown some success. On its website, BofA says its Community Homeownership Commitment has "helped more than 36,000 people and families become homeowners, having provided more than $9.5 billion in low down payment loans and over $350 million in non-repayable down payment and/or closing cost grants. To date, two-thirds of the loans and grants made through the Community Homeownership Commitment have helped multicultural clients to achieve homeownership."[3] It isn't entirely clear what "multicultural clients" means—it seems decidedly vague.

Also noteworthy is that one-third of the previous Community Homeownership Commitment participants were not "multicultural." Presumably that means white. Here's the math: More than $3 billion in loans and over $100 million in grants potentially went to non-multicultural homebuyers. Hence, as many (or maybe more) white persons could plausibly benefit from the bank's new loan program that targets Black and Latino neighborhoods. The result would be gentrification and the displacement of long-time residents of color.

Given the criteria, significant numbers of white applicants who pay their bills on time, meet the income threshold, and satisfy the other program requirements could take over certain communities under the guise of equitable home ownership opportunity. This has already occurred in numerous cities across America as white early career professionals (usually in their 20s and early 30s) moved into neighborhoods that had been long underresourced. High-end coffee shops, craft breweries, co-working spaces, CrossFit facilities and boxing gyms, dog parks, boutiques that sell $80 t-shirts, and lots of expensive restaurants swiftly followed these white urban gentrifiers.

Two other outcomes: Real estate developers seduced low-income residents of color into selling their homes below what would quickly become skyrocketed market values, and those Black and Latino families were ultimately displaced from communities they'd long called home. These surely aren't the results that BofA wants. But deliberately raceless approaches to launching and administering the new loan program make this well-intended effort susceptible to reproducing the gentrification that has occurred through its and other banks' previous initiatives that were reportedly intended to expand home ownership for low-income people of color. Imagine a Bank of America branch in downtown Detroit with few Black and Latino customers. Versions of this have already occurred for businesses in Oak Cliff, a rapidly gentrifying Dallas community.[4]

There are numerous actions BofA can take to minimize unintended racial consequences. First is directing communications about the program aggressively and multidimensionally to Black and Latino residents in the target neighborhoods. It can't be assumed that everyone has the same information literacy or equitable access to details about the availability of these new loans. The bank is going to have to strategically confront skepticism that lingers from the 2008 housing crisis that disproportionately devastated Black and Latino families who were tricked into subprime mortgages they couldn't afford.[5] BofA has to earn the trust of racially diverse long-term residents and explicitly assure them that this new program is different from prior predatory lending efforts. Duping loan recipients with outrageously high interest rates is one guaranteed way to erode this trust.

Predominantly Black and Latino churches and other religious institutions, alumni affairs offices at local HBCUs (Charlotte, Dallas, and Miami have them), NAACP and Urban League chapters, and alumni chapters of historically Black sororities and fraternities are some organizations with which BofA could partner to disseminate information about its new loan program. These communication partnerships ought to be expansive and ongoing. The bank also has to somehow systematically ascertain that Black and Latino residents in target communities received information and know about the loan program. Simply placing postcards in their mailboxes will be insufficient. Hosting community forums and having trustworthy representatives canvas neighborhoods to talk with individual families are likely to yield better outcomes. All these efforts must be followed up with surveys that offer insights into who knows what about the program. The surveys shouldn't be raceless. One question has to be about the demographic makeup of the homes in which survey respondents live.

"Prospective buyers must complete a homebuyer certification course provided by select Bank of America and HUD-approved housing counseling partners prior to application," the website indicates. Both the course completion and application stages offer additional opportunities to collect racial and ethnic demographics, and make immediate changes to program marketing approaches if there's an underrepresentation of Black and Latino participants. Transparent reporting about the loan program's beneficiaries is also key. Monthly or quarterly, as opposed to annual reporting of the data would help keep the bank honest about its progress in expanding home ownership opportunity to Black and Latino people. These numbers should be shared on the program's externally facing website.

Even if they're relatively small in number, BofA has some Black and Latino executives and senior-level leaders across the country. Its Black Professional Group has more than 13,000 members, and its Hispanic/Latino Organization for Leadership & Advancement (HOLA) has more than 14,500 members. Influential leaders of color, along with members of the two employee resource groups, must hold the bank accountable for ensuring that this new loan program doesn't further push Black and Latino persons out of communities that have long been theirs. These diverse employees also should insist that loan program administrators share the numbers internally on a monthly or quarterly basis and seek their ideas for improvement. Additionally, they could be helpful in facilitating external access to predominantly Black and Latino community leaders with whom BofA might partner to maximize information distribution about its new loan program.

HENRY'S PRODUCTIVE DISAGREEMENT

In the modern development of cities, a profound tension seems to constantly exist between capital investment in historically underresourced neighborhoods and who ultimately enjoys, reaps the benefits of, and makes a profit off of these investments. It is expected that once a neighborhood has been identified to receive this kind of financial attention, its development ends up pushing out the very residents the capital was meant for. Though I agree with Dr. Harper's arguments that a loan program for property ownership targeting Black and Latino neighborhoods, but yet is race-neutral in terms of individuals who receive these loans, will only perpetuate the same, often-repeated development and gentrification cycles, I think he can go much further with this critique.

A corporate bank as large, powerful, and omnipresent as Bank of America should be held to the highest standard for innovation when developing a program meant to alleviate the vast gap in real estate ownership between white people and people of color. In fact, before offering a loan program such as this one, Bank of America has the responsibility to reshape the structure that undergirds and makes possible this perpetual gentrification machine. Bank of America should first use its immense political network to collaborate with federal and more local governments to develop codes, ordinances, and legislation that would collectively redefine how real estate is developed—and who develops—in low-income neighborhoods. According to their website, Bank of America has relationships with all levels of governmental policymakers, public officials and regulators "in order to promote and advance the long-term goals and interests of our company, customers, stockholders, and economy." They should use these networks to structurally examine and propose changes that will actively support purported goals of The Community Affordable Loan Solution (TCALS). Surely this kind of initiative would also fall under the interests of current and future customers that Bank of America hopes to reach.

The express goal of this work should be to keep current residents in their neighborhoods and to help pave ways for home ownership for renters in communities earmarked for significant capital investments so that they get to enjoy the benefits and financial upsides of changes in their neighborhoods. Only when the customers expressly targeted by TCALS are supported by policy can a more well-honed version (which would also mean specifically engaging Black and Latino residents, not the nebulous neighborhoods) of the program be rolled out effectively and successfully. While I agree that the existing program is extremely limited and will further encourage speculative development and gentrification, I propose a solution that goes a bit further than redefining who gets access to these loans and makes the very development of neighborhoods more equitable. Only a corporation as well connected as Bank of America could work toward such a foundational rethinking of the systems that perpetuate the same old homogenization and resident churn in neighborhoods facing redevelopment.

PRODUCTIVE RESPONSE FROM HENRY'S PROFESSOR

Henry's perspective makes me wonder what would be the incentive for Bank of America to do what either of us is recommending. Altruism, access, opportunity, integrity, and corporate social responsibility are too often undermined by growth targets and other manifestations of capitalism. Like Henry, I would love for BofA and other big banks to leverage their political capital to get inequitable policies revised and new regulations implemented. But I worry that demographic, socioeconomic, and residential mismatches make doing so unlikely. Bank executives who possess the political influence that Henry advocates are overwhelmingly white and male—what would compel them to protect Black and Latino people? And most politically wealthy persons in banking also are wealthy; their financial circumstances are much different from those of low-income Americans of color. Also, those wealthy persons tend not to live in ungentrified, predominantly Black and Latino neighborhoods. These realities therefore make me doubtful of bank executives placing themselves at the forefront of legislative changes that would make home ownership more equitable and gentrification less common. Unfortunately, professionals who work at lower levels in banks (including the diverse ERG members I referenced) typically don't have enough power to actualize the systems and policy revisions that Henry suggests.

CHAPTER 17

Adidas Gets Transphobic Backlash for "Woke" Pride Month Swimsuit Marketing

Adidas has for sale on its website a new swimsuit to celebrate LGBTQ+ Pride Month. Several people are communicating disapproval via social media. Hundreds of posts include the hashtag #AdidasHatesWomen. The colorful one-piece has "Love Unites" printed on it. Resistance doesn't seem to be about the swimsuit itself. Like other companies, Adidas has marketed and sold Pride Month merchandise in previous years without this level of condemnation. The problem this time is who the company chose to model the garment.

The swimsuit is listed in the Women's Sportswear section of the Adidas website. But the two people modeling it present as gender nonbinary. This is what critics are calling attention to on social media. One of them is former NCAA women's swim star Riley Gaines, who has been a vocal opponent of the inclusion of trans athletes in women's sports.[1] In a tweet she noted, "I don't understand why companies are voluntarily doing this to themselves. They could have at least said the suit is 'unisex,' but they didn't because it's about erasing women. Ever wondered why we hardly see this go the other way?"[2] Like Gaines, concerned others are misunderstanding the inclusion of gender nonbinary models as an effort to erase women.

"I'm old enough to remember when women actually modeled women's bathing suits, not men," Congresswoman Nancy Mace (R-SC) wrote on Twitter.[3] The clear implication here is that trans women are not women. Similar to Mace, outraged others on social media are declaring that Adidas is the latest example of a company that has become "too woke." In a tweet, Congresswoman Marjorie Taylor Greene (R-GA) asked, "Who is telling these major corporations to alienate women, half the population, in order to market to trans which are less than 1%?"[4]

On its website, Adidas has 45 pages of women's clothing; almost all of the 2,139 garments have models wearing them. Clicking and scrolling through every page—which I did—irrefutably confirms that the company is neither erasing women nor drowning itself in so-called wokeness. There are thousands of clothing items for purchase on the site that aren't being modeled by gender nonbinary persons. Anyone who takes time to scroll through every page of the women's section will also discover that the Pride swimsuit appears twice: once with the two gender nonbinary models and again with what the company categorized as a plus-size model.

Would Gaines and others argue that the inclusion of this one larger swimsuit model is an attack on women who weigh less and have smaller body frames? Probably not. So, why are they so upset about the other page where this same garment is being sold? Gaines offers one possible explanation in her tweet: "Women's swimsuits aren't accessorized with a bulge." In addition to being transphobic, this claim is also quite disputable—certain body parts on many women do indeed create what could be characterized as bulges. Historically, apparel companies have chosen cisgender women to represent swimsuits like the one for sale on the Adidas website. This doesn't mean that men and gender nonbinary people cannot or don't wear one-piece garments. Instead, it's that marketers have chosen not to represent such persons in this type of swimwear.

Mace, Gaines, and others who are opposing gender-inclusive marketing on the Adidas website likely misunderstand gender to be a binary with a restricted range of corresponding behavioral and presentation parameters. Furthermore, they fail to recognize how including and affirming one group of people doesn't necessarily require the exclusion or erasure of another. Again, the evidence is clear that cisgender women are neither excluded nor erased in the women's apparel section of the Adidas website. In fact, my thorough examination of every garment on all 45 pages of women's clothing reveals the severe underrepresentation of gender nonbinary models.

Marketers and corporate leaders elsewhere may be spooked by the backlash that Adidas is receiving and decide against including gender nonbinary people in their advertisements. They'll likely view it as too risky. Adidas didn't take a risk. Instead, the company chose to disrupt narrow conceptualizations of gender during LGBTQ+ Pride Month. It would be great if Adidas and other companies expanded and sustained their inclusion of transgender, gender nonbinary, and genderqueer persons all year long and beyond one-time Pride Month marketing efforts.

SLOANE'S PRODUCTIVE DISAGREEMENT

After reading several of your *Forbes* articles, one singular line took me by surprise on your work titled, "Adidas Gets Transphobic Backlash for 'Woke' Pride Month Swimsuit Marketing." I completely agree with your stance that Adidas is not erasing women from their website. They are doing the opposite through expanding representation of what women's clothing means. Everything was amazingly written by calling out the facts, quoting the opponents, and addressing their comments in a nonaggressive nature. I almost didn't find anything to critique until you wrote one small sentence at the end of the article.

In the last paragraph, you said, "Adidas didn't take a risk." However, I believe they did. I agree with you that other marketers and corporate leaders may see the

Adidas backlash and get deterred from also disrupting Pride Month promotions. Since there is such a dramatic response from celebrities and congresswomen, there is significant risk associated with breaking down, as you so eloquently said, "the narrow conceptualization of gender pertaining to Pride Month." If you agreed that the backlash Adidas encountered could deter others from including nonbinary people in their advertisements, I believe that is the main argument as to why Adidas *did* take a risk.

Transgender and nonbinary people have received tremendous backlash and real estate in the news pertaining to athletics, apparel, and simply living their true lives. An example is Lia Thomas, a trans women athlete at the University of Pennsylvania. I remember the spark of debate that resulted during her 2021 swim season. She was not the first and not the last to receive negative press. There was an article recently written by Zack Jewell in *The Daily Wire* titled, "Here Are the Men Who Have Dominated Women's Sports."[5] Jewell, Gaines, and Mace are not exceptions. There are lots of people who are transphobic, vocal about their views, and have a large platform to communicate those views. It is no surprise that people like Mace and Gaines made public disagreement with Adidas.

According to *USA Today*, there were also "hundreds of negative reviews left for the swimsuit," including a comment stating, "People stop offending, biological women by having men wear women's suits."[6] The article also details how conservatives were calling for a boycott of the brand. Adidas had to have known they would receive negative feedback, loss of customers, and lots of press debating why they had a seemingly nonbinary model in the women's section. Knowing this and continuing to double-down on their core brand values, Adidas took a risk.

The act of risk taking doesn't always mean potential backlash. In this case, Adidas took a risk to effectively communicate to the people who they want to be their customers that they are willing to take risks with them. Those people are the ones who support representation of transgender people, gender nonbinary, and genderqueer persons in fashion and lifestyle. As Jay Brown said in *USA Today*, "Businesses that stand up for what's right not only prove their support to LGBTQ+ shareholders and employees, they also send a powerful message that bullying and discrimination will not go unchecked."[7]

I believe that the risk that Adidas took was one that is needed and respected by not only myself but other customers, employees, and stakeholders who are proud to support Adidas and companies alike that are disrupting Pride Month campaigns and beyond. Even though I understand why you could say Adidas did not take a risk, I believe that they did, and I respect them for it.

PRODUCTIVE RESPONSE FROM SLOANE'S PROFESSOR

Sloane changed my mind. What Adidas did *was* risky; I just wish it weren't. Including trans, genderqueer, and gender nonbinary persons in ads and on websites shouldn't be deemed risky for any company, yet transphobia makes it so.

Like Sloane, I am grateful that Adidas took the risk. Until and unless more businesses (large and small) become deliberately more trans inclusive, activities like the one Adidas took will be perceived as radical, anti-women, and dangerous. There's a real chance, though, that other companies will misinterpret the transphobic response that Adidas received as clear guidance that they shouldn't undertake similar inclusion efforts in advertising. In my opinion, that's awful. Sloane and I agree that Adidas seized the opportunity to send a powerful message. I think they did so reasonably. Doing so didn't tank their business. Many people point to Anheuser-Busch's profit loss following the backlash the company received in response to featuring Dylan Mulvaney, a transgender influencer, on a Bud Light can.[8] Anheuser-Busch remains one of our country's most profitable beverage manufacturers. As was the case with Adidas, any negative consequences that Anheuser-Busch endured were far from fatal. Ultimately, inclusion is a far more positive consequence for companies and their trans, genderqueer, and gender nonbinary customers and employees.

CHAPTER 18

Target Fumbles Black History Month, Pulls Offensive Item From Stores

A Black woman who teaches U.S. history posted a TikTok video insisting that Target immediately discontinue its sale of a magnetic sticker kit intended to honor civil rights icons and significant moments in Black history.[1] The teacher's critique isn't a too-woke, debatable culture war attack on one of America's largest retailers. Instead, it's about an unacceptable misrepresentation of historical facts. It's one of many reasons why teaching and learning about race in schools and workplaces is essential.

In the kit, the face of W. E. B. Du Bois appears on a magnet labeled Carter G. Woodson. Booker T. Washington's face appears on a magnet labeled W. E. B. Du Bois. And Carter G. Woodson's face appears on a magnet labeled Booker T. Washington. Many Americans would excuse this as a harmless mistake. But there are several noteworthy implications for schools, product manufacturers, retailers, and other workplaces.

First, children are introduced to only a small handful of Black inventors, leaders, and icons in most K–12 schools. It's usually Rev. Dr. Martin Luther King Jr. and Rosa Parks, sometimes Thurgood Marshall, and more recently Barack Obama and Kamala Harris. In some contexts, Harriet Tubman makes it into the curriculum, even though the horrific enslavement that she and others escaped usually gets sanitized and minimized. Many students get confused about the Underground Railroad—they think Tubman was an actual choo-choo train conductor. She's also mistaken for Sojourner Truth far too often.

Parents and families across racial groups have to compensate for what their kids aren't learning about Black history in schools with sticker kits, coloring books, and other materials they buy from retail outlets. Hence, it's especially vital to ensure content accuracy. Ironically, Carter G. Woodson authored the classic book *The Mis-education of the Negro*,[2] published in 1933. Disappointingly, too much of what was characteristic of Black children's educational experiences then still occurs in today's schools.

But it isn't just Black students who are continuously miseducated about Black people, Black history, Black culture, Black excellence, and Black contributions. Their Asian American, Indigenous, Latino, and white classmates also learn far too little about Black topics. Students across every racial group are often taught too many inaccuracies, stereotypes, and generalizations about Black Americans. The erroneous magnet kit situation therefore compounds our nation's existing, longstanding miseducation problem.

In addition to being inaccurate, the face-name sticker mismatch debacle is also offensive. It helps sustain the centuries-old trope that all Black people look alike. Du Bois, Washington, and Woodson shouldn't have been confused for each other—they weren't triplets. They don't resemble each other in photos. They did, however, have two things in common: (1) They were Black men, and (2) their contributions were extraordinary. Mixing them up is a careless way of minimizing their significance. Put differently, they were seemingly so unimportant that connecting the right face with the correct name wasn't worth triple-checking.

In my workplace climate research and corporate DEI consulting, countless Black professionals across companies and industries tell me they've been repeatedly mistaken for other Black colleagues whom they look nothing like. When I ask how that impacts them, they almost always express that it makes them feel unimportant to their coworkers. People don't suddenly begin devaluing Black folks when they enter the workforce; they learn how to do so in schools, by watching television and movies, and through books and learning resources such as magnet kits. Furthermore, few Black professionals have their first-time encounters with devaluation in their workplaces; it starts much earlier.

The logo for Bendon, a company that has been making coloring books and learning materials for children over the past 23 years, appears on front of the now disgraced civil rights product. Evidently, no one who works at Bendon knew enough about the Black people whom they chose to showcase. Was it just one Target employee who unilaterally made the decision to sell Bendon's magnet kits in stores across the country? Probably not. It likely had to be reviewed and approved by multiple Target employees. It appears that none of those people caught the mistake. This is one of numerous compelling reasons why racial diversity in the workplace matters.

Target has Black employees. Were they invited to offer input on this product? If so, how many were consulted, and was their feedback taken seriously? Companies can and should compensate Black employees for performing extra work like this and sharing their expertise. The cost of such bonuses is worth the risk management expense. Having meaningful numbers of Black people involved in product creation, product review, and product selection processes would've significantly reduced the likelihood of Target's fumble in February 2024 (as well as Walmart's highly criticized commercialization of Juneteenth in 2022).[3]

Also essential is ensuring that employees who aren't Black possess the racial literacy required to help companies avoid racial mistakes that become financially and reputationally costly. Had the one Black teacher not posted the TikTok video, how long would it have taken for someone who isn't Black to point out inaccuracies in the magnet kit? How many white schoolchildren and white adults are able to differentiate Du Bois, Woodson, and Washington from each other? How many can accurately articulate the contributions these men made to America?

How many other influential Black Americans are they able to correctly identify and talk about with accurate fluency?

Miseducated students grow up to become miseducated workers, managers, and executives. Some become educators—professional, inadvertent spreaders of misinformation about Black people. Nearly 80% of K–12 teachers across our country are white; the overwhelming majority are white women. How many of them would've been able to do what their Black teacher colleague did on TikTok?

DEI opponents have recklessly convinced themselves, state legislators, parents, and social media followers that too much attention is being devoted to teaching students about race and divisive concepts in schools. This is disinformation. Kids barely learn about Black history and other racial groups in classrooms. In most places, the curriculum—like Bendon's magnet kit that Target yanked off its shelves—denies kids across all racial groups accurate lessons about our nation's racial past and present. And certainly, not enough remediation of racial illiteracy occurs in workplaces through necessary DEI professional learning experiences.

SAMANTHA'S PRODUCTIVE DISAGREEMENT

While I mostly agree with all that was said in your article, there are a few additional perspectives worth considering. First, it seems unlikely Target had malicious intent; rather, this appears to be an oversight by the product team like you mentioned. Large retailers like Target develop thousands of products, and imperfect vetting likely led to these offensive items slipping through. You mentioned, "Target has Black employees," and asked, "were they invited to offer input on this product?" While I understand the value in bringing the perspective of Black individuals to this topic, it also seems unfair that they should be called on to perform quality control just because they're Black. This logic assumes that all Black people know all Black historical figures like the back of their hand. I doubt it's a fair comparison, but as a Mexican American woman I don't think I could accurately point to cartoon versions of historically significant Chicano figures and wouldn't feel qualified to weigh in on it for a major corporation like Target. When it comes to culturally significant merchandise, I would recommend Target implement stronger review processes and pray that they learned their lessons from this embarrassing mishap. I would also have liked to have seen Target announce a new Black-owned publisher to replace the one that made this grave error.

Second, Target's quick action to remove the products and issue an apology indicates the company acknowledged its error and did not actually intend to promote racial stereotypes. Though still disappointing, this incident seems more of an unintentional mistake rather than blatant disregard. This single incident does not necessarily reflect Target's overall commitment to diversity and inclusion. For example, the company has received high scores on the Corporate Equality Index for LGBTQ-friendly policies. No person, business, or corporation is perfect. While I agree that we should hold Target to a higher standard when it comes to honoring civil rights activists, we should also acknowledge that they are putting in efforts when so many other businesses aren't. I believe continued dialogue, dollars invested in Black-owned publishing partners, and continued employee education offer the best path forward for Target.

PRODUCTIVE RESPONSE FROM SAMANTHA'S PROFESSOR

In reading Samantha's critique, I realized that I inadvertently neglected to make two things clear. First, the onus should not be placed entirely on Black professionals to save their predominantly white employers from making reputationally and financially costly racial mistakes. As Samantha insisted, I agree that's an unfair expectation. However, I do know from experience that for myriad reasons, Black representation matters in the workplace (as does the representation of women professionals and colleagues who are Latino, Asian, Indigenous, Muslim, and Jewish, to name a few). The availability of in-house cultural intelligence and having opportunities for cultural input are just two of many reasons. Samantha is right: Simply having diversity represented in a company doesn't guarantee that employees who make those workplaces diverse know any more than their co-workers from other racial groups. I should've been clearer about this. In public K–12 schools, students of color are exposed to the exact same curriculum and textbooks as are their white peers. It's entirely possible that many (perhaps even most) Black kids and adults would mix up W. E. B. Du Bois, Carter G. Woodson, and Booker T. Washington, or confuse Harriet Tubman with Sojourner Truth. That's a problem for companies that honestly aim to get DEI right.

CHAPTER 19

Why a "Lay Low" DEI Strategy Is Especially Bad Right Now

Politicized attacks on diversity, equity, and inclusion have frightened many educational, military, and corporate leaders. Executives don't want their organizations to be targets of unnecessarily polarizing, headline-grabbing schemes to mislead the public about DEI. Some are therefore running scared, renaming, and not calling attention to their DEI initiatives. This strategy isn't what our democracy needs right now.

Why are leaders suddenly so interested in deemphasizing certain programs, policies, and accountability systems? Since January 2021, 44 states have introduced legislative bans on the teaching of topics related to DEI in K–12 schools, according to data published in *Education Week*.[1] Those efforts have succeeded in 18 states thus far. Local school boards across the 32 remaining states have enacted assorted DEI suppression policies. Also, a *Chronicle of Higher Education* legislative tracker shows that DEI initiatives have been defunded at colleges and universities in Florida, Texas, Tennessee, and other states.[2]

In summer 2023, Republicans in the U.S. House of Representatives demanded that all DEI activities be stripped from the annual military budget, which delayed passage of the National Defense Authorization Act for months.[3] Other DEI opponents are intentionally and recklessly mischaracterizing all DEI programs and policies as too-woke, divisive indoctrination. For example, in a recent tweet, Tesla and SpaceX CEO Elon Musk dubbed DEI initiatives racist and sexist. Musk didn't specify which ones, thus his assertion presumably applies to all of them.[4]

Across industries, businesses have significantly rolled back their internal DEI efforts.[5] Some, but definitely not all of this is attributable to the negative press DEI has received since 2021. Too many leaders have been duped by extraordinarily effective misinformation and disinformation campaigns; they actually believe what obstructionists baselessly allege. And then there are those who were never truly committed to DEI—any convenient excuse to abandon and disinvest is fine with them.

Fortunately, lots of leaders know better. They understand how people and our nation benefit from organizations that are diverse, equitable, and inclusive. They know the price of DEI initiatives is only a tiny fraction of what discrimination and harassment lawsuits cost. There are some white male CEOs, specifically, who recognize the importance of having leadership teams that reflect the diversity of their customers and the demographics of America. Notwithstanding such appreciation for DEI, many leaders are spooked right now.

"Let's just do the work without calling unnecessary attention to ourselves" is one popular response. Renaming programs and positions to make them not so obviously tied to DEI is another protective sustainability tactic. This is the wrong strategy for numerous reasons. First, when organizations don't show their work, people presume that DEI initiatives therein are versions of the extremism they hear about on conservative broadcasts and read on social media. Leaders who know that children aren't being taught pornographic content in K–12 classrooms, that white workers aren't being told in every campus or corporate DEI training that all of them are racist, that only people of color are being hired and promoted, and that other ridiculous DEI myths aren't universally (or even mostly) true have a professional responsibility to counter such harmful misinformation and disinformation with facts about what *actually* is occurring.

In the absence of public information about high-quality, reasonable, and totally appropriate DEI efforts, significantly more Americans will be poisoned by lies that are being aggressively spread through well-coordinated, well-funded campaigns. What sense does it make to know something is a lie and to have examples of what's actually true yet deliberately hide those truths for fear of what liars might do? This is a paradoxical, peculiar brand of dishonesty that gives too much power to liars.

A "lay low" DEI strategy also strongly conveys to women, people of color, queer people, persons with disabilities, people from nondominant religious groups, and others who make organizations diverse that they aren't worth fighting for and protecting. Hiding DEI efforts also conveys the same disappointing message to diverse customers, clients, partners, investors, and community members. It also weakens trust among the very people that DEI initiatives are intended to protect and serve.

Furthermore, keeping quiet about DEI is bad role modeling for current and future leaders. Today's employees and managers who witness executives mute an essential part of the business are being taught that it's fine to mistreat it as a disposable imperative when they become senior leaders someday. Spinelessness runs the risk of becoming a cultural leadership behavior in those settings. Loudly declaring that DEI was among the organization's highest priorities immediately after George Floyd's murder (one of many performative actions executives took in June 2020), then subduing it now signals to current and aspiring leaders that it's okay to contradict themselves.[6]

Lastly, institutions and industries need inspiring examples of DEI effectiveness. Laying low denies colleagues elsewhere access to adaptable, replicable, and scalable models of success. The "as long as we do the work" and "it doesn't matter what we call it" logics undermine internal and external opportunities for organizational learning. If diversity, equity, and inclusion are indeed the ultimate aims, then they should be called by their name—not by cryptic, imprecise, politically palatable synonyms. Good DEI efforts that eliminate individual harm, improve teams, reduce risks, and strengthen organizations in numerous other ways must be proudly showcased and defended.

MERON'S PRODUCTIVE DISAGREEMENT

While the chilling effect of politicization on diversity, equity, and inclusion (DEI) initiatives raised in the article is a valid concern, placing the sole responsibility of showcasing efforts on companies creates several challenges. Instead, fostering genuine DEI progress requires a multipronged approach where independent research plays a key role. Additionally, navigating complex social issues necessitates careful consideration to avoid unintended consequences.

Shifting the Focus From Showcase to Impact

The article advocates for companies to counter misinformation through public declarations. However, this can be counterproductive, potentially amplifying negativity and alienating stakeholders with differing views. Companies navigating a politically charged landscape risk jeopardizing progress by drawing unnecessary attention to their initiatives. Instead, the focus should shift to demonstrating the tangible benefits of DEI through independent research and analysis. Third-party institutions, free from corporate pressures and biases, can conduct comprehensive studies comparing companies with robust DEI programs to those without. Analyzing metrics like employee satisfaction, innovation, talent acquisition, and financial performance would provide objective evidence of DEI's positive impact on the bottom line, ultimately benefiting the entire business landscape.

Beyond Public Pronouncements

Companies should be cautious about entering the complex territory of publicly taking stances on social issues, especially those without a clear business impact. Doing so can create expectations for future engagement on any emerging social issue, regardless of its relevance to the core business. Furthermore, navigating ethical and ideological complexities without clear-cut "right" or "wrong" answers can be fraught with challenges. Deciding company stances on diverse social issues can be divisive internally and externally, potentially alienating groups based on differing viewpoints. Therefore, companies should prioritize internal action over public pronouncements on unrelated social issues. Focusing on fostering inclusive cultures, equitable practices, and ethical sourcing directly aligns with their core functions and responsibilities. Additionally, advocating for positive change within their industries, especially on issues directly impacting them, can be a more effective and less controversial approach.

Independent Research: The Key to Credibility

The article expresses concerns about silence implying guilt and eroding stakeholder trust. However, this overlooks the potential harm of performative pronouncements lacking concrete action. Companies can demonstrate their commitment through genuine implementation, fostering inclusive cultures, and equitable practices. Meanwhile, independent research plays a crucial role in showcasing the positive outcomes objectively, without the biases inherent in self-promotion. Furthermore, emphasizing data-driven decision-making addresses concerns about role modeling for future leaders. By highlighting the value of independent research in guiding DEI efforts, companies encourage future leaders to prioritize evidence-based approaches over public-facing activism.

A Multipronged Approach for Sustainable Progress

The fight for DEI requires a multipronged approach. While companies have a responsibility to implement effective initiatives, the burden of public advocacy and countering misinformation should not rest solely on their shoulders. Empowering independent institutions to conduct objective research and showcase the positive impact of DEI creates a more sustainable and effective path toward a truly inclusive society. This allows companies to focus on genuine implementation, fostering trust with diverse stakeholders through concrete action rather than public pronouncements, ultimately leading to more meaningful progress on the path to equity and inclusion.

PRODUCTIVE RESPONSE FROM MERON'S PROFESSOR

"Yes, if only" is what I repeatedly thought as I read what Meron wrote. Yes, if only people valued evidence about what is and isn't happening in the name of DEI in companies. Yes, if only the decades of published, extremely credible research on the benefits of DEI were taken more seriously and used to defend those activities during this era of baseless, politicized attacks. And yes, if only companies did more with the independent research that executives commissioned and paid for. The last one especially resonates with me. Over the past 2 decades, I have been continuously engaged in the assessment of campus climates at colleges and universities, as well as workplace climates for corporations and other organizations. As Meron notes, rigorous assessments like those I conduct can and should be leveraged to showcase the effectiveness of DEI policies and programs. Companies shouldn't keep quiet about the availability of such evidence or about what it says. It can be used internally and externally to justify DEI efforts. Business leaders must also be transparent about the less flattering, at times more alarming findings from culture and climate surveys. Those data show where problems, vulnerabilities, and unfulfilled expectations are, which could be used to justify the need for sustaining, improving, and creating new DEI strategies.

Part III

PRODUCTIVE DISAGREEMENTS ABOUT AMERICAN POLITICS AND ELECTED OFFICIALS

CHAPTER 20

They're Saying He's Too Old: Ageism in Media Discourse About Joe Biden's Reelection

Cable news journalists and commentators keep reminding us that if he's reelected, Joe Biden will be 82 years old at the start of his second presidential term. For months, they've been asking themselves and the American people if Biden is too old to continue in the presidency. The constant interrogation of this question in such a public fashion is blatantly ageist. It's neither uncommon nor unreasonable for the press to inquire about a presidential candidate's fitness to lead. They typically probe and highlight potentially troublesome findings from physicians' reports. In recent years, no health information has threatened to disqualify a presidential candidate (that, by the way, would be a different form of bias and discrimination). David Frum, a staff writer at *The Atlantic*, posited that Biden's health between now and the next presidential election is likely to be his "X Factor."[1] Yet the current public discourse isn't about what Biden's medical records say. It's almost entirely about his age.

Some commentators occasionally note that Biden has fallen three times since being elected in November 2020: once while playing with his dog, which resulted in hairline fractures in his foot; again while riding his bike; and more recently, on stage at the Air Force Academy graduation, where he tripped on a sandbag. Clumsiness may or may not be attributable to Biden's age. Concerns about this trio of slip-and-falls isn't what most of the age-focused commentary is about. Instead, the discussions focus more on the number of decades he's spent in public service, how old he'd be at the end of his second term, and what will happen if he passes away before January 2029. There's a constitutional answer to the death question, which Frum argues exacerbates concerns about Biden's likelihood of making it through a full second term.

Fascination with Biden's age compelled media organizations to ask everyday Americans about it explicitly in polls. In an ABC News/Washington Post survey conducted in May 2023, 68% of respondents said Biden is too old for another term.[2] Similarly, in an April 2023 NBC News poll, 70% of respondents felt the president shouldn't seek reelection—among them, 71% attributed their reasoning to his age.[3] These results make clear that it isn't just journalists and pundits who are concerned about the 81-year-old leader's desire to serve four more years. Might it be, though, that constant conversations about his age in the media are significantly shaping public opinion?

Ageism has become surprisingly acceptable in press coverage about Biden's pursuit of a second term. In a one-on-one interview at the White House,[4] MSNBC's *The 11th Hour* host Stephanie Ruhle told the President of the United States, "there's not a Fortune 500 company in the world looking to hire a CEO in his 80s." That statement was ageist, even if it's true. Ruhle then asked, "Why would an 82-year-old Joe Biden be the right person for the most important job in the world?" That question also was ageist. "I have acquired a hell of a lot of wisdom and know more than the vast majority of people," Biden replied. "And I'm more experienced than anybody that's ever run for the office. And I think I've proven myself to be honorable, as well as also effective."

The president's response to Ruhle's question is what the press should be talking about, not hypothetical predictions of his leadership fitness in January 2025. When he took office, Biden was already the oldest person to assume the American presidency. According to recent Pew Research Center analyses,[5] he is the world's ninth-oldest national leader. The ages range from mid-30s to 90. Biden exceeds the median by 18 years. Compared to younger government CEOs around the globe, does he perform less effectively because of his age? There's no evidence that leaders of other countries make better decisions or are otherwise more successful than Biden because they're younger. If broadcast journalists and others insist on continuing to talk about Biden's age, their questions should focus on whether the current 80-year-old president is effectively doing his job. Unfortunately, how people appraise Biden's performance will depend largely on whether they're Republicans or Democrats.

Here's a specific set of objective, nonpartisan questions: Because of his age, does Biden often miss or fall asleep in meetings, has he been unable to travel domestically and internationally to execute his responsibilities, are cabinet members and others in the White House complaining that he moves too slowly on getting things done, is he stuck in the past and only surrounding himself with other people his age, was he out of work for extended time periods after falling off his bike and tripping on a sandbag (he was president-elect when he fractured his foot), did 58-year-old House Speaker Kevin McCarthy wear him out in the debt ceiling negotiations, and does his behavior pose a credible threat to national security? The answer to each of these questions is no. Hence, the unsubstantiated, inappropriate ageism really should stop.

DELANEY'S PRODUCTIVE DISAGREEMENT

In the article, you write, "For months, they've been asking themselves and the American people if Biden is too old to continue in the presidency. The constant interrogation of this question in such a public fashion is blatantly ageist." I argue that this is not ageism. Many times, those statements are based not solely on his age but on surrounding events and actions involving the president—from aggravated behavior to slurred and incoherent speeches. His age becomes more pronounced due to concerns regarding his ability to perform the functions and responsibilities of the presidency.

While discussing surveys of the American population and their opinion of Joe Biden's age, you asked, "Might it be, though, that constant conversations about his age in the media are significantly shaping public opinion?" While I am always on the lookout for potential bias in media, specifically surveys and the biases of those responding to these questions, I don't believe it's fair to fully correlate the responses of the American population with conversations in the media. I don't believe Biden is too old simply because he is over 80. I firmly believe that the person elected to the presidential position should be more reflective in age of the American population they represent. Reported in June 2023, the median age of the American population is 38.9 years old, according to the Census Bureau, which is approximately half of Biden's current age.[6]

I also disagree with your characterization of Ruhle's questions as ageist. According to the World Health Organization, "Ageism refers to the stereotypes (how we think), prejudice (how we feel), and discrimination (how we act) toward others or oneself based on age."[7] In terms of how we think about Biden, the argument isn't that he's 81 and therefore he cannot be president. The concern is that Biden is demonstrating behaviors that may impact his ability to perform presidential duties. In reports following a January 2024 campaign event in Virginia, Biden was actively caught mumbling, slurring his words, or acting confused. He also has come under fire for illegally taking classified documents, similar to what Trump did. Following the investigation, "Special Counsel Robert Hur said in a report that he opted against bringing criminal charges following a 15-month investigation because Biden cooperated and would be difficult to convict, describing him as a 'well-meaning, elderly man with a poor memory.'"[8]

And regarding the point of ageism and discrimination and how we act toward Biden, no one is impeding him from running again at this point in time. He is not being discriminated against in his ability to run for office—in fact, many people still plan to vote for him. Finally, you end your article with a series of nonpartisan questions to which I have included some of my own answers. Does his behavior pose a credible threat to national security? Yes, his incoherent speech and confusion at several events and in various public addresses lead to concerns over his coherent nature when meeting with other political individuals and his ability to understand key issues facing our nation. Additionally, the 15-months-long investigation of his misuse of classified documents leads individuals to wonder about other lapses of judgment regarding information security. Therefore, while I agree there may have been some ageism in the media discourse surrounding Biden, the stem of these comments is primarily regarding his actions and his ability to perform the role of president while also representing the values of the current American population.

PRODUCTIVE RESPONSE FROM DELANEY'S PROFESSOR

In the months following Delaney's critiques of my article, more Americans became concerned about President Biden's reelection bid. Delaney helped me realize something I hadn't considered: It was Biden's behaviors, not his age, that engendered worries, doubts, and calls for him to step aside. Nancy Pelosi and Maxine Waters, for example, are both in their mid-80s. While some feel they have been in Congress long enough and it's time to make way for a new generation of leaders, performance concerns haven't been raised about them in ways they have been about Biden. When I teach qualitative research methods courses and advise doctoral dissertations, I stress to students the importance of disclosing biases they bring to their projects. I'll model that here: I'm biased toward President Biden because I was on his education policy team during the 2020 campaign and he subsequently appointed me to the National Board for Education Sciences. I think he's a great man and a truly patriotic American. Given this, I looked past the behaviors that Delaney, journalists, and many others saw. Despite my deep expertise on discrimination, I appreciate how Delaney challenged me to see that no one was technically discriminating against Biden. I'm ultimately grateful that he selflessly discontinued his reelection pursuit and created the pathway for the potential of a Kamala Harris presidency.

CHAPTER 21

Who Told Nikki Haley and Ron DeSantis That America Has Never Been Racist?

In a Fox News Channel interview, then-Republican presidential candidate Nikki Haley confidently proclaimed that America "has never been a racist country."[1] She went on to say, "I faced racism when I was growing up, but I can tell you today is a lot better than it was then." Florida governor Ron DeSantis, another presidential hopeful, was subsequently asked in a CNN Town Hall if he agreed with Haley.[2] "The U.S. is not a racist country, and we've overcome things in our history" was his response. Neither Haley nor DeSantis disclosed the data sources on which their declarations were based. With whom have they spoken specifically about this? What are the racial demographics of their informants?

"America has always had racism, but America has never been a racist country," Haley's campaign spokesperson AnnMarie Graham-Barnes said in a statement. "The liberal media always fails to get that distinction." Beyond the critique of journalists, there was no acknowledgment that Americans who have historically and contemporarily experienced racism often have a very different appraisal of our nation. Instead, both Haley and DeSantis determined that centuries of racist acts don't necessarily mean America is or ever has been racist. There are a few potential explanations for how they reached such conclusions.

Despite DeSantis's war on so-called woke education in Florida,[3] there's no evidence to confirm that K–12 teachers (nearly 80% of whom are white) are aiming to convince schoolchildren that America is racist. Instead, some (not even most) have attempted to teach full truths about our nation's racial past and present. The whitewashing of American history; the minimization of slavery, Jim Crow, redlining, racist policies, and color-blind approaches to teaching and learning aren't new phenomena; they probably existed when DeSantis and Haley were students. Because they were likely exposed to only a limited, largely raceless version of our country in their own K–12 and collegiate schooling experiences, what the two presidential candidates believe to be universally true is what they themselves were taught.

Haley's comments were in response to a prediction Joy Reid, host of *The ReidOut* on MSNBC, made about her likelihood of emerging as the Republican party's nominee. In a panel conversation about Haley's third-place finish in Iowa, Reid said the racially homogeneous GOP was unlikely to have an Indian American woman at the top of its ticket in the 2024 general election. Nationally, 85% of Republican voters in the 2022 midterm elections were white, according to Pew Research Center data.[4] As has always been the case, people of color remain woefully underrepresented among Republican governors and congresspeople, as well as in powerful party leadership roles.

Given the demographics of their party, it's entirely plausible that Haley and DeSantis received their intel primarily from Americans who've had few firsthand encounters with interpersonal, structural, and systemic racism. DeSantis proudly touted that he visited all 99 counties in Iowa ahead of the state's 2024 GOP primary caucus. It's unlikely that he asked those residents explicitly about racism. Even if he had, they probably would've affirmed his stance. ABC News entrance poll results show that 98% of caucusgoers were white.[5] Engagement with so little racial and ethnic diversity across all levels within the GOP surely influences what candidates—not just DeSantis and Haley—come to know about how people of color experience and characterize America.

Haley served 6 years as governor of South Carolina. DeSantis has been Florida's governor since 2018. Both states are considerably more diverse than is Iowa. Census data show that whites comprise 68.9% and 76.8% of South Carolina and Florida residents, respectively. During their tenures, did the two governors specifically ask people of color in their states about racism? If so, how many people, how often were they asked, in what settings, and using what methods? Are DeSantis, Haley, and others in the GOP able to offer perspectives beyond a handful of cherry-picked anecdotes solicited from conservatives of color?

Governors usually commit themselves to being leaders of all the people in their states, including those who belong to the opposite political party. Had they been explicitly asked, democrats of color (and maybe some republicans of color, too) surely would've offered Governors DeSantis and Haley more complex understandings of racism within their states and across America. An ours "has never been a racist country" proclamation, especially from two leaders vying to become president of the United States, deserves significant and meaningful input from citizens whom racism has and continues to harm.

The most significant leadership implication isn't limited to insufficiently informed U.S. presidential candidates. It's professionally irresponsible for school principals and superintendents, college and university administrators, high-ranking military officers, CEOs, and other executives to insist the organizations they lead aren't racist without first asking ample numbers of diverse stakeholders. People of color who are invited to offer examples of racism they've experienced likely will do so if they believe the leaders who are asking won't attempt to gaslight or retaliate against them, are genuinely interested in knowing the truth, and will take corrective actions in response to what they hear.

RACHAEL'S PRODUCTIVE DISAGREEMENT

I appreciate the approach taken in this article, which is to question the underlying basis for Haley's and DeSantis's statements. Asking what information the candidates relied on to reach their conclusions is valid because there is ample evidence that America has and continues to be a racist country. Where I respectfully disagree is that I do not believe it is ultimately effective to solely take the candidates' statements at face value and assume they are genuine. It gives too much power to these statements to attempt to debate them as if they were diligently formulated and honestly offered. Instead, it is important also to examine the true motives for these statements.

I believe these kinds of negating statements are common among political conservatives and specifically designed to uphold power structures that benefit specific demographics over others (namely, heterosexual white men and women who identify as part of the Christian religion). Fundamentally, conservatives in the United States want to minimize any acknowledgment or recognition that certain groups experience privilege and that this privilege is at the expense of other groups.

The old adage is that recognizing a problem is half the solution. This is the exact reason why conservatives want to perpetuate the notion that racism (and other forms of discrimination and oppression like sexism and ableism) do not exist in any significant, structural, or institutionalized way that requires redress. Refusing to admit that a problem has existed or currently exists and working hard to convince others that this is the case is the most effective way to avoid change. "Nothing to see here" is their first line of defense.

The next line of defense is to discredit those who believe in the reality of racism. If America is not racist, then those who raise the issue of racial inequalities must be completely misguided. The intent is to try to discredit any mention of "racism," "race," or "racial inequality" as a petty and vindictive attack against innocents. The question is, what would inspire and fuel such persistent "invalid" race-based grievances if no significant institutional, legal, or governmental racism has ever existed? Are entire groups of people this petty and vindictive? Unfortunately, many conservatives feel this way about entire groups in the United States, which is itself a racist view.

The irony is that many of the same people who deny the existence of institutionalized racism in America often try to argue that somehow there is "reverse racism" and that the world is "against them" for being white and male. They simultaneously cast doubt on the reality of racism while employing the concept to frame themselves as victims.

PRODUCTIVE RESPONSE FROM RACHAEL'S PROFESSOR

In some places, quantifiers are needed in Rachael's response—a few, some, many, a lot, most conservatives. I think it's important to not paint all conservatives with the same broad brush. Other aspects of what Rachael wrote make sense to me. I'm open to the strong possibility that some GOP candidates and elected officials know full well that America has long had and continues to have problems with racism, but they intentionally avoid saying so for their political self-preservation. Also, Rachael is right in pointing out how refusing to acknowledge racism and racial inequities upholds power imbalances. It's easier, politically safer, and in some instances, financially more profitable to ignore or refute racial realities. As a social scientist, I had obviously thought about some of what Rachael argued, even though I didn't highlight it in my article. Some racism denial is surely attributable to political strategy. I still maintain, though, that miseducation explains other parts of it. Too few adult citizens (myself included) learned enough truths about our nation's racial past and present in K–12 schools, colleges, or graduate degree programs, thereby making us all susceptible to minimizing its severity when we speak about America in conversations regarding politics at work and elsewhere.

CHAPTER 22

Kevin McCarthy's Failed Bids for House Speaker Expose the Ironies of Ideological Diversity and Homogeneity in the GOP

For the first time in a century, members of the United States House of Representatives didn't elect a Speaker in its first round of voting. Kevin McCarthy (R-CA) failed in 10 additional rounds over 3 days to secure the 218 votes needed for him to become Speaker. A month prior, New York Democrat Hakeem Jeffries, a Black man, was elected leader of the House Democrats, succeeding outgoing House Speaker Nancy Pelosi (D-CA).[1] It's unsurprising that colleagues from Jeffries's party placed his name into nomination for House Speaker in the 118th Congress. They all voted for him in every round but knew he wouldn't win because House Republicans held a 222 to 212 majority.

In the first round of voting, Texas Republican Chip Roy was the only member to cast a vote for Byron Donalds (R-FL), a Black man whose name hadn't been officially placed on the ballot.[2] The next day, on the fourth ballot, Roy formally nominated Donalds for Speaker and noted, "for the first time in history, there have been two Black Americans placed into the nomination for Speaker of the House." His Republican and Democratic colleagues rose for a thunderous standing ovation. Roy then followed up with a conveniently overutilized Martin Luther King Jr. quote: "We do not seek to judge people by the color of their skin, but by the content of their character."

Moments later, 20 Republicans voted for Donalds, thereby delivering McCarthy his fourth defeat. Just a few minutes after that, Ohio Republican Warren Davidson nominated McCarthy, California Democrat Pete Aguilar nominated Jeffries, and Colorado Republican Lauren Boebert nominated Donalds. The outcome didn't change. Again, exactly 20 Republicans voted for Donalds. Shortly thereafter, Florida Republican Kat Cammack nominated McCarthy for the sixth ballot. He lost, again. The House adjourned and tried five additional times the next day. McCarthy failed on all 11 ballots. In his passionate advocacy for Donalds in the sixth round, Pennsylvania Republican Scott Perry reminded his colleagues that Frederick Douglass also was a Black man and a Republican. This garnered no additional votes for Donalds.

Diversity offers a fascinating, paradoxical explanation for the defeats McCarthy suffered in his bid to become Speaker. In November 2022, New York voters elected George Santos, a Republican, to serve in the House. Multiple media outlets subsequently uncovered numerous lies Santos told in his bios, tweets, speeches, and interviews.[3] Assuming he isn't lying about his sexual orientation, Santos is the first openly gay, nonincumbent Republican candidate to win a congressional election.[4] Hence, he added diversity to the House Republicans.

In comparison to the Democratic Party, the GOP has long lacked both racial and gender diversity. In the 117th Congress, only 27% of women in the House were Republicans, according to a December 2022 Congressional Research Service report.[5] Republicans were just 2 of the 56 Black, 13 of the 45 Latino, and 3 of the 19 Asian American and Pacific Islander House members. Half of the 6 Native American House members were Republicans.

White members comprise approximately 70% of the House; their representation among Republicans is even larger. Given its lack of racial diversity and the underrepresentation of women, it would seem that the GOP would more easily reach consensus. There are at least two explanations for why, in 11 rounds of voting, a group mostly comprised of white heterosexual men refused to cast their votes for McCarthy, another white heterosexual man.

On its website and in on-air broadcasts, CNN highlighted what it called "Five Families" inside the House GOP.[6] Accordingly, they are the Freedom Caucus, chaired by Perry; the Republican Study Committee, chaired by Oklahoma Rep. Kevin Hern; the Main Street Caucus, chaired by South Dakota Rep. Dusty Johnson; the Problem Solvers, cochaired by Pennsylvania Rep. Brian Fitzpatrick; and the GOP Governance Group, chaired by Ohio Rep. David Joyce.

Even though each leader of these so-called families is a white man, the existence of five (or more) cliques in the Republican Party showcases a particular brand of diversity. *Forbes* contributor Carrie Lukas wrote an article in 2019 titled "One Type of Diversity Never Seems to Matter."[7] She was referring to what's called ideological diversity. Presumably, GOP members think it's good that not all members feel the exact same way about the leadership of their party.

Compelling empirical evidence of the organizational benefits of diversity are presented in a 2020 McKinsey report.[8] The business case for diversity has also been established in hundreds of other studies over the past few decades. One thing, though, that researchers, executives, and employees across levels and industries have made clear is that diversity complicates workplace interactions. Reaching consensus is easier when there's homogeneity; there's less conflict over which direction to take an organization and over which ideas are worth pursuing.

Ironically, the political party that has considerably fewer women, people of color, and LGBTQ+ members than does its opponent issued a historic 11-time defeat to a white heterosexual man. It therefore seems that the ideological diversity that conservatives often champion in lieu of compositional diversity has brought complication to the Republican Party and conflict to the House floor. Notwithstanding that fact, diversity in all its forms adds value to organizations and political parties alike.

MARIESSA'S PRODUCTIVE DISAGREEMENT

Today more than ever, ideological diversity seems to be a significant point of contention evident from the tension within the Republican Party and their lack of support for Kevin McCarthy as he was seeking to become Speaker of the House. When a person of color identifies with opposing views from their in-group, this tension can become a valid reason to be uninvited from the proverbial "cookout." Just as people of color are not a monolith who share similar views, nor are Republicans.

The article highlights the lack of diversity in the GOP and the overrepresentation of white heterosexual men, apparent by viewing the Congress floor. I postulate that the nuance in ideological differences is embedded within the "Five Families of the House GOP" and a lack of respectful political discourse throughout our country. The Five Families may have conservative political agendas potentially misaligned with McCarthy's, resulting in the lack of votes in his favor and subsequent losses. As McCarthy is from California, a historically liberal state, one might question whether any significant ideological differences are discernable between a Republican from a liberal state versus conservative state. Could this breed mistrust within the party? Is McCarthy not "Republican enough" to be accepted and worthy of votes?

Carrie Lukas's article argues, "Cultural leaders today make sure to feature people with a variety of backgrounds and life experiences, but somehow never manage to consider political or ideological diversity . . . our culture has become more conformist in depicting one ideology as good and the other as not."[9] Happening on both sides of the aisle, as progressivism intensifies, the more conservative the right becomes. Both groups become inevitably more excluded and ostracized from the other.

Additionally, the saying "the squeaky wheel gets the oil" explains why we only hear the most extreme voices dominating each party. An inability to be heard or fear of judgment could motivate people toward a conservative social media platform like Truth Social. A subset of conservatives holding extreme views may feel safer and validated on Truth Social in contrast to Instagram, a more left-leaning platform. A key question remains: Is there space in mainstream media for respectful political debate between parties without resorting to blatant lies and personal attacks? The current environment of mockery and bullying of government officials against each other and the citizens they represent leaves our country divisive and dangerous.

From social media to Congress, a broader range of thoughts and opinions must be represented to accurately reflect the diverse views of the American people.

A conscious effort to think outside of oneself and engage with an opposing perspective without hostility is required for our ideal of having a country representative of all people. Until ideological diversity in both parties is valued alongside our broader definition of diversity, equity, and inclusion, we are doing a disservice to those with differing opinions, ourselves, and our country.

PRODUCTIVE RESPONSE FROM MARIESSA'S PROFESSOR

In response to what Rachael (another former student of mine) wrote, I indicated the following in Chapter 21 of this book: "I think it's important to not paint all conservatives with the same broad brush." Mariessa reinforced this stance by pointing out that even though the GOP is one political party, there's tremendous diversity within it. I suppose it would be somehow unfair of me to prioritize certain kinds of diversity (gender, race, socioeconomic origins, sexual orientation, etc.) over other aspects of difference that's reflected in the House GOP's so-called "Five Families." The response from Mariessa also compels me to disclose the frustration I feel when viewpoint diversity is used to diminish the kinds of diversity about which I care most. This is indeed a paradox, I acknowledge. Ultimately, I want the leaders we elect to public service to be more reflective of Americans in every way that makes our nation diverse. I don't want ideological diversity to prevail at the exclusion or minimization of everything else. To be sure, I very much value a range of viewpoints. As indicated in the preface of this book, ideological echo chambers, especially in my classrooms, are undesirable (in fact, unacceptable) to me. But I also wouldn't find teaching courses that are homogeneous in many other ways as fulfilling as the multidimensionally diverse learning environments we have at USC.

CHAPTER 23

If George Santos Were Black, There'd Be Harsher Consequences for the Congressman's Lies

George Santos, a New York Republican, was elected to the U.S. House of Representatives in November 2022. Several inconsistencies in Santos's resumé were exposed in a *New York Times* article published weeks after the election.[1] Multiple media outlets subsequently revealed additional fabrications in his website bio, social media posts, and claims he'd made in campaign speeches and interviews. Constitutionally, it seemed nothing could be done to stop Santos from being sworn into Congress. In the 1969 *Powell v. McCormack* U.S. Supreme Court case, justices ruled that the House cannot refuse to seat a candidate whom voters in that person's state have duly elected.[2] It would require a two-thirds House vote to remove an elected member, and expulsion could only occur after that person has been officially seated and an investigation has been conducted. Republican Congressman-elect Nick LaLota, a Navy veteran who's also from New York, wrote this in a statement he shared via Twitter: "I believe a full investigation by the House Ethics Committee and, if necessary, law enforcement, is required."[3] It took the Republican-majority House nearly a year to expel Santos.

The same year Santos was elected, the GOP tokenized Herschel Walker, a former Heisman Trophy winner and pro football athlete who had no political experience, as it attempted to secure Georgia's coveted seat in the U.S. Senate.[4] Weeks before the election, two women accused Walker of pressuring them to have abortions.[5] He denied those allegations. It wasn't enough to compel pro-life conservatives to withdraw their support of Walker. But what if Walker or any other Black man had lied as elaborately as Santos did about his credentials?

If Santos were a Black man, he wouldn't have gotten elected. He would've been more thoroughly vetted prior to being allowed to run for the seat to represent New York's 3rd Congressional District. If not prior to the primary, his lies definitely would've come out before the November 2022 general election. Even if he somehow managed to escape an "October Surprise" (a bombshell that has high potential of tanking a political campaign), someone surely would've come forward with facts about him before a majority of misinformed New York residents entered voting booths to cast their ballots for a fraud.

Even if, under the unlikeliest of circumstances, a lying Black political candidate miraculously got elected to Congress and then his fibs were revealed 4–6 weeks later, the opponent he beat or someone else would've found some way to get the results immediately overturned in the courts. Maybe even the voters themselves would've sued, as they were duped into voting for a candidate who presented fake credentials and made-up stories. Plans to swear him into a congressional office on January 3 wouldn't proceed.

Washington Post journalist Aaron Blake analyzed and aggregated several Santos falsehoods.[6] Accordingly, Santos lied about having earned a bachelor's degree from Baruch College and a law degree from NYU; he hasn't graduated from any higher education institution. He also lied about working for Goldman Sachs and Citigroup. Santos reported that he and his family own 13 homes they lease as rental properties; neither his nor any immediate family members' names showed up in public housing records. In an interview on *Police Off the Record*, a YouTube show hosted by two former NYPD officers, Santos claimed that he attended Horace Mann, an expensive private school in the Bronx, but had to drop out 4 months before graduation because his family couldn't afford the tuition.[7] Horace Mann's records don't show that he was ever a student there.

Santos tweeted, "It was an honor to address fellow members of the Jewish community," along with photos of himself and two rabbis.[8] The keyword in this tweet is "fellow." Santos had previously and repeatedly claimed to be a "proud American Jew" and said his grandparents were Holocaust survivors. Those were lies. He later explained that he's "*Jew-ish*," because his mother's family is from a Jewish "background."[9] Santos later admitted that he's Catholic. Federal prosecutors investigated Santos's finances because the math about more than $700,000 in contributions to his congressional campaign didn't add up; it also didn't match his tax records.[10] "The numerous fabrications and inconsistencies associated with Santos are nothing short of stunning," Anne Donnelly, a Republican who serves as the Nassau County district attorney, said in a statement. "No one is above the law and if a crime was committed in this county, we will prosecute it."[11]

Speaking of a crime, Blake reports that Santos was allegedly charged with signing someone else's name to stolen checks he wrote in Brazil in 2008 but wasn't convicted because he never showed up in court. Of course, Santos made no mention of having a criminal history on another continent to New York voters. "I made a mistake, and I think humans are flawed and we all make mistakes," Santos declared in a Fox News interview with former congresswoman Tulsi Gabbard (D-Hawaii).[12] "In order to move past this and move forward and be an effective member of Congress, I have to face my mistakes."

Here's the thing: Black men don't get away with "mistakes" of this magnitude. The racialized double standard starts early. Research shows that Black boys are suspended and expelled from K–12 schools far more frequently than are white boys whose misbehaviors are the same or worse. In our study of 3,022 public school districts across 13 Southern states, Dr. Edward J. Smith and I found that

Black boys were about 12% of students enrolled, yet they comprised 47% of boys who were suspended and 44% of boys who were expelled.[13]

"Consequence inequities" (a new term I'm debuting here) follow boys from school to work. Across industries, many Black men who participate in my workplace climate studies frequently talk about how there's a different standard for them. It isn't just a feeling. Most have examples of inappropriateness or policy violations their white male coworkers got away with in the workplace, yet they and other Black male professionals were penalized or fired for doing the same or less egregious versions thereof. This racialized double standard impacts Black men's careers across all levels, from custodial workers to C-suite executives to the American presidency.

Barack Obama would've been impeached and swiftly evicted from the White House had he behaved like Donald Trump. In fact, Obama never would've been elected had an audio recording emerged of him bragging about sexually assaulting women, or if he said even a fraction of the outrageously offensive things Trump said while campaigning for the presidency. The overwhelming majority of Americans who participated in the January 6 attack on the U.S. Capitol were white men. Imagine if they'd been Black. Undoubtedly, they would've been swiftly gunned down at the scene of the crime. Or at very least, they would've been met with the same force they encountered when Trump walked through a mostly peaceful protest near the White House following the murder of George Floyd.[14]

Because he's lied so much, there really is no telling how Santos identifies racially or ethnically at this point. Perhaps Brazilian American, who knows? There's a chance that many voters read Santos as white; he therefore benefits from white privilege and its corresponding protections. Few, if any, mistook him to be a Black man. If they had, there's no way Santos would've gotten away with so many lies prior to or after his election to Congress.

MATHEW'S PRODUCTIVE DISAGREEMENT

While I in no way would argue against the facts outlined in this article that Black people are unfairly and unjustly punished disproportionately to white people, I am not convinced that if George Santos were Black the outcome of the New York 3rd Congressional District election would have turned out differently. I am skeptical of the U.S. government's standards as a whole and believe that a political party's agenda and need for control outweigh the improvement of the lives of the American people, at least in the eyes of our elected officials.

I cannot begin to explain how George Santos was able to compound lie after lie without getting caught prior to his election, and while it is highly likely that if he were Black, he would have faced additional scrutiny, I can point to at least one other non-Black politician this past election cycle who was caught for embellishing his background after becoming the lead Republican candidate for his district but who eventually lost significantly to his Democratic counterpart. That individual is J. R. Majewski, who campaigned for an Ohio congressional seat, and who I assume identifies as a white male. Majewski lied about the extent of his service in the military, exaggerating about where he served and fabricating many stories about the conditions he endured.[15] Again, unlike Santos, Majewski was caught before the election.

In my opinion, what happened to George Santos, a minority, has nothing to do with race, but with the vetting process of each political party of its candidates. I think it's a stretch to say that George Santos benefited from white privilege. The commonality between the Santos and Majewski investigations is that both were done independently by national news reporters. There appears to be no accountability from political leaders on either side for who can represent their parties and what information about their candidates they choose to disclose to the public, nor are there serious repercussions when candidates or elected officials get caught for their controversies.

The political system is especially good at forgiving and forgetting when it comes to elected officials. Over the past several decades, elected officials have been accused of lying about their backgrounds, sexual misconduct, racism, and various crimes. And despite getting caught, many of those officials remain in office today regardless of race. Two of those individuals sit in arguably the most important positions in the country as members of the Supreme Court. Those two individuals are Brett Kavanaugh, a white man, and Clarence Thomas, a Black man. There are even more of these examples within the Senate and the House. In my opinion, this shows that there is not inequitable punishment between political figures based on race but a broken political system that cares more about party control than the integrity of those who represent the people of this country.

Based on this and history, I think it is unfair to say, for example, that Barack Obama would have been impeached and removed from the White House had he behaved like Donald Trump. There is no precedence to support this since no president has ever been removed from office, and Donald Trump was in fact impeached twice. History shows that despite the extent of a crime and regardless of race, political figures rarely are removed from office. In total, 20 members of Congress have been expelled from office, the last of which occurred in 2002.[16] I will not argue with the fact that Black people receive harsher punishments than white people across school and work in general, and that it's completely unacceptable, but I am not sure how well that translates to politics just based on a lack of evidence for that specific sector. In this case, the biggest issue to me is that the people we choose to represent us, regardless of race, can continue to operate in a position of power despite evidence of unethical and sometimes illegal behavior.

PRODUCTIVE RESPONSE FROM MATHEW'S PROFESSOR

I often push my students to provide evidence to substantiate their claims. Mathew's critique fairly pushes me to do the same. I was theorizing and speculating based on racialized and gendered "consequence inequities" in other contexts. But Mathew is right: It's seemingly different in politics. I furnished no evidence of Black candidates or elected officials being swiftly or more harshly punished for engaging in the same behaviors as their white counterparts. Journalistic speed explains my negligence. I remember writing this article—it was during the time when all the news outlets were abuzz about Santos. The unfortunate reality of traditional press outlets like *Forbes* is that the news cycle moves fast; stories quickly become old news. Had I more time, I would've done a thorough search of peer-reviewed journals to see if studies had been published about consequence inequities in American politics. I may have even contacted a few of my friends and colleagues who teach in political science departments at universities across the country. One clear takeaway from Mathew's response is that time and data strengthen claims about racial inequities. I'm still convinced, though, that Black insurrectionists would've been treated very differently on January 6, 2021. Even though overtaking the U.S. Capitol isn't something that had occurred in my lifetime, there've been far too many other tragic instances of law enforcement officers killing Black Americans for actions that were considerably less violent than what occurred in our nation's capital on January 6.

CHAPTER 24

How Karen Bass Beat a Billionaire to Become First Woman and Second Black L.A. Mayor

Los Angeles voters elected six-term Democratic congresswoman Karen Bass to serve as the city's 43rd mayor. She was the first woman and only the second Black person to lead our nation's second-largest city. The mayoral race was called in Bass's favor 1 full week after election day. Bass received 53% of votes, defeating billionaire real estate developer Rick Caruso. *The Los Angeles Times* estimates that Caruso spent more than $100 million on his campaign, significantly more than Bass.[1] Why didn't outspending Bass work for him? I'll leave it to my faculty colleagues here in the University of Southern California political science department to do the research and present evidence-based explanations. But in the meantime, I'll offer several possibilities.

Both candidates crafted plans to fix the city's homelessness and unaffordable housing crises,[2] as well as its crime problems. Some voters inevitably liked Bass's plans better than Caruso's. Hiring 1,500 additional LAPD officers was one thing Caruso promised during a time that Americans were fiercely calling for funds to be redirected from law enforcement to multisector efforts that will address the larger systemic forces that lead to crime and violence.[3] Some voters said no thanks to putting more cops on the city's predominantly people of color streets. It could also be that voters were annoyed by the avalanche of Caruso brochures that flooded their mailboxes just about every day, as well as too many television and radio ads urging them to put their trust in a billionaire. For some, it felt like he was trying to buy the election. Stark campaign wealth inequities might've inspired some to vote for the financially underprivileged, economically more relatable candidate.

Caruso, a longtime Republican, switched his political party just a few days prior to jumping into the mayoral race.[4] It's really hard for a Republican to be voted LA mayor, especially one who'd helped finance the campaigns of numerous GOP candidates and for years publicly opposed abortion. In an interview, Caruso explained that he no longer agreed with the direction in which the Republican Party was going. It's plausible that many voters didn't buy it. They likely thought of him as a conservative conveniently masquerading as a Democrat just to get elected. It also seems that some voters valued Bass's deep political experience over the business background Caruso brought to the race. Bass has served on the House Committee on Foreign Affairs and on the House Judiciary Committee. She also has been chair of the Congressional Black Caucus, founder and cochair of the Congressional Caucus on Foster Youth, and a member of 20 other congressional caucuses.

Before being elected to the United States House of Representatives in 2008, Bass served three terms in the California State Assembly. She was elected Speaker of the Assembly in 2008, making her the first-ever Black woman in U.S. history to serve in that role for any state. Because of her deep political experience, Bass was reportedly on the shortlist of prospects whom Joe Biden seriously considered to be his vice presidential running mate in the 2020 national election.[5] He ultimately chose California senator Kamala Harris. Biden, Harris, and President Barack Obama endorsed Bass in the L.A. mayoral race. Maybe, just maybe two U.S. presidents and the sitting VP wouldn't have endorsed a weak, inexperienced candidate whose track record in Congress failed to impress them. Two-time presidential hopeful and Vermont senator Bernie Sanders endorsed her, too. Perhaps some loyal Democratic voters were more persuaded by Obama, Biden, Harris, and Sanders than they were by Snoop Dogg, Elon Musk, Kim Kardashian, Katy Perry, Gwyneth Paltrow, Chris Pratt, and other celebrities who publicly declared their support for Caruso.[6]

I'll conclude with one additional noteworthy possibility: Some voters thought it was finally time to elect an extraordinarily qualified woman to serve as the city's chief executive officer, and some felt that having just one Black mayor in the 241-year history of L.A. wasn't enough. This mayoral contest occurred in one of our country's most racially and ethnically diverse cities. Diversity is highly valued here. Telemundo journalist Dunia Elvir referred to Caruso as white in a debate she moderated a few weeks before the election.[7] He swiftly corrected her by saying, "I'm Italian . . . that's Latin." Evidently, that wasn't enough to compel some voters to view him as distinguishably different from the overwhelming majority of men who've served as L.A. mayor. Bass's victory is incontestably a huge win for both racial diversity and gender diversity in California's largest city.

NICOLETTE'S PRODUCTIVE DISAGREEMENT

I respectfully disagree with some of the points brought up in Shaun Harper's *Forbes* article. I agree that Karen Bass is well deserving of the position and that she will serve Los Angeles as an exceptional mayor. However, I do not agree with the point made in the article that Rick Caruso was thought of as a "conservative conveniently masquerading as a Democrat just to get elected." I know a countless number of conservative individuals whose political preferences have evolved over the recent past, especially following President Donald Trump's election.

Politicians and political parties preferences change year over year, and it is unfair to state that an individual would change their political preference solely for show. For example, since high school my best friend had always supported the Republican Party. However, after Trump's first presidency and the overturning of *Roe v. Wade*, she has for the past year supported the Democratic Party. I know many people who considered themselves fiscally conservative and socially liberal who may have supported the Republican Party in the past but have made the deliberate switch to supporting the Democratic Party in recent years. For that reason, I believe that Caruso no longer agreed with the Republican Party's stances and made the honest decision to run for L.A. mayor as a Democrat. I also believe he will continue to support the Democratic Party even after his loss. I do not think it is fair to say that someone would make such an important decision solely for the optics.

Another point that I disagree with is that voters valued Bass's deep political experience over Rick Caruso's business background. I argue that many individuals have grown weary of politicians and their inability to give direct, to-the-point, and truthful answers. However, I also believe that most individuals have been severely traumatized by the notion of a businessman entering politics because of Trump's first presidential term. I think the issue with Caruso running for mayor was that people were skeptical of his intentions. I think many people thought that Caruso wanted to become mayor of Los Angeles to gain power to increase his own wealth.

I believe the majority of voters were largely turned off by the fact that Caruso had very wealthy individuals and celebrities endorsing his campaign and assumed he would be a mayor for the rich instead of a mayor that supports all L.A. residents. I personally disagree with people who take that stance, but I understand where their skepticism is coming from. Trump's first presidency was filled with unbelievably inappropriate conduct (something that people from any political party should be able to agree on). I believe that Los Angeles residents were so disgusted and turned off from Trump's term that they did not believe any of Caruso's initiatives during his campaign, which may have been unfair to Caruso.

PRODUCTIVE RESPONSE FROM NICOLETTE'S PROFESSOR

Noteworthy is that Nicolette's response began with, "I respectfully disagree with some of the points." It's a great demonstration of how it's okay to disagree with certain aspects of an argument without engaging in wholesale rejections of people's perspectives about politics and other contested issues. I also appreciate Nicolette's acknowledgment of how some candidates' political stances can evolve over time. Such shifts may even necessitate changing political parties, which very well could have been the case with Caruso. Nicolette also highlighted what could be characterized as the "Trump effect" in this particular mayoral race. According to Fox News, "'What do we know about Rick Caruso?' asked the narrator in a

Bass campaign commercial. 'We know he was a registered Republican for decades and not just any kind of Republican. Caruso served as a senior adviser to President Trump.'"[8] Perhaps it wasn't the mere switching of political parties that ignited skepticism and resistance among some L.A. voters, but instead Caruso's prior association with Trump and the fact that both of them are wealthy businessmen. Lastly, I appreciate Nicolette highlighting how some policy priorities (e.g., fiscal conservatism) can indeed coexist alongside some other values (e.g., inclusion and social justice) within the same voter or political candidate.

CHAPTER 25

Brittney Griner, Paul Whelan, or Nothing? Why the Biden Administration Chose the Black Woman

With her wife Cherelle by his side, President Joe Biden announced that six-time WNBA All-Star Brittney Griner had just been released from a Russian penal colony.[1] Griner was serving a 9-year prison sentence for carrying less than 0.7 grams of cannabis oil through a Russian airport in February 2022. Not everyone is thrilled that the Biden administration prioritized the release of a Black American woman who earned two Olympic gold medals for Team USA.

Paul Whelan, a U.S. Marine Corps veteran who completed tours of duty in Iraq, was serving a 16-year prison sentence in Russia for espionage when Griner was jailed. During his visit there for a wedding in 2018, Whelan was given a flash drive that contained classified information, and was subsequently deemed guilty of spying on the Russian government. He spent 6 years behind bars. Some critics are asking why Griner instead of Whelan. If there is a line, how did a Black lesbian basketball star who was imprisoned just under 10 months get to skip ahead of the former active-duty reservist who generously served our country for many years?

"We never forgot about Brittney, we've not forgotten about Paul Whelan, who has been unjustly detained in Russia for years," Biden stated in a White House briefing on the day Griner was released. "This was not a choice of which American to bring home." Secretary of State Antony Blinken reiterated the same message in his remarks to the press later that same day.[2] "Despite our ceaseless efforts, the Russian government has not yet been willing to end [Whelan's] wrongful detention," Blinken contended. "Russia has continued to see Paul's case through the lens of sham espionage charges, and they are treating him differently than they treated Brittney Griner."

"We made every possible offer available to us to secure Paul's release," White House Press Secretary Karine Jean-Pierre insisted in her briefing.[3] "Of course, we would have preferred to see them both released . . . but we did not want to lose the opportunity before us to secure the release of one of them. And so that was the choice: one or none, and not which one." Despite Biden, Blinken, and Jean-Pierre all saying that releasing Whelan was not an option the Russians extended them and that their choice was to either free Griner or no American at all, critics swiftly began forcing an either/or choice. Opponents also argued that Biden negotiated a bad deal. Viktor Bout (who is known as the "Merchant of Death") had served nearly half of a 25-year prison sentence in the United States for selling weapons to Al Qaeda, the Taliban, and Rwandan murderers. The Biden administration swapped Bout for Griner. The not-so-subtle subtext of the critics' responses is that Bout was too valuable a trade to waste on a WNBA player.

Republican lawmakers were among those who criticized the swap.[4] In a social media post, former President Donald Trump called the trade a "stupid and unpatriotic embarrassment for the USA." Congresswoman Marjorie Taylor Greene (R-GA) suggested it was a reason to impeach Biden. Democratic strategist and CNN political contributor James Carville believes these negative responses were largely about Griner's race and sexual orientation. "Does anyone in their right mind think that if Brittney was a blonde Chi Omega from SMU that the reaction would've been the same?" he asked in a CNN interview. "Of course not," Carville insisted.

In a Fox News interview, retired Marine Lt. Colonel Stuart Scheller told host Tucker Carlson, "We released an arms dealer that starts wars in places that Marines and service members respond to. And right now, we place the priority of the famous basketball player over the Marine." Scheller and Carlson seemed unwilling to believe what the Biden administration officials said their options were. They and others erroneously claimed that Whelan was an option on the table and that Griner didn't deserve to be the choice.

Even if what White House officials said wasn't true (though I'm convinced they weren't lying), some other things are absolutely irrefutable. Here's one: More than 90% of Black women voted for Biden in the 2020 presidential election. Hence, if there was in fact a choice to make, would it have been entirely wrong of the president to demonstrate loyalty to an often taken-for-granted group who was the most loyal to him?

Also, in another prisoner swap with Russia, the Biden administration brought home Trevor Reed, an American citizen and Marine veteran who was detained for 3 years.[5] Reed was serving a 9-year sentence for allegedly attacking a Russian police officer. Griner was sentenced to the same amount of time for being in possession of, at most, a misdemeanor quantity of cannabis oil. Reed was released and reunited with his family in the United States 8 months ago. If there was just one choice between Griner and Whelan, why couldn't it have been a Black woman this time? It was Reed last time.

But what about those who protected the United States through their military service? Shouldn't they be higher priority than a Black woman who plays on a professional basketball team? These two questions could be met with this important one: What about Black women who bravely serve in the U.S. military but are systematically denied opportunities for promotion, who aren't believed when they report their experiences with sexual harassment and sexual assault, who are forced to hide or lie about their sexual orientations if they're queer, and whose contributions are routinely overshadowed by those of their white male counterparts? Griner hasn't served in the U.S. military, but perhaps putting her ahead of a man who has is one act of restorative justice on behalf of all those Black women servicemembers who've been mistreated over time.

Lastly, as I noted in another *Forbes* article about Griner's release, across the globe, there was a 17% increase in the number of incarcerated women between 2010 and 2020.[6] Here in the United States, Black women's representation in prisons exceeds that of white women by more than twice. Undoing the systemic forces that lead to mass incarceration and the overrepresentation of imprisoned Black American women requires a robust, complex set of policy corrections that extend far beyond one president's authority. Had he a choice, perhaps Biden would've decided to do the thing that he alone had the power to do in December 2022: get one wrongly detained Black woman released from an overseas penal colony.

It's worth noting one final time that Biden and other top officials on his team maintain there was no choice to make between Griner and Whelan. But even if there was, the president certainly had several compelling justifications for bringing the Black American woman home. To argue that the Biden administration shouldn't have accepted any deal from the Russians that didn't include both Griner and Whelan—meaning they should've terminated negotiations and walked away with no deal—strongly conveys disregard for a Black woman's life and freedom. It says she isn't enough. Griner is enough. Black women are enough. Fortunately, Biden refused the "or nothing" option.

Jean-Pierre assured reporters that the White House will continue to pursue every option and opportunity to get Whelan freed. "The U.S. government continues to encourage the Russian government through every—every contact with them, through every channel to secure his release," she maintained. For all the right reasons, a wrongly imprisoned Black American lesbian was set free this time. It certainly beats the alternative, which was nothing.

TODD'S PRODUCTIVE DISAGREEMENT

You concluded the article writing, "for all the right reasons a wrongly imprisoned Black American lesbian was set free this time." I don't believe that her release was done for the right reasons, although I do strongly believe that Griner should've been released much sooner. If the reasons were in fact right, it would not have taken almost 10 months. The right reasons for Griner's release are that she committed a totally victimless crime and that Russia was utilizing her celebrity status as a bargaining chip around the Russia–Ukraine war and U.S.–Russia relations.

Another reason she should've been released is that female basketball stars should not have to work two jobs and play basketball in Russia in the first place, but they do, because the WNBA does not pay them their worth. I believe Griner was released because of the mounting pressure that came from the WNBA and its stars, in addition to pressure from the men's basketball league, the NBA, which owns half of the WNBA. This pressure also came from well-known white people, like NBA commissioner Adam Silver and WNBA star Breanna Stewart.

It should be noted that the WNBA also received its first-ever funding round in 2022, valuing the league at $1 billion. There were a lot of rich, liberal, white people campaigning for Griner's release. If she didn't play basketball at a high level, she would likely still be in a Russian cell, which is wrong. While I wish Griner came home for the right reasons, I believe her celebrity status, rich white people campaigning for her release, and Biden's desire for votes in the next election led to her release.

Another point you made that I'd like to add more nuance to is that since 90% of Black women voted for Biden in the 2020 election, there's nothing wrong with demonstrating loyalty to those who are loyal to him. I'm happy Biden ultimately negotiated her release, but I'm weary of this reasoning. When the situation is reversed and a president is supported by mostly white men, I do think there is something wrong with showing extra support to those constituents who supported that elected official.

I wholeheartedly agree that "undoing the systemic forces that lead to mass incarceration and the overrepresentation of imprisoned Black American women requires a robust, complex set of policy corrections." While Biden may not have the power to make all those corrections, I would not want any U.S. president to free one single famous Black person instead of pursuing those policy corrections that have a wider impact. For instance, while Trump got praise for helping exonerate A$AP Rocky, many Americans have deemed him racist for a host of other documented actions.

I loved your point about how a Black lesbian woman in the military wouldn't have had the same opportunities as Whelan did and would have a tougher time reaching his status. I agree that those Republicans comparing them "strongly conveys disregard for a Black woman's life and freedom." Overall, I agree with your viewpoint that it is very positive she was released, I just respectfully disagree about it being done for the right reasons and that it symbolizes progress.

PRODUCTIVE RESPONSE FROM TODD'S PROFESSOR

I couldn't agree more with Todd's excellent point about the problematic privileging of donors and loyal voters. Every 4 years, we elect someone to be the president of all Americans, not just those who supported them during the campaign. When I wrote this article, I felt that our country (including the Democratic Party) owes a tremendous debt to Black women. I still feel this way. Notwithstanding that fact, I would be outraged if Donald Trump privileged wealthy white men above all others during his second presidency. Oh wait, will he not? It might not be in a prisoner swap with some other nation, but could it occur in myriad other ways?

Would doing so be massively inconsistent with how lots of other U.S. presidents over centuries demonstrated who was most important to them and their administrations? Todd and I are on the same page about how privileging loyalists is wrong. I just don't think it should be deemed situationally inappropriate and most unacceptable when it pertains to a Democratic president deciding to show gratitude to Black American women.

Part IV

PRODUCTIVE DISAGREEMENTS ABOUT ENTERTAINMENT AND SPORTS

CHAPTER 26

Beyoncé Wins the Most Grammy Awards, Becomes the Actual GOAT

Beyoncé made history at the 65th annual Grammy Awards. The singer, songwriter, and actor walked away with four awards for *Renaissance*, the deliciously inclusive, genre-blending dance album she released in July 2022.[1] She's earned more of the Recording Academy's highly coveted golden trophies than any other musician. The late music conductor Georg Solti previously held the record with 31 wins. This isn't the first time Beyoncé snatched a Grammy record. Two years prior, she became the woman with the most wins.

"Alien Superstar," the third track on *Renaissance*, includes these lyrics: "I'm one of one. I'm number one. I'm the only one." The Recording Academy has corroborated these claims. Technically, Beyoncé really is one of one as it pertains to the most Grammy wins. There isn't a tie or any declaration-weakening caveat. She's the only one.

In a short but emotional acceptance speech for one of the awards she received at the 2023 Grammy ceremony in Los Angeles, Beyoncé thanked her late Uncle Jonny, a gay man whom she referred to as "Godmother" in the *Renaissance* credits. His life and love of dance inspired many tracks on the album and its overall vibe. She also saluted in the Grammy acceptance speech a community of which her uncle was part, one of the most loyal sectors of the BeyHive (as her fans call themselves, including me). "I would like to thank the queer community for your love, for inventing the genre. God bless you."

Of the 88 nominations Queen Bey earned over 22 years, here's a list of her 32 career wins:

- 2023—Best Dance/Electric Recording; Best Dance/Electronic Music Album; Best Traditional R&B Performance; and Best R&B Song
- 2021—Best R&B Performance: "Black Parade"; Best Rap Performance: "Savage" (with Megan Thee Stallion); Best Rap Song: "Savage" (with Megan Thee Stallion); and Best Music Video: "Brown Skin Girl"
- 2020—Best Music Film: *Homecoming*
- 2019—Best Urban Contemporary Album: *Everything Is Love*
- 2017—Best Urban Contemporary Album: *Lemonade*; Best Music Video: *Formation*

- 2015—Best R&B Performance: "Drunk in Love" (with Jay Z); Best R&B Song: "Drunk in Love" (with Jay Z); Best Surround Sound Album: "Drunk in Love" (with Jay Z)
- 2013—Best Traditional R&B Performance: "Love on Top"
- 2010—Song of the Year: "Single Ladies"; Best Female Pop Vocal Performance: "Halo"; Best Female R&B Vocal Performance: "Single Ladies"; Best Traditional R&B Vocal Performance: "At Last"; Best R&B Song: "Single Ladies"; Best Contemporary R&B Album: *I Am . . . Sasha Fierce*
- 2007—Best Contemporary R&B Album: "B'Day"
- 2006—Best R&B Performance by a Duo or Group With Vocals: "So Amazing" (with Stevie Wonder)
- 2004—Best Female R&B Vocal Performance: "Dangerously in Love 2"; Best R&B Performance by a Duo or Group With Vocals: "The Closer I Get to You" (with Luther Vandross); Best R&B Song: "Crazy in Love"; Best Contemporary R&B Album: *Dangerously in Love*; Best Rap/Sung Collaboration: "Crazy in Love"
- 2002—Best R&B Performance by a Duo or Group With Vocal: "Survivor" (with Destiny's Child)
- 2001—Best R&B Performance by a Duo or Group With Vocal: "Say My Name" (with Destiny's Child); Best R&B Song: "Say My Name" (with Destiny's Child)

Comedian Trevor Noah hosted the 2023 awards show; he was great. He declared Beyoncé the GOAT, an acronym for Greatest of All Time. With her recent Grammy record-grabbing success, Beyoncé enters another elite club: extraordinarily talented and accomplished Black artists, entertainers, athletes, and influencers who've been deemed the GOAT. Her husband Jay Z has earned membership in this super-exclusive club, alongside Aretha Franklin, Patti LaBelle, Michael Jackson, Prince, Richard Pryor, Whitney Houston, Oprah Winfrey, Michael Jordan, Denzel Washington, Serena Williams, Tiger Woods, LeBron James, and Michelle Obama. And of course, it includes a pair of musical geniuses with whom Beyoncé has collaborated: Luther Vandross and Stevie Wonder.

It's important to note that Black Americans don't haphazardly confer the GOAT status, hence the low number of people who've earned membership. Induction is reserved for only the most exceptional. It's subjective yet exceedingly defensible. Beyoncé undeniably belongs in this stratospheric league. Having earned more Grammy awards than every other musician in history is but one indicator. The incontestable quality, originality, and global reach of her music is another. In "Alien Superstar," Beyoncé says, "I'm the bar." She is.

SYDNEY'S PRODUCTIVE DISAGREEMENT

While I agree with the fact that Beyoncé is one of the most talented musical artists of our time, I disagree with her qualification of the GOAT to be undisputed based on her number of Grammy awards. The fairness of the Grammy awards process has been criticized for years, with some arguing that it is not a fair representation of the best music or artists. Winners are determined by the voting members of the National Academy of Recording Arts and Sciences.

Naturally, as all humans do, these members will have their own biases. Art is subjective and every genre is different, and while electronic dance and classical music are largely defined by composition, rap is focused on lyrics, and pop is more of a mixed bag. It is hard to compare different types of music that are not so comparable. In sports, we can more objectively proclaim winners, leaving little room for interpretation. LeBron James and Michael Jordan are the GOATs in objective metrics, tied directly to their records of points scored or games won.

Similarly, the Grammys are not representative of all music due to this subjective selection process. There are many examples of GOAT status artists that have not been appropriately decorated with Grammy awards. Some include Kendrick Lamar and Drake. Kendrick has received many Grammy nominations but has yet to win many awards despite being considered one of the GOAT rappers in the industry. Drake is in a similar position as Kendrick and is one of the most successful and popular musicians of the decade. Historically, rap has been underrepresented as a genre in the Grammys, largely due to the lack of diversity and bias in the Academy. Historical prejudice against rap is another important consideration when we think of the Grammy-recognized GOAT artists versus those who are applauded in other ways. While Beyoncé is both, it is critical to see the bias within the Grammy Awards that cannot be representative of an artist's status and respectability within the industry.

GOAT status in art should come down to the impact that artists have had in their genres, innovation, and community response to their contributions, not an industry metric that is inherently subjective and largely tied to the capitalistic nature of the entertainment industry. The Grammy Awards are financed by corporate sponsorships, and these financial partners have influence over the awards presented. The Grammys are partially determined by record sales and are market driven—artists that are signed with major labels have commercial appeal. I would rather see Beyoncé's GOAT status tied to her innovative music and raw performance talent and the ability of her music to transcend global boundaries and connect with millions, arguably billions of people.

Beyoncé's GOAT status should factor in not only her musical talent but her profound impact for all women, namely Black women. Her advocacy and activism to lift the Black community by encouraging political activism through voting, utilizing her platform to promote Black Lives Matter, and philanthropic giving through the BeyGOOD initiative that supports organizations working to improve the lives of Black people are all profound. Additionally, Beyoncé has also advocated for more Black representation in media and entertainment. Therefore, her GOAT status is justified not by her Grammys but by the legacy she leads through impact and innovation in the industry.

PRODUCTIVE RESPONSE FROM SYDNEY'S PROFESSOR

It seems that Sydney and I at least agree that Beyoncé is indeed the GOAT. As long as there isn't an attempt to take this indisputably well-deserved status from her, I will concede the point about having the most Grammy awards being an important determinant. I'm a staunch, longtime Beyoncé loyalist. When I'm at one of her concerts, or watching a televised performance of hers, or crushing my fitness goals as her musical brilliance penetrates my eardrums in the gym, I'm not thinking about how many awards she's gotten. When she's nominated for awards but doesn't receive them, her musical prowess and impact are in no way diminished for me. So in other words, Sydney is right. I also very much appreciate her point about voter subjectivity. I've served on dissertation of the year and book of the year award committees for professional associations, as well as on selection panels for other highly coveted honors in my fields. In every instance, highly qualified people have been nominated and recognized. But there also are numerous others who are just as talented whose contributions weren't lauded. This doesn't make their work any less valuable. I teach my students that every one of us (including me) has implicit biases; sometimes, our biases are explicit. I therefore appreciate that Sydney raised the point about the biases that Academy voters bring with them to the annual Grammy selection process. I'm nonetheless thrilled that they've smartly chosen to recognize my favorite artist more times than anyone else.

CHAPTER 27

Megan Thee Stallion Supporters Call Out Misogynoir in Hip-Hop Industry— What It Is and Where Else It Exists

For more than 2 years, it felt like hip-hop superstar and three-time Grammy Award winner Megan Thee Stallion was on trial. She wasn't. A jury recently found rapper Tory Lanez guilty of shooting Megan multiple times in both feet as they left Kylie Jenner's pool party in Los Angeles in 2020.[1] Lanez was convicted of assault with a semiautomatic firearm, carrying a loaded unregistered firearm in a vehicle, and discharge of a firearm with gross negligence. He was sentenced to 10 years in prison.[2]

Nearly 53,000 people signed a Change.org petition calling for the Lanez verdict to be appealed.[3] Misogynoir, a distinctive cocktail of misogyny and racism that's specific to Black women, largely explains why in the court of public opinion the shooting victim has been scrutinized much more severely than has the man who shot her. It also helps explain the status and experiences of Black women across professional industries, including hip-hop.

Weeks after the incident, Megan revealed on Instagram that Lanez was her shooter.[4] She explained in considerable detail what happened the night of the shooting and repeatedly called on Lanez to stop lying about it. The viral video garnered tremendous attention. Numerous fans, domestic violence survivors, and others sympathized with Megan and called for Lanez to be held accountable. However, an alarming number of people on social media, podcasts, and elsewhere accused Megan of lying. Megan subsequently posted a photo of one of her wounded feet to Instagram.[5] Apparently, photographic evidence still wasn't enough for some people, including men in her industry.

In November 2022, rappers Drake and 21 Savage released *Her Loss*, a collaborative music album. In their song "Circo Loco," Drake said, "This bitch lie 'bout gettin shots, but she still a stallion."[6] Many outraged listeners deemed the lyric an obvious and disgusting mockery of Megan.[7] In a tweet, Megan demanded that the rappers stop using her name for clout.[8] She also asked when it became cool to joke about women being shot. In addition, she highlighted how rappers use their platforms to protest other things, "but dog pile on a Black woman when she say one of y'all homeboys abused her."

In many songs, music videos, and media interviews over the course of her career, Megan has proudly expressed her sex positivity. Doubters used this to unfairly discredit her claims about the shooting. Her sexuality was absolutely irrelevant in the Lanez case. Inconsistencies in what she reported to police officers and hospital workers on the night of the assault and later in a *CBS Mornings* interview with Gayle King also intensified the skepticism.[9] In her August 2020 Instagram Live post, Megan explained that she didn't originally tell the truth about Lanez shooting her because she was afraid they both would be arrested for having a firearm in the vehicle they were driving.

Moya Bailey, a professor in the Department of Communication Studies at Northwestern University, coined the term *misogynoir*. It captures the unique intersectionality of racism, sexism, and misogyny that Black women experience. In her 2021 book *Misogynoir Transformed: Black Women's Digital Resistance*,[10] Bailey furnishes numerous examples of how Black women are hypersexualized and misrepresented as unattractive, unhealthy, and deviant.

Expert scholars in women's, gender, and sexuality studies attribute much of the skepticism and online abuse that Megan has experienced to misogynoir. Among them is Treva B. Lindsey, a professor at The Ohio State University and author of the book *America, Goddam: Violence, Black Women, and the Struggle for Justice*.[11] "Since she was shot, Meg contended with misogynoir within the media, in the criminal legal system, and from far too many of her rap industry peers," Lindsey notes.

City University of New York professor Marc Lamont Hill agrees with Lindsey. "Throughout this ordeal, Meg has experienced stunning levels of misogynoir within the hip-hop community," he observes. "From social media posts to rap lyrics, hip-hop artists have responded to her shooting with cruel levels of mockery, dismissiveness, denial, and victim-blaming." Hill says he isn't surprised by the way Megan has been mistreated because "hip-hop culture has consistently demonstrated particular hatred for Black women and girls."

Other scholars have documented the hatred that Hill references, but in very particular ways. Academic analyses and social critiques of hip-hop have focused mostly on song lyrics, music videos, and the sexualization of Black women dancers in men's live hip-hop performances. To a lesser extent, attention has been paid to the terribly lopsided coverage of Black women hip-hop artists on the radio and in various forms of media, as well as gender disparities in the artists whose music DJs play and promoters amplify. Even less focus has been placed on the underrepresentation of Black women leaders and executives on the business side of hip-hop.

The way that many men in her industry have responded to Megan's shooting reveals another aspect of misogynoir in hip-hop: a disregard for Black women no matter how accomplished, talented, and powerful they are. To be sure, no Black woman deserves to experience misogynoir, regardless of how she's positioned in her industry. But the point here is that Megan has achieved more success and mainstream exposure than most other women, men, and genderqueer hip-hop artists over the past 5 years. Notwithstanding that fact, the considerably less well-known Canadian rapper who shot her, a man, has enjoyed a surprisingly strong benefit of the doubt from peers in their industry. Versions of this happen in other professions.

"Misogynoir doesn't start or end with hip-hop; rather, it is a microcosm of a broader white-supremacist society that refuses to see Black women and girls as worthy of love, care, protection, safety, and dignity," Hill argues. "Frankly, nearly every sector of society hates Black women and girls. This hatred is intensified within hip-hop culture, however, because it is such a male-dominated space at every level. As a result, we have a world that rewards hip-hop artists—through money, attention, and awards—for hating Black women and girls."

My research in organizations across industries (including but not limited to entertainment companies) shows that Black women professionals experience misogynoir in numerous ways. In women's employee resource groups (ERGs), it occurs via the erasure of Black members' ideas and cultural interests, disregard for intersectionality in their career acceleration, and minimization of their racialized workplace concerns. Many Black women have told my research team members and me over the years that women's ERGs almost always default to white women's needs and concerns.

Misogynoir also helps explain workplace stratification and positional segregation. In many workplaces, Black women are disproportionately represented in secretarial, food service, custodial, and call center customer service roles. They're seemingly not good enough to occupy mid-level, senior, and executive leadership roles. And when the few of them reach those top positions, they're often silenced and aren't given the same power, authority, and resources as men.

In addition, business leaders reportedly respond less urgently to Black women's reports of gender discrimination, sexual harassment, and racism than they do to white women's. As has been the case with Megan Thee Stallion, a disappointingly high number of leaders and coworkers doubt Black women colleagues who come forth with examples of professional abuse. There are men who have no Black women on teams they lead and others who stifle Black women's careers in myriad ways. These leaders often get rewarded for their success on other metrics that are seemingly more valuable than anything pertaining to Black women.

Because misogynoir is so persistent and pervasive in professional industries, a one-time Black History Month or Women's History Month panel on the topic will do little more than raise consciousness about it and affirm Black women who've experienced it in any workplace. The outcome in Lanez's trial will do far too little, if anything at all, to address the hip-hop industry's deeply entrenched misogynoir problems. Lindsey wants, but unfortunately doesn't anticipate, an immediate ending to the misogynoir against Megan. "Even with a guilty verdict for Tory, she will still be subjected to the wrath of abuse from apologists who refuse to see Black women survivors as worthy of care and protection," she predicts. "The road ahead in an industry that remains rife with misogynoir will not be an easy one, but I hope this verdict gives Meg some peace as she pushes forward in her already stellar career."

The eradication of misogynoir in hip-hop and every other industry first requires acknowledgment of its existence. It demands believing Black women. Ongoing, not one-time interrogations of its root causes and the factors that sustain it are also necessary steps. Restorative justice and monetary investments into the reparation of historical and contemporary harms against Black women professionals are also essential. What does this look like? Leaders must ask Black women in their industries. Surely, those whom misogynoir has affected will have some suggestions about what constitutes justice and equity for them. Executives and other leaders must then act swiftly, seriously, strategically, sustainably, and transparently on the ideas that Black women professionals generously offer them.

WAYNE'S PRODUCTIVE DISAGREEMENT

Megan Thee Stallion's fierce, unapologetic persona and infectious hits like "Captain Hook" propelled her to the top of the rap game. She's even given her "hottie" fans a strong voice, popularizing the catchphrase "real hot girl shit." However, in the aftermath of the shooting incident involving Tory Lanez, she has been subjected to intense scrutiny and skepticism. While it is undeniable that Black women like Megan face a unique form of discrimination known as misogynoir, and Megan has been hypersexualized and misrepresented in specific ways, these issues may not be the sole or primary cause of her skepticism and online abuse.

One factor contributing to the disbelief surrounding Megan's shooting incident is the presence of inconsistencies in her reports to police and hospital workers on the night of the incident, as well as in her subsequent interview with Gayle King. Dissociative amnesia, a condition characterized by the inability to recall important personal information due to a traumatic or stressful event, may have played a role in Megan's case, as trauma survivors frequently have trouble recalling events accurately or at all. However, it is understandable that these inconsistencies may have caused some individuals to harbor doubts.

In addition, Megan's celebrity status and the media attention the incident has received should be taken into account. In high-profile cases such as this one, it is common for individuals to take sides, disagree, and engage in debate regarding the event in question. This is not necessarily the result of misogynoir but rather the natural human tendency to become emotionally invested in and opinionated about a widely reported event.

Finally, while it is true that male rappers such as Drake and 50 Cent have made inappropriate comments about Megan, it is important to note that not everyone who has expressed skepticism about Megan's account of the shooting has done so maliciously or abusively. It is possible to disagree with or question someone's version of events without launching a personal attack or insult. The term for this is "constructive questioning." Since more evidence has emerged, particularly the phone call between Tory and Megan's former friend Kelsey, 50 Cent has apologized to Megan, implying that his scrutiny was based on skepticism due to Megan's inconsistencies rather than misogyny.

Even though the misogynoir framework helps shed light on Megan's experiences, it's possible that other factors are also at play. Some possible logical fallacies can be found in Dr. Harper's evaluation of Megan's experience. Insinuating that the skepticism toward Megan's claims is solely due to the gender of those questioning her, he commits the ad hominem fallacy. In addition, he commits a strawman fallacy by asserting that skeptics were only attempting to discredit Megan by highlighting her sex positivity rather than recognizing other possible explanations for the inconsistencies in her statements, such as the need to protect her reputation. Finally, he uses a false dilemma by suggesting that Megan's contradictory statements were motivated by her fear of the police rather than any other possible explanations.

PRODUCTIVE RESPONSE FROM WAYNE'S PROFESSOR

To be honest, I didn't really like Wayne's response when I first read it. I stepped away, reflected on his viewpoints, and then reread what he wrote two additional times. I found this approach helpful and instructive. Many debates about sexism, racism, homophobia, anti-Semitism, and other -isms and -phobias usually engender strong feelings that compel people to immediately tune out perspectives that are inconsistent with theirs. I still largely disagree with Wayne, but revisiting his words afforded me the opportunity to at least consider factors that I hadn't previously. I had reduced the online abuse of Megan to misogynoir. Wayne fairly points out that other factors were at play for some critics and doubters. I can now see how my interpretation conveyed absolutism. I also appreciate Wayne's acknowledgment of people's rights to engage in constructive questioning. He and I agree on that, especially since "innocent until proven guilty" is supposedly a fundamental principle in our nation's judicial system. Where Wayne and I might disagree, though, is on whether the questioning was constructive. For weeks, I spent far too much time reading social media posts and associated comments about the Megan and Tory situation. So many of them were beyond disgusting. Being so routinely referred to as "this bitch" or "that hoe" didn't qualify for me as constructive questioning and instead were clear expressions of misogynoir.

CHAPTER 28

Kanye West Could Lose Everything If Someone Doesn't Help Him

Musical genius and fashion icon Ye, formerly known as Kanye West, has made several inexcusable anti-Semitic remarks, mocked the Black Lives Matter movement, said untrue things about George Floyd's murder, and harassed his ex-wife and her now ex-boyfriend. Those words and actions hurt and angered lots of people. They also pose serious threats to the survivability of his brand. In October 2022, Hollywood talent agency CAA dropped him from its client roster.[1]

I'm one of Kanye's biggest, most loyal fans. Despite his disgraceful comments and erratic behaviors over the years, I refuse to give up on Ye. The 24-time Grammy Award winner has been public about his bipolar disorder.[2] Fans and others in his industry have understood this and therefore excused some of his behaviors, but many are running out of patience.[3]

My sense is that a lot of people don't think of bipolar disorder as a disability. They should. The Americans with Disabilities Act and the United States Social Security Administration have officially declared it so. I often argue to friends, fleeting fans, and critics that we ought not abandon a person who has this particular disability. Increasingly, fewer people are willing to stand alongside me in support of West. I'm losing credibility. As it pertains to all artists (not just Ye) who behave recklessly, I've stopped trying to convince myself and others to separate the art from the artist, as doing so results in complicity and the sustainability of harm. Ye's self-destruction is public and painful to watch. It's worsening. He's surely on the brink of being canceled. Someone, anyone please help before he does irreparable harm to his legacy and billionaire empire.

To be sure, Kanye and I have never talked or met each other; I've only been in the audience at six of his concerts. I nonetheless care deeply about him as a person, a brilliant artist, and a Black man who has to navigate two racist industries (music and fashion) that systematically disadvantage creatives of color. I must admit that I was so deeply disappointed when I saw photos of him wearing a White Lives Matter t-shirt at Paris Fashion Week.[4] Appearances in his Make America Great Again hat[5] and his bizarre bromance with President Donald Trump,[6] as well as his own failed campaign to become president of the United States,[7] so repeatedly confused other fans and me.

Also quite disturbing was Ye's harassment of ex-wife Kim Kardashian and actor Pete Davidson, her now ex-boyfriend.[8] Tweeting that he'd go "death con 3 on Jewish people" was horrific;[9] so too was the disgustingly inaccurate explanation he offered for George Floyd's death. Floyd's family subsequently sued West for $250 million for remarks he made on the podcast *Drink Champs*.[10] In a live interview with Piers Morgan, Kanye said that President Joe Biden's refusal to accept advice from Elon Musk is "fucking retarded."[11] West then maintained that his mental health issues gave him license to use those words.

Ye recently agreed to purchase Parler, a conservative social media platform that aims to be an "uncancelable" alternative to Twitter.[12] Freedom of speech is incontestably important, yet a platform like Parler will be more harmful than helpful to West. He needs more accountability, not less. Being canceled everywhere but on Parler ultimately won't be good for his long-term mental and emotional wellness, and certainly not for his career.

Kanye's downward spiral is extremely difficult to watch. He deserves empathy and help, but also has to be held accountable for the destruction he's causing in other people's lives and in his industries. He doesn't seem to care. Is it because he *actually* doesn't care, or is it because of his bipolar disorder? I believe it's the latter. Are there really no friends, family members, influential industry colleagues, doctors, therapists, legal team members, trusted financial advisors, business partners, or sponsors left who can persuade Ye to get the help he needs?

I watched the docuseries *jeen-yuhs: A Kanye Trilogy* on Netflix, which received a Primetime Emmy nomination.[13] It was mostly an inspiring, musically exciting reminder of why I fell in love with Kanye. But I also experienced deep sadness as I saw what happened to Ye's mental and emotional health after his mother, his most trusted accountability partner, died. Seeing the erosion of Ye's friendships over time also saddened me. As I suspect was the case for most documentary viewers, I wonder who he has left. I want his friends and colleagues to step in before he totally loses everything and everyone, including himself.

I care foremost about Kanye and the people whom his behaviors harm, but let's get down to business. Too few American billionaires are Black—according to *Forbes*, Ye is one of them.[14] His deal with Adidas is reportedly worth $1.5 billion. Online shoe retailers say Kanye's recent controversies haven't negatively affected sales of his Adidas Yeezy sneaker line,[15] at least not yet. Despite this, the partnership appears to be at risk of collapse. "FUUUUUUCK ADIDAS I AM ADIDAS ADIDAS RAPED AND STOLE MY DESIGNS" is what West posted to Instagram in response to a CNBC article about Adidas reviewing and potentially terminating its relationship with him.[16] If the company drops Ye, he will no longer be a billionaire, *Forbes* reports.[17]

The luxury fashion brand Balenciaga is done with West.[18] Following his anti-Semitic remarks and the Paris Fashion Week white lives matter apparel fiasco, a *Vogue* spokesperson announced that neither the magazine nor its editor in chief Anna Wintour will work with Ye again in the future.[19] While not attributed to any specific incident, his very public breakup with JPMorgan Chase,[20] our nation's biggest bank, is another recent example of a highly publicized dissolution of a business relationship. In September 2022, Ye told the retail apparel giant Gap he was ending their contract for a business partnership that was supposed to last through 2030 because the company failed to fulfill its obligations.[21] In a memo to employees, Gap CEO Mark Breitbard offered a different explanation. He noted that West and the company "share a vision of bringing high-quality, trend-forward, utilitarian design to all people . . . how we work together to deliver this vision is not aligned."[22]

The shakiness of his Adidas deal, combined with the collapse of other business partnerships, is likely to result in significant financial troubles for one of the world's most talented creatives. If he doesn't receive the challenge, support, and treatment that he so obviously needs, I'm afraid his music is going to stop being played on radio stations and elsewhere. Because I love him and recognize that he's not in control of his mental illness, I desperately want someone to help save Kanye from himself. I most certainly would if I could.

ELENA'S PRODUCTIVE DISAGREEMENT

People have long known that Kanye deals with mental illness and willingly used it to excuse his behavior for far too long. In the *Forbes* article, Professor Harper also uses Kanye's mental illness as an excuse for his behavior and calls on his inner circle to help him before he loses his "billionaire empire." Kanye West absolutely needs proper treatment, but it does not excuse his behavior; taking away his platforms in the meantime does not equate to cancellation.

When discussing mental illness in the United States, we have taken to using it to explain or excuse bad and extreme behavior. Commonly, during the 2010s, when discussing gun violence, the conversation evolved into a discussion about mental illness and ascribing these heinous acts to people living with mental illness. In fact, the National Institutes of Health conducted a study in 2015 to determine the correlation between mental illness and gun violence, and ultimately found that "the large majority of people with serious mental illness are never violent."[23] Just as mental illness does not inherently lead to violence, mental illness does not inherently lead to, or excuse, racism.

By continually ascribing Kanye's racist and anti-Semitic statements to his bipolar diagnosis, we do not hold him, as a person, accountable for his actions. If we were to do the same to someone who committed an extreme act of gun violence against another, we would be excusing horrific behavior and willingly enabling these acts without any repercussions. Isha Metzger, professor of clinical psychology at the University of Georgia, told a *Washington Post* reporter, "'Those beliefs [racist statements] are not a symptom of having bipolar disorder."[24] While those living with mental illness should be given grace when it comes to erratic behavior; to continually do so means allowing the behavior to persist, and that is ultimately what causes the greatest damage.

To prevent further damage, to both himself and the communities he targets, Kanye's platforms should be taken from him, at least temporarily. While this may seem like it supports cancel culture, it does the opposite in his case. With Kanye being in the public eye, he likely gets approached regarding any form of drastic behavior he exhibits, so much so that he writes it off. As long as he has followers and people interested in what he says, he will likely not feel compelled to get help or realize the gravity of the situation. By taking away his platforms, it will alert Kanye to how unacceptable his behavior is. The overarching problem with all this, though, is that Kanye can only get the help he needs if he wants it. His inner circle can make the difficult decision to have him hospitalized involuntarily, but that only guarantees his care in the short term. For treatment to have lasting effects, Kanye needs to want help, and it is unclear if he does. By taking away his platforms, it pushes him to realize how drastic measures need to be taken for him to salvage his life and career.

PRODUCTIVE RESPONSE FROM ELENA'S PROFESSOR

What Elena recommended seems to have occurred: Most platforms have been taken away from Kanye West. Hopefully this is as good for his mental wellness as it is for the people whom his words and actions harmed over the years. I appreciate Elena's reliance on perspectives from experts who know much more than I do about mental illness broadly and bipolar disorder specifically. One of the first emails I received in response to my article was from a woman who has bipolar disorder. Consistent with what Elena wrote in her critique, the woman insisted that being bipolar doesn't make people do what Kanye was doing. She is more expert than me on this; thus I believed her. I also believe my Jewish friends who wrote to convey their disappointment in my advocacy of Ye. Given my unshakable commitment to DEI, they said they were surprised that I would excuse his anti-Semitism and instead advocate for the preservation of his career and protection of his wealth. They said this hurt them. I feel strongly that when people we care about (as well as those whom we don't know well) tell us that something we said or did was hurtful to them, we ought to listen with an open heart. In the weeks that followed their honest feedback to me, I published a second *Forbes* article titled "Businesses Ended Their Relationships With Kanye West—I Must, Too."[25] Inasmuch as I love his music, my values and commitments are more important. I often tell my students that it's okay to walk back and sincerely apologize for hurtful statements; I insist that doing so won't weaken their leadership. I attempted to model that for them by writing the second article about Mr. West.

CHAPTER 29

The Color Purple Cinematic Remix Expands Cultural Contribution and Financial Impact

Alice Walker's classic 1982 novel *The Color Purple* inspired the production of a 1985 film with the same title. The movie earned more than $94 million in its initial run. Walker's book and the now 40-year-old film persist as extraordinary works of art, as sacred Black cultural jewels. The story was adapted for a Broadway musical that ran from 2005 to 2008, then again from 2015 to 2017. The 1,360 live shows in New York City grossed nearly $148 million. A 2023 reinterpretation of the movie grossed $18.15 million on opening day, the highest for a Christmas film release since 2009.[1]

With nearly all-Black casts on stages and screens, *The Color Purple* has had an enormously positive financial impact on Black actors. And with Oprah Winfrey as one of the executive producers of the newest version, surely lots of Black crew members were paid for important contributions they made behind the cameras. Also, more than 5 million copies of the original book have been sold, many by bookstores in predominantly Black communities. Walker's classic has therefore long contributed to the financial sustainability of these Black-owned businesses.

On social media during the 2023 holiday season, Black families and friends posted group photos of themselves gathered at movie theaters to see the film. These groups were strikingly and beautifully intergenerational. In many pictures, every group member was wearing purple. Black moviegoers and everyone involved in the new film ensured the brilliance that Walker gifted in her Pulitzer Prize–winning novel more than four decades ago continues to cross generational boundaries and multiplies in reach.

The Color Purple earned a National Book Award in 1983. "Simply put, Alice Walker penned a classic story and Celie is an extraordinarily beautiful character," notes 2022 National Book Award winner Imani Perry, who holds the Henry A. Morss Jr. and Elisabeth W. Morss Professorship at Harvard University. "The context is Jim Crow and poverty, but the story itself is about love, heartbreak, trauma, endurance and ultimately spiritual triumph. So, it resonates so deeply across multiple formats and generations."

I watched the new movie in the same hometown cinema where I saw the original film with my family as a 10-year-old boy. Because I had seen so many group photos on social media, I wasn't surprised by the expansive generational diversity that awaited my family and me at the theater. "We're here to see the movie," one older Black woman exclaimed to the young white box office worker. The customer didn't specify which one, but the employee somehow knew what film she and her two sisters were there to see. Perhaps their identical matching purple outfits offered a clue. After the show, one sister in the group told me it was important for them to watch it together because their mother had recently died. The cinematic cultural experience aided in their healing as sisters.

A different group of older Black women sat directly behind us. They talked nearly the entire movie. Normally, I would've been extremely and justifiably annoyed. In this instance, though, their commentary and real-time analysis added color to what was occurring on screen. Their chatter was culturally familiar, unexpectedly satisfying to me. It was also quite hilarious, even though no one would characterize the film itself as a comedy. A baby in the row in front of ours (who couldn't have been more than 6 months old) slept through most of the film. The space was that intergenerational.

The most noteworthy difference between the 1985 and 2003 versions is the significant increase in song and dance. The latter is parts traditional film, parts musical. The two coexist without discarding elements that made its originator so culturally resonant. "*The Color Purple* has endured because it taps into identities and themes that are culturally specific to the African American experience," explains Gil Robertson IV, cofounder and president of the African American Film Critics Association. "Audiences find the story's emphasis on the value of family, hard work, and faith validating because it mirrors their own worldview. Featuring robust musical numbers, the latest iteration is deeply satisfying because the music effectively punctuates the film's salient moments."

One of those audience members is Sharon Brown, a Georgia native and retired educator who has seen the original film multiple times, gone twice to NYC for the Broadway show, and watched the latest iteration a day after its release. She instantly determined that the newest is her favorite. "The reimagined version of *The Color Purple* harkens back to the rich African American tradition of messaging through song," Brown says. "The powerful, soul-stirring voices delivered in every way. The transmission of moods, feelings, and emotions was accomplished and elicited tears of joy and pain."

Not everyone will agree with Brown's selection. Fierce debates about which version of *The Color Purple* is best are guaranteed to ensue during spades matches, family reunions, holiday gatherings, and post-funeral repasts. These arguments will be good for the culture. For people who haven't yet seen it, I would advise against expecting the latest version to be a mere replica of the original. That would be a mistake. It's more of a remix than a remake. Plus, Oprah Winfrey, Whoopi Goldberg, and Danny Glover (some of the 1985 cast members) aren't in the same generation of actors as Fantasia Barrino, Colman Domingo, Taraji P.

Henson, Danielle Brooks, and Halle Bailey. The generational handoff, plus the musical elements and some storyline amplification differences, makes the two projects not quite right for apples-to-apples juxtapositions.

"Despite being drawn from the same intellectual treasure, both films stand as valuable pieces of Black art in their own right that highlight different aspects of one powerful story," notes Jade Holmes Christian, a Los Angeles-based producer and director. "What I appreciate most about the new version is how it clearly centralizes the triumph, sisterhood, and faith of Black women over their pain. The levity of the music aids in its placement as a universal story of resilience, not just for Black women, but for anyone who has ever survived their own traumas. It's church."

BILL'S PRODUCTIVE DISAGREEMENT

Professor Harper's article rightfully celebrates the film's achievements, particularly noting its financial success and cultural impact among Black communities. However, it glosses over a critical DEI dimension: the scarcity of such large-scale productions helmed by Black artists. This gap could become an oversight and might miss a chance to probe the systemic challenges in the entertainment industry, where achievements like these are outliers, not norms. By spotlighting this rarity, we could engage in a richer critique of the industry's sluggish inclusivity. An in-depth exploration of the systemic hurdles Black artists encounter in realizing large-scale projects could enrich the conversation, emphasizing the need for equitable opportunities and representation.

My focus on the infrequency of major productions led by Black artists stems from a commitment to uncovering systemic inequities in the entertainment industry. This isn't merely about celebrating isolated successes but questioning the rarity of such achievements and identifying the systemic barriers that hinder more stories like *The Color Purple* from reaching a grand scale. It's an invitation to dismantle the obstacles that restrict the visibility and opportunities for Black artists and narratives in mainstream media. Addressing these issues can shift the dialogue from individual success stories to broader systemic reform, advocating for an industry where diversity in storytelling is standard.

If tasked with rewriting Professor Harper's article, I'd highlight *The Color Purple*'s pivotal role in paving the way for more diverse narratives in mainstream media while critiquing the industry's slow march toward inclusivity. This version would ponder the film's success implications for future projects, questioning how the industry might capitalize on this momentum to break down longstanding barriers and cultivate a genuinely inclusive space where diverse voices are celebrated. I'd urge audiences not just to consume these narratives but to engage with the broader societal themes they mirror. Moreover, I'd propose actionable industry steps, like mentorship programs for underrepresented artists and promoting diverse leadership within studios, to encourage broader story support.

These narratives play a crucial role in shaping societal attitudes and fostering understanding among diverse audiences.

In conclusion, it's a great article, and Professor Harper adeptly highlights *The Color Purple*'s immediate cultural and financial impact. A broader approach could deepen the DEI discourse. By confronting systemic challenges and championing inclusivity, we can steer the conversation toward creating a more equitable and diverse entertainment landscape. The different narrative isn't just my perspective, it isn't just about acknowledging progress—it's also about continuing to push for change where it's most needed.

PRODUCTIVE RESPONSE FROM BILL'S PROFESSOR

Bill gets no pushback from me on his rightful acknowledgment of the need for more Black-focused and Black-led movies in Hollywood and everywhere else that filmmaking occurs. I love and tremendously respect Oprah. On the one hand, it's commendable that she leveraged her capital and relationships to bring the 2023 version of *The Color Purple* to theaters. Also praiseworthy is the film's incredible financial success. But on the other hand, these opportunities shouldn't be isolated to Black filmmakers who have achieved Oprah's stratospheric status. Put differently, others deserve the budgets, promotion, and investments from which the most recent version of *The Color Purple* benefited. Oprah makes excellent art—so too do lots of other Black geniuses whose visions don't become fully actualized because of racism in the movie and television industries. Bill calls for mentoring programs for diverse creatives. I like those but only when they're well designed and ultimately poise Black professionals to showcase their work, attract funding, and cultivate relationships with powerful industry insiders who ultimately invest in their current projects and long-term careers. Here are three realities: (1) The industry is extraordinarily white; (2) too few white insiders see the value in Black scripts and Black representation; and (3) not enough executives who aren't Black actually know how to meaningfully invest in Black creatives and their high-potential projects. It's therefore clear to me that those industry insiders need rigorous mentoring, coaching, and guidance.

CHAPTER 30

Viola Davis Makes Compelling Case for Darker Skin Black Women in *The Woman King*

The highly anticipated movie *The Woman King* was released in theaters in September 2022. It stars Emmy, Grammy, Oscar, and Tony Award winner Viola Davis and numerous other darker-skin Black women actors. The film is visually stunning, substantive, action packed, and inspiring. Its significance extends beyond its extraordinary cinematic contribution. This movie is about the Agojie Warriors, an all-women military unit who protected the African kingdom of Dahomey during the 18th and 19th centuries. They forfeited marriage, sex, and motherhood for the defense of their kingdom. Davis's character, General Nanisca, becomes the first woman king and leader of the Agojie fighters. True events that inspired this movie are described in Smithsonian magazine.[1]

In a *CBS Mornings* interview, Davis said that for Black women like her who have darker skin, "from the moment you come out of the womb—it's in language, it's in behavior—that you're ugly, you're more masculine, you're overly strong, you could take pain, your nose is too wide, your lips are too big—[it's] constant, constant, constant."[2] *The Woman King* disrupts not only narrow conceptualizations of Black women's beauty but also their power. It complicates narratives and tropes about strong Black women that are traceable to their enslavement here in the Americas. Relative to lighter-skin enslaved Black women, those with darker skin were usually considered more durable and more capable of hard physical labor. Contemporarily, these perceptions persist in ways that harm, and in some instances kill, Black women.

Studies show that Black women are prescribed fewer pain medicines than are women from other racial and ethnic groups because doctors presume Black people have a higher tolerance for pain.[3] In too many instances, Black women die in childbirth at disproportionately higher rates because of this presumption and other racialized medical errors experienced throughout their pregnancies. According to CDC data, they are more than three times likelier than are white women to die from pregnancy-related causes.[4]

For some, *The Woman King* might reinforce the notion that darker-skin Black women are unbreakably strong because Davis and her costars are impressively fierce fighters. Such an interpretation is too unidimensional. Beyond their strength and resilience, the film at several junctures also shows Black women as vulnerable and nuanced. It humanizes them beyond the warriors they become in combat. It invites viewers to understand Black women more holistically.

The Woman King should ignite difficult conversations about when, where, and how we see darker-skin Black women. It pushes beyond ongoing discussions about colorism within Black communities and the sometimes corresponding tensions between lighter- and darker-skin Black women. Those are important discussions. But less talked about is the underrepresentation of darker-skin Black women in entertainment and other industries, and how they are normally restricted to stereotypical and least-powerful roles.

Across skin tones, Black women often experience a unique convergence of racism and sexism that severely limits how many are allowed to advance to positions of leadership and authority. These limits are exacerbated for darker-skin Black women and are often accompanied by hurtful (at times violent) racial epithets directed toward them on city streets, on college campuses, in workplaces, on dating apps, on social media, in video game chats, and elsewhere. Michelle Obama endured such public violence during her 8 years as First Lady[5]—so too have Venus and Serena Williams throughout their careers as tennis megastars.[6] Viola Davis has as well.

Darker-skin Black women deserve to be seen as multidimensionally as Davis and her costars brilliantly represent them in *The Woman King*. Doing so requires studio execs, corporate leaders, doctors and nurses, and professionals across industries to confront their implicit and explicit acts of racism, sexism, and colorism that systematically disadvantage Black women across the color spectrum, most especially those with darker skin. It demands honest grappling with which Black women are deemed beautiful, strong, deserving of leadership opportunities, and worthy of lifesaving medical care. Also, which Black women routinely get cast and in which roles, which Black women get put in front of clients, and how Black women's experiences within and beyond workplaces vary based on their skin tones are additional questions that are worthy of ongoing exploration.

In the *CBS Mornings* interview, Davis, who is also a producer of *The Woman King*, talked about how hard it was to get studio executives to finance the project. "They don't think that Black women can lead a global box office in a major motion picture action historical drama because when has it ever been done?" She went on to note how other action movies like *Lara Croft: Tomb Raider* weren't tested in front of largely Black audiences, yet films like hers are expected to appeal to white audiences in order to be greenlit. This reality calls for decision-makers in Hollywood as well as those on Wall Street, in Silicon Valley, and everywhere else to recognize and ultimately do something about the inequitable performance expectations that are placed on professionals of color in general, Black women in particular, and darker-skin Black women most especially.

ALLISON JOYCE'S PRODUCTIVE DISAGREEMENT

I want to first thank you for writing this article. As I mentioned in my personal DEI history paper, my experiences with colorism were some of the most memorable moments I had when coming to understand how the world viewed me as a Black woman. I believe the harm that colorism causes for Black women needs to be addressed and called out, so I deeply appreciate the perspective you raise in this article. While I do agree with your overall premise that Viola Davis and the rest of the cast did an incredible job of showing beautiful, Black women as leaders, I would not agree that this film is as compelling as it was intended to be.

While the film aimed to show Black women as multidimensional people who are strong, fierce, beautiful, vulnerable, etc., I think this genre and storyline do not lend themselves well to telling a different story about Black women than the one constantly told by society. I think the film inadvertently reinforces some of the existing stereotypes and tropes about Black women. You mentioned you believe the notion that the film reinforces old notions about Black women is unidimensional. I would respectfully disagree with that point. I think that is a valid interpretation that has various nuances. To truly disrupt stereotypes about Black women, their strength, power, and beauty, it would be important to have media representation in which darker-skinned Black women are portrayed as vulnerable, where they are loved, and where strength and resilience are not the qualities they are most praised for.

While we do see many of the characters in vulnerable moments, we, for the most part, saw that through their trauma experiences such as Nawi being abused by her father and potential spouses, and Nanisca's vulnerability as a reaction to her rapist, and reuniting with the child she bore from him. We see these women as vulnerable humans who are harmed by others and harmed by the societal norms of the time. Showing that Black women experience hurt and emotions because of trauma isn't revelatory, so much as typical and a common theme in media. Instead, it would be novel to see them as vulnerable in situations not centered on their abuse or trauma.

There is a common stereotype that Black women are not soft or feminine, and the fact that the women in the film are seen as worthy because they chose to abstain from love, marriage, sex, etc. plays into that narrative. The warrior depiction further advances the angry, hard, Black woman trope. These women are written as strong enough the fight for a king and kingdom, not soft enough to be loved or have families. Leaning further into that point, I believe the love stories we do see have problematic undertones as well. While Shante, King Ghezo's wife, is a Black woman who is loved, we often see her depicted as jealous of Nanisca, which pits two Black women against each other. The other love story arc we see is between Nawi and Malik. While it was very important to see Malik's biracial identity and homecoming story, his interest and pursuit of Nawi seemed off. It appears she is much younger than him, and her sneaking off to see him was an act of disobedience, which in some ways reinforces the harmful stereotype about the promiscuity of young Black girls. To see darker-skin Black women as leading women who are desirable wives, nurturing mothers, and women who are generally protected would've been more appealing in terms of changing the narrative.

Finally, because the story had levels of historical significance, one would hope it would push white audiences to consider the harm caused by abusive histories of slavery and violence against African people, and how those harmful histories trickle into the experience of modern Black people today. I do not think that point landed. As we mentioned in class, when witnessing Black trauma on camera, whether in fictitious films or horrifying bodycam footage, seeing the abuse or vulnerability of Black people doesn't necessarily encourage empathy or action from white viewers. I think this proved to be true as we saw *The Woman King* be excluded from the Academy Award nominations. The film, while cinematically lovely and inspiring in terms of showing Black resistance and power, was in a way another Black trauma film. I don't think the film pushed boundaries or told a disruptive narrative to counteract the existing narrative about darker-skin women; rather, it leans into the idea that darker Black women are strong, capable of taking more pain than one should bear, and not seen in a romantic or sexual lens. A more compelling story would be one in which we truly see the multidimensional aspect of Black women and their identities being valued holistically, beyond strength and trauma.

PRODUCTIVE RESPONSE FROM ALLISON JOYCE'S PROFESSOR

Allison Joyce is a Black woman; I am not. I therefore respect and honor her viewpoints on *The Woman King* above my own. The critiques she offers seem reasonable to me. As Allison Joyce and I both noted, the film is based on true events. Perhaps Viola Davis and everyone else involved in its production felt compelled to make the cinematic interpretation as proximal as possible to the original story, thereby making some of the presentation alternatives that Allison Joyce recommended seemingly out of bounds. It is clear to me, though, that her larger point extends far beyond this one film. I join Allison Joyce in calling for Hollywood executives, writers, producers, and others engaged in the cinematic arts ecosystem to deliver movies and television shows that show the fullness of Black women's lives beyond narrow, predictable stereotypes. And those projects should showcase Black women across the skin-tone spectrum, including major productions that include darker-skin leads. She did not say this explicitly, but my sense is that Allison Joyce is tired of seeing only particular presentations of herself on screens. I know for sure that my mother, aunts, best friend, and other significant Black women in my life share this frustration. I do, too.

CHAPTER 31

What the Porn Industry Teaches Teens, Especially Guys, About Sex

Most American teenagers have consumed pornography, according to a recent report from Common Sense,[1] a nonprofit organization that aims to improve the impact of media and technology on kids and families. Common Sense partnered with Benenson Strategy Group to administer a survey to teens ages 13 to 17. Of the 1,358 people who responded, nearly three-fourths said they'd either accidentally or intentionally encountered online pornography. Most had recently done so.

Teens aren't simply watching porn to satisfy their curiosities or as a stimulant for self-pleasure. Seventy-nine percent of survey respondents who'd consumed porn said doing so taught them how to have sex. Just over half had viewed content that depicted actors choking, assaulting, or otherwise inflicting pain on costars. Researchers have long contended that what porn watchers see in films oftentimes shapes their current and future sexual expectations and behaviors. Men, women, and genderqueer people can be harmed by this, including those who themselves aren't porn consumers but are in relationships with partners who are or have been.

"Exposure to pornography at too young an age can lead to poor mental health, sexual violence, and other negative outcomes," notes Jim Steyer, founder and CEO of Common Sense. "The overexposure by teens identified in our report can normalize unhealthy views and behaviors about sex and sexual relationships that we don't want young people to think are commonplace. In addition, with so much exposure to violent pornographic material, a major concern is how this might impact the sensitivity levels of teens to other types of violence." Teens across all genders are susceptible to these negative outcomes, but research shows the risks are more pronounced among young men.

Exposure and consumption rates presented in the Common Sense report varied by gender. Boys comprised 48% of the respondents, girls were 46%, and the remaining 6% were genderqueer. Despite the fairly even number of cisgender teens in the sample, there were differences on a survey question about intentionality. Fifty-two percent of boys said they'd intentionally watched porn, compared to just 36% of girls. In some ways, this is neither new nor unexpected. Think back to pre-Internet times. Teenage boys were considerably more likely than were girls to have pornographic magazines hidden beneath their mattresses.

Even though the Common Sense report is focused on teens, the consumption differences among cisgender respondents presented therein are consistent with other research that is inclusive of teens and adults. In a 2022 study published in *Sexuality Research and Social Policy*, a peer-reviewed academic journal, researchers found that more than 97% of boys and young men had consumed pornography, compared to approximately 77% of girls and young women.[2]

San Diego State University professor Frank Harris III is one of the most respected and highly cited experts on college men and masculinities. "A consequence of porn consumption among teenage boys is their tendency to pursue inequitable and oppressive sexual relationships during their young adult years," he says. "For example, some young men may seek to assert themselves as men in sexual relationships by mimicking the aggressive or violent sexual acts that are often depicted in pornography." Harris and other social scientists also acknowledge that porn consumption can result in some young men objectifying and engaging in abusive emotional, verbal, and physical interactions with their partners. This includes but isn't limited to heterosexual men's relationships with women.

In addition to discovering higher consumption rates among boys, there were also sexual orientation and racial differences in the Common Sense survey. Just over 74% of respondents identified as heterosexual; 7 out of 10 said they'd been exposed to porn. Among LGBTQ+ teens in the sample, it was 89%. In addition, 69% of Black teens who'd watched porn indicated they'd viewed films that portrayed their racial group in stereotypical ways. It was 61% among Latino survey respondents.

The Common Sense report doesn't offer a three-way intersectional analysis of the survey results by gender, sexual orientation, and race. I've watched 150 pornographic films on a website that has thousands of videos showing men having sex with men. Obviously, I did so entirely for research purposes. Obviously. These videos did not involve boys, teens, "twinks," or any men who appeared to be under the age of 18. I did an analysis of these videos by race. Specifically, I watched 50 videos in each of these three racial groupings: white men having sex with white men, Black men having sex with Black men, and Black men having sex with white men.

One set of findings from my analysis are particularly relevant to the Common Sense report. Films with white guys having sex with each other often had plots and storylines, the actors talked to each other more often before and during sex, and there was more emotional intimacy between partners (gazing in each other's eyes, gentle caressing, and kissing). Videos involving Black men had less of this—even less so when the videos included only Black men. Undoubtedly, some women and heterosexual men have either accidentally or intentionally watched gay porn. But queer guys are the overwhelming consumers of this specific genre. These production differences teach powerful, unfortunate, and oftentimes racist lessons to consumers. The Common Sense report confirms that queer teens are among these consumers.

"The ways in which dominant male partners appear in pornography—usually with impeccably fit bodies and well-endowed penises, along with the ability to simultaneously please multiple partners and perform sex for long periods of time without climaxing—are unrealistic," Harris adds. "This may lead some young men to develop negative perceptions of themselves as sexual partners if they cannot meet these expectations."

The Common Sense report concludes with three recommendations. The first is to resist the presumption that teens will avoid porn, especially since so many of them accidentally encounter it online. Second, the report suggests parents and family members should talk with teens about porn, regardless of how awkward those conversations are. Third, the report advocates for age-appropriate sex education curriculum that includes learning about porn, as well as stricter legislation to protect kids from accessing online sexual content.

Because its profits are so massive, I believe that as an act of corporate social responsibility, the porn industry ought to invest a portion of its billions into organizations that seek to eradicate violence against women and LGBTQ+ persons. There is also a role for porn production companies in helping men become considerably more mindful of the dangers associated with internalizing or attempting to reenact what they see in porn. Through billboards, television commercials, print and digital ads, and other mediums, many alcoholic beverage companies discourage drunk driving. Casinos and online sports-betting platforms warn players against developing gambling addictions; they sometimes even include the telephone numbers of places to call for help. These are just two examples the porn industry might consider following.

MAX'S PRODUCTIVE DISAGREEMENT

You speak to pornography's dangerous side effects, specifically leading to more abusive physical and emotional relationships among partners. Your article also calls out that pornography's explicit use of men with fit bodies and well-endowed penises will cause adolescents to develop negative perceptions of themselves over time. Despite the adverse violent effects of porn, I have developed a different solution to address the problem. I argue for pornography's positive effects, specifically among LGBTQ+ individuals, where it can be a source of comfort and acceptance with one's sexual orientation and lead to increased self-awareness and validation of sexual identity.

In the Common Sense study that you reference, pornography consumption is highest among LGBTQ+ respondents (66%), six percentage points higher than any other group. This data lead me to believe that these individuals are seeking out pornography to help them realize or make sense of their sexual preferences and desires. The Common Sense study also cites that among all teen respondents, not just LGBTQ+ individuals, almost half (45%) believed online pornography gave helpful information about sex. These pieces of data suggest there are clear benefits and educational information from pornography. Fifty-four percent of LGBTQ+ teens stated that they watched pornography to "find out what arouses and excites them" (not simply to experience arousal or excitement).

Amidst the chaotic, and at times confusing teenage years, especially for LGBTQ+ teens, pornography can be validating and provide a respite for teens who don't necessarily receive the support and guidance from systems to nurture their sexual experience. As an LGBTQ+ teen, not once in middle school or high school did I receive any sexual education about same-sex relations or same-sex intercourse. All my education was entirely geared toward heteronormative adolescents, and I felt confused and ostracized for seeking information that I wasn't sure existed. There was a sense of comfort and validation I got from consuming pornography in realizing I wasn't alone, and it allowed me to realize that my sexual preferences and desires didn't need to exist entirely in my head.

To address the problematic features of pornography, which can include abusive emotional and physical relationships, I also wanted to argue another solution. You advocate that (1) parents should talk to their kids at a younger age about pornography and (2) the pornography industry should make people aware of the dangers of sexual violence in pornography through billboards, television and print ads, and other mediums. While I do agree that parents talking to their kids about pornography at a young age can be helpful, I think that a mass-marketing campaign illustrating the dangers of violence in pornography is far too passive. Like any addiction or vice, whether it be alcohol, cigarettes, or gambling, pornography can also be incredibly addicting, so the mere mention of the side effects I find way too passive to properly address the dangers.

My suggestion is that a governing body in Congress be created and administer a $1 million fine on any pornography film that promotes violence in any manner. This board will review and fine those films. The board will review breaches of the rule periodically as well as be required on every pornography site, the addition of a user-interface button that reads "Report Video" for users if they believe the video promotes violence. This button will send videos to this board to review. I believe this system will more effectively address the dangers of porn while allowing individuals, especially adolescents, to benefit from learning and exploring their own desires and preferences.

PRODUCTIVE RESPONSE FROM MAX'S PROFESSOR

Max's suggestion regarding the establishment of a congressional oversight board sounds unrealistic. Arguably, members of Congress ought not be the arbiters of what constitutes violence in pornography. How will they know if something is actually violent? Where will the line be? And who will determine where the line is? It's possible that the "Report Video" button will be clicked by lots of people, perhaps even sometimes accidentally. Will everything that gets reported go straight to the congressional board? That won't work. Also, what about consumers who actually enjoy various depictions of violence in pornographic scenes? The Common Sense report is focused on teens, but what about adults who are mature enough to make determinations about whether something they've watched is too violent? Aside from placing warning labels and ratings on packages, most prior congressional attempts to ban or otherwise regulate violence in video games have failed.[3] What Max is recommending surely will, too. Now, Max did shift my perspective a bit on the potential helpfulness of queer adolescents watching pornographic films. He's right that too little formal sex education is available to teens, and too much of it focuses on heterosexuals. I still worry, though, that if young LGBTQ+ consumers and their heterosexual peers are exposed to only particular genres and storylines, their expectations of what's supposed to happen in their own sexual experiences could be dangerously misshaped.

CHAPTER 32

NCAA Basketball Champ Angel Reese Was Called "Classless" Because She's Black

Louisiana State University defeated the University of Iowa in the 2023 NCAA Women's Basketball Tournament. The celebration of LSU's first-ever national championship was met with unfair criticism of Angel Reese, one of the team's star players. Near the end of the game that LSU won 102–85, Reese first waved her hand in front of her face (a taunt WWE wrestler John Cena popularized to signify "you can't see me"),[1] she then pointed to her ring finger. The gesture was directed at Caitlin Clark, the Iowa Hawkeye's leading scorer. Critics deemed the move unsportsmanlike.

Sports and political commentator Keith Olbermann referred to Reese as a "fucking idiot" in a tweet.[2] He further argued, "doesn't matter the gender, the sport, the background—you're seconds away from a championship and you do something like this and overshadow all the good." In addition, Barstool Sports founder David Portnoy tweeted "classless piece of shit" in response to Reese's gesture.[3] Others on social media argued that Reese stalked Clark during the matchup. Some suggested the referees should've given Reese a technical foul.

The biggest problem with condemnations of Reese's gesture is that Clark did the exact same thing in Iowa's tournament win over the University of Louisville just a few days prior. It wasn't a move that was somewhat or perhaps disputably similar—it was the exact same "you can't see me" hand motion. Most sports commentators and fans praised Clark for it. They didn't criticize her like they did Reese. Even the taunt's architect, Cena, tweeted a video of Clark along with the words, "Even if they could see you . . . they couldn't guard you!"[4] Why did so many people treat the two tournament ballers so differently? Here's one explanation: Clark is white, Reese is Black.

In a postgame interview, Reese talked about how she'd been the target of double standards throughout the season. She said the media and others told her that she's "too hood, too ghetto." Reese proudly declared that her championship game performance was for other women who look like her. North Carolina State University professor Joy Gaston Gayles, an expert on intercollegiate athletics, maintains that Reese's treatment is a clear example of anti-Blackness. "Angel's response is a good representation of resistance to anti-Blackness. She's intentionally deciding to be herself regardless of society's refusal to recognize her humanity as a Black woman."

Gayles further maintains, "to call any human a 'classless piece of shit' is never okay, but for a Black woman, it's steeped in what Moya Bailey termed misogynoir[5]—the unique and specific type of violence that happens to Black women at the intersection of racism, sexism, and anti-Blackness." Gayles went on to explain. "Reese is experiencing the intended outcomes of misogynoir, which function to discredit her, subject her to heightened scrutiny, hold innocent a white woman, and ultimately misrepresent her as a threat to white women in college basketball."

The threat to which Gayles refers isn't about just any white woman. It's about Clark, who made history during March Madness. With 191 points, she became the highest-scoring college basketball player of any gender in the history of the NCAA women's and men's tournaments. Therefore, Reese doing to Clark what Clark did to a Louisville player just days prior was likely interpreted as a petty Black woman unnecessarily disrespecting the tournament's biggest star. But despite her individual success, Clark's team lost the championship contest. Reese's team won.

It's worth noting that men taunt each other all the time in college sports in ways that are far more outrageous than the hand gesture that Clark and Reese both used throughout the tournament. But the women's taunting disrupted sexist expectations of how they're supposed to behave in sports. "We are socialized to understand femininity through a white-normed lens," says Michigan State University professor Dorinda Carter Andrews. "White women and girls are inherently viewed as sweet, gentle, and docile. Even when they perform 'aggressive' or 'assertive' acts, it's not viewed as problematic." Carter Andrews notes that when Black women behave in the same ways as white women, "they are perceived as barbaric and disrespectful. The standard for femininity is racialized in ways that penalize Black women and girls."

Julie Rousseau, an associate athletic director at the University of Southern California, has been a college basketball player, as well as a head coach of multiple college basketball programs and a WNBA team. "Here we are in 2023, with two highly competitive teams facing each other surrounded by a record-breaking crowd, and the spotlight quickly shifts to Angel Reese and the kind of bravado gesture that we have come to expect in men's basketball, that Caitlin Clark also exhibited in a previous game," Rousseau observes. "Some called Angel's gesture classless, but this term was misapplied to Angel when it more appropriately describes the response of media to Black women who play this game. It seems the press cannot resist promoting the racist trope when it finds itself incapable of acknowledging skill and pride expressed by all women, especially Black women."

DESTINY'S PRODUCTIVE DISAGREEMENT

The article highlights the discourse that erupted after Louisiana State University's Angel Reese imitated University of Iowa's Caitlin Clark's gesture near the end of the 2023 NCAA Women's Basketball Tournament. This response will further the argument that the differential treatment between Reese and Clark was not only because she is Black but because she is Black and a woman.

In men's sports, there is rarely a dramatic narrative woven into the playing of their sport. Most times, male athletes enjoy the luxury of playing their sport without being juxtaposed around some media-driven story. Men get to be notorious for trash talking and be physical on the court without being called "classless idiots." Most times they are praised for their physicality and trash talking. Kevin Garnett and Kobe Bryant were some of the most notable for their trash talking while playing. That praise was extended to Caitlin Clark when she started using the "you can't see me" gesture coined by John Cena. White women often get praised for the very same things that Black women get criticized for.

Not only was Caitlin Clark, as a white woman, praised for her trash talking, but the Iowa team, which was comprised of mostly white players, were portrayed in a storybook manner as they were excelling in the tournament. Angel Reese and the LSU team got the scrappy underdog narrative. This difference in the media portrayal was not isolated to the LSU Tigers. The South Carolina Gamecocks, who won the tournament the year prior, were criticized for their physicality, with the Iowa coach describing them as "bar fighters." South Carolina's team is made up of a majority of Black players, similar to the LSU Tigers. This demonstrates the ideology around Black women in basketball and the stereotypes that harm Black women in sports through the media portrayal.

The intersection of being Black and a woman predisposes people in these identities to harmful stereotypes. These stereotypes are usually the assumption of having a domineering persona or being overly aggressive, especially when Black women are playing male-dominated sports like basketball. The backlash that Angel Reese received has happened to countless Black female athletes, such as Serena Williams and Brittney Griner.

So, to further the argument made in the *Forbes* article, the intersecting identities of Angel Reese being a Black woman in basketball is the reason why she got differential treatment compared to Caitlin Clark, a white woman. This new argument better encompasses how the media further perpetuates racial stereotypes in women's sports.

PRODUCTIVE RESPONSE FROM DESTINY'S PROFESSOR

Kimberlé Crenshaw, one of our nation's most brilliant legal scholars, introduced the term *intersectionality*. The concept is one of my favorites to teach; I do so annually in just about every course. I therefore appreciate how Destiny amplified the intersectionality of race and gender in the responses to Angel Reese. Also praiseworthy is how Destiny, like my colleague Julie Rousseau, pointed out the gendered expectation differences in women's and men's sports. This is traceable back to early play and schooling experiences. Research shows that young boys, more often than girls, are given rugged toy trucks, plastic soldiers, and fake guns; a "boys will be boys" explanation is offered when they behave rambunctiously in play groups and classrooms; and they are more frequently urged to participate in rough contact sports like football and wrestling.[6] Destiny rightly extends these trends to intercollegiate (and presumably professional) sports. We agree that these gendered expectations get racialized in unique ways for Black women athletes. This intersection unfairly places them at risk of being given inequitable penalties from referees; receiving racist and misogynistic comments from fans and commentators; getting passed over for lucrative shoe, apparel, and endorsement deals; and potentially being deemed undesirable for the WNBA and other professional sports drafts, as well as for membership on national teams that compete in the Olympics and FIFA Women's World Cup.

CHAPTER 33

What to Do When Drunk Fans Say Inexcusably Offensive Things at Sporting Events

Intoxicated people sometimes make racist, sexist, homophobic, and otherwise deplorable statements at sporting events. There's a chance they wouldn't say such things if they were sober—maybe in private, but probably not in a public venue surrounded by thousands of strangers. Unfortunately, their friends and nearby fans sometimes laugh or otherwise affirm the inappropriateness. Some others do nothing because they respect the drunk person's freedom of speech, even if they personally find the jokes, statements, or chants offensive. The "let's ignore him, he's just sloppy drunk" response is also common in sports arenas, bars, and other public spaces. In too many instances, nearby people hear something they know is wrong, but they really just want to avoid confrontation and enjoy the event. Many who reach the point of disgust simply don't know what to say or do.

At a recent college football matchup between rivals USC and Notre Dame, fans for one reason or another didn't know what to say to a drunk guy in their section who repeatedly yelled terrible obscenities. I arrived to their section after halftime and immediately found myself in an uncomfortable position that required me to transition from USC Trojan fanboy to disruptive consciousness-raiser. Like everyone else around me (including the obnoxious drunk dude), I really just wanted to have a good time. My friend and I were there for a thrilling, enjoyable sporting experience—Professor Harper was supposed to have the night off. For context, Notre Dame is a Catholic university. Our drunk neighbor repeatedly chanted, "pound those altar boys' asses." It was a shocking reference to the sexual assault of children in the Catholic church. I convinced myself that there was no way I heard what I thought I heard the first time he said it. But then he said it again, and again.

After hearing it three times, I turned around to ask drunk dude if he was calling Notre Dame's football team altar boys because they are Catholic. He said yes. I then asked if the pounding he was calling for was a reference to forceable anal sex. He said yes. I then told him that joking about Catholic boys being raped was absolutely terrible. I insisted he stop. He didn't stop. Instead, he doubled down with another despicable statement about the Trojans (my university's mascot) behaving like priests and bringing "those altar boys to their knees." He continued by maintaining, "At a certain point when your ass is being pounded, you might as well just relax and enjoy it." I kept pushing him to understand that he was being an advocate for rape and pedophilia. I finally somehow broke through to him. Thankfully, he discontinued the horrific altar boy comments.

After some time, drunk dude became annoyingly apologetic and surprisingly reflective. "I'm not *that guy*," he repeatedly attempted to convince me. He shared a personal story about a family member whom he believes is gay because he was sexually assaulted as a young boy. Yikes, I really just wanted to enjoy the game. I honestly didn't have it in me to educate him on his problematic causation thesis: the presumption that his family member is gay *only* because of sexual abuse suffered earlier in life. The friend who accompanied me to the game is a heterosexual man. I don't know if the intoxicated fan seated behind us sensed that I'm gay. Oddly, he began touching my friend and me excessively. Perhaps he was trying to prove he's not homophobic. My friend and I kept removing his hands from our shoulders. At one point, he was so close that he accidentally spat in my face and in my wine. He tried to fix it by going to buy me a new glass—but, sigh, the stadium stopped selling alcoholic beverages at the beginning of the fourth quarter. I just wanted to enjoy the game, and I did. Others around me did, too. The two women next to me said he'd been saying offensive things all night. They seemed grateful that someone finally got it to stop.

The point of this story isn't to embarrass the intoxicated man who made me work during a really amazing football game. Self-righteousness also isn't my aim here. I'm not congratulating myself for doing in my personal time what I call for in my everyday DEI work with business professionals and educators. Once I confirmed what I thought I heard, it instantly occurred to me that my students would expect of me the same that I expect of them. This experience occurred during my 19th year as a professor. For many years, I required graduate students I've taught at USC and the University of Pennsylvania to do an assignment in which they find three disruptive opportunities throughout the semester to raise consciousness among friends, family members, significant others, coworkers, and strangers about sexist, homophobic, transphobic, racist, Islamophobic, and other problematic things those persons said. They had to do this in real time, not later. In their journals, my students described the situation, what they did to disrupt it, how it made them feel, how the other person(s) reacted, and what they would've done differently in hindsight. Almost always, students describe being terrified in the first journal entry. But by the third disruption, they're noticeably more confident and comfortable. Encounters like the one I had with the man seated behind me at the football game require not only courage but also practice, which is the intended outcome of the assignment I give my students.

Sometimes, we just want to have a good time, even if someone is saying or doing offensive things; but doing nothing makes us complicit in the continuation or exacerbation of terribleness, injustice, and violence. On the one hand, it's important to recognize people's free speech rights. But on the other, it's critical to exercise one's own First Amendment rights by seriously attempting to raise a drunk or sober person's consciousness about inexcusable words and actions. Failing to do so makes us bystanders.

"She was drunk" is often used to explain away a colleague's racist statement at a happy hour with coworkers. "He's really not *that guy*" is also used to minimize the severity of a friend's or colleague's jokes about sexual assault. Disrupting these actions doesn't necessarily require making a big scene or getting into a physical altercation with someone. At no point did I want to fight drunk dude—even when his spit disgustingly landed in my right eye. As professionals work on becoming more comfortable with uncomfortable topics and situations in their places of employment, we must also do so in situations that demand constructive confrontation outside of workplaces. It takes consciousness, courage, rehearsal, and intentionality, including in social settings where we just want to have a good time.

PAXTON'S PRODUCTIVE DISAGREEMENT

Crafting a nuanced response to offensive behaviors at sporting events, especially when alcohol is involved, necessitates a multifaceted approach that prioritizes safety, effectiveness, and long-term impact. The incident described in Dr. Shaun Harper's *Forbes* article illustrates the complexity of directly confronting intoxicated individuals who engage in offensive chanting. In this case, Dr. Harper felt obligated to confront a nearby intoxicated fan chanting offensive and insensitive references to rape and pedophilia. However, research by Parrott and Eckhardt,[1] Sundin et al.,[2] Heinz et al.,[3] and Giancola[4] provides a basis for understanding the heightened risk of aggression and the diminished cognitive function in intoxicated individuals, suggesting that immediate confrontation may not only be unsafe but also ineffective in fostering any meaningful change or learning in the offender's behavior.

The aggressive tendencies exacerbated by alcohol, as highlighted by Parrott and Eckhardt,[5] suggest that direct intervention, especially in the heat of the moment, could escalate the situation, potentially leading to physical violence. This risk is further underscored by Sundin et al.'s findings, which link heavy episodic drinking to increased instances of harm from others' drinking-related aggression.[6] Therefore, while Dr. Harper's intention to address the offensive behavior is spot-on and on par with promoting a culture of decency and respect, the method of direct confrontation under these circumstances poses significant risks to personal safety and the efficacy of the message being conveyed.

Moreover, alcohol's impact on cognitive functioning, including the narrowing of attention and suppression of inhibitions as detailed by the referenced research, implies that the offender's capacity to understand and remember the confrontation may be significantly impaired. This limitation not only challenges the immediate effectiveness of such interventions but also raises questions about their long-term impact on behavioral change.

An alternative approach involves leveraging the stadium's security and management to handle the situation, coupled with imposing substantial fines in the ballpark of thousands of dollars as deterrents. This method not only ensures the safety of individual spectators, but also utilizes existing event management protocols to address such behavior efficiently. The imposition of fines, scaling with the severity of the offense, serves as a tangible consequence that has the potential to deter future incidents, by directly impacting the offender financially and signaling the seriousness with which such behavior is viewed by society and sporting communities.

In conclusion, while the instinct to confront offensive behaviors directly is understandable, the complexities introduced by alcohol consumption require a more strategic approach. Utilizing venue management and security channels, alongside imposing financial penalties, offers a safer and potentially more effective means of addressing and deterring offensive behavior at sporting events. This strategy not only aligns with the research on alcohol's effects on aggression and cognitive function but also with broader societal efforts to create inclusive, safe spaces for all spectators.

PRODUCTIVE RESPONSE FROM PAXTON'S PROFESSOR

In the midst of this incident, I didn't consult the studies that Paxton referenced. Reading research in real time isn't something most people, including nerds like me, do at sporting events. I was fully aware that confronting "drunk dude" (as I referred to him in the article) could've led to physical violence. Even though I haven't been in a fight since 5th grade, I suppose it was a risk I was willing to take in the moment. In retrospect, a distinguished professor fighting at his university's football game would've been outrageously inappropriate and terrible for a multitude of reasons. Even though I was aware that drunk dude may have gotten upset and responded with physical violence, I chose an approach that likely would've taken a while to get him to that point. I didn't call him names, yell at him, or get in his face. I asked confirming questions before accusing him of behaving inappropriately. I made sure that he knew how I felt about what he was saying and insisted he stop, but I didn't threaten to beat him up if he didn't. I took a calm, reasonable, educator's stance. Maybe, just maybe this is one reason why drunk dude began gently and apologetically touching me after I got him to stop making the offensive statements. Paxton and the researchers are right, though: I should've just gotten stadium security personnel to come handle this situation. According to one of the studies Paxton referenced, there's a chance that drunk dude didn't even remember any of this the following day. Yikes.

Part V

OTHER PRODUCTIVE DEI DISAGREEMENTS

CHAPTER 34

White Guy Says He'll Bring Fried Chicken to the Black Cookout—How to Recover From Racial Microaggressions

It was an awkward moment on *CBS Mornings* when Tony Dokoupil, a white cohost, told his two Black colleagues that he'd bring fried chicken to a Black cookout. This is a racial microaggression, even though Dokoupil didn't intend for it to be. In moments like these, people of color on the receiving end of subtle, seemingly innocuous racial insults often don't know what to say. And microaggressors usually don't even realize they've said something offensive. In response to Dokoupil's statement, Jericka Duncan, a Black woman and CBS national correspondent, asked, "Why it's gotta be fried chicken, though?" She laughed it off and said she was kidding. The other Black co-host, Nate Burleson, later explained that Dokoupil had visited his home where they made pasta, burgers, and fried chicken. "So for everybody at home that's hearing that statement and is like, 'did Tony just say fried chicken to Nate,' that's what he actually made . . . that's the only food that he made." As Burleson was speaking, Dokoupil repeatedly emphasized in the background that it was a cookout. Duncan attempted to lighten the moment with laughter. "It's all good," she insisted three times.

Racial microaggressions are perceivably harmless. On its own, each microaggression seems insignificant. Anyone who makes a big deal out of it is typically viewed as being too sensitive and advised to get a thicker skin. Or worse, they're told to stop making everything a racial issue. This is often the viewpoint of people who aren't the same race as the person or group being microaggressed. Stereotypes and unconscious biases undergird racial microaggressions. One of them is that Black people love to eat watermelon and fried chicken, hence Duncan's reaction to her white colleague's comment. To be sure, some Black people do love fried chicken (it actually happens to be my favorite), but it isn't the only thing we eat. Many white people love fried chicken, too, yet it isn't stereotypically associated with their cultural eating habits.

Speaking slang to no one else at work besides Black colleagues is another example of a racial microaggression. Others include confusing two Black people who look nothing alike for each other; referring to Black folks as ghetto; white women being visibly frightened and clutching their purses when Black men enter elevators with them; and assuming that Black shoppers are store employees (despite not being dressed in uniforms) or they're going to steal something and therefore should be followed around. These are just a few examples. There are hundreds, perhaps thousands more, and they aren't limited to race—there are also microaggressions based on gender, socioeconomic status, country of origin, accent, and religion, to name a few. Columbia University professor Derald Wing Sue and Arizona State University professor Lisa Spanierman offer an expansive list in their book *Microaggressions in Everyday Life*.[1]

My research, as well as findings from studies conducted by Sue, Spanierman, UCLA professor Daniel G. Solórzano, California State University Long Beach professor Lindsay Pérez Huber, and other scholars make clear that individual, one-time encounters with microaggressions can be, but usually aren't, all that harmful. It's the everyday repeated encounters with them that produce negative psychological, emotional, physiological, academic, and occupational outcomes. Critics who accuse microaggressed persons of being too sensitive fail to understand the cumulative effects of those exact same or similar statements and experiences over time. Even though she raised it jokingly, surely this wasn't Duncan's first time hearing a white person associate fried chicken with Black people.

Sometimes, when people of color hear microaggressions, they ask themselves, "Was that statement about race?" It can become a distracting question they contemplate for hours, sometimes days. In other instances, people are fairly certain that what they heard was a microaggression, but they say nothing in the moment. This is because some don't know what to say. Others fear retaliation or they aren't in the mood to hear microaggressors tell them it wasn't a big deal and that the situation has nothing to do with race. And then there are white tears: moments that white women start crying because they've been told that something they said or did landed on a person of color in an offensive way. Guilt, shame, regret, and exhaustion typically ensue when a microaggressed person decides against calling out a microaggression.

Duncan responded exactly the right way. Instead of accusing Dokoupil of being racist or taking on the labor of educating him about the problematic "all Black people love fried chicken" trope, she made him do the work. Again, Duncan asked a question: "Why it's gotta be fried chicken, though?" In addition to taking the consciousness-raising pressure off of herself, this approach also ensured that she didn't leave the studio regretting that she'd let a problematic comment slide, especially as a Black woman journalist appearing in front of 3 million viewers (some of whom are Black and have reasonably high expectations of her to responsibly use such an important TV platform to disrupt stereotypes about Black people). Dokoupil spoke for himself and offered an explanation. Burleson also helped by adding more context.

When someone calls attention to a microaggressive statement or action, the offender should first attempt to understand before immediately and desperately aiming to be understood. If there's more context to give (as was the case with Burleson's cookout for which Dokoupil prepared fried chicken), it's fine to give it without becoming defensive or feeling attacked. Telling the person who likely experiences various forms of microaggressions far too frequently that they're wrong isn't the right response. Censoring oneself or being too afraid to say anything else that could be interpreted through a racialized lens also isn't the best way to recover from making a racial mistake. Apologizing is good. Reflecting on the feedback and being more mindful in the future is even better.

For the record, I watch *CBS Mornings* almost every day. I really love Tony Dokoupil's approach; he's one of my favorite journalists. This isn't an attack on him. I'm not accusing him of being racist, especially since we don't know each other. And I'm definitely not advocating for him to be canceled. However, I do think this situation is a powerfully illustrative example of how a seemingly harmless comment connects to a longstanding stereotype about Black people and why Dokoupil's Black woman colleague said something about it. As is the case in other instances of human communication, intent and impact aren't the same.

SEAN'S PRODUCTIVE DISAGREEMENT

I feel it is important to note that I do not disagree with much of Dr. Harper's analysis. I believe his explanation of the events taking place in the article, as well as the potential responses, align well with real-world application. However, I do take issue with some of the examples given as microaggressions and the general use of the word to categorize racialized interactions. For the purpose of this response, I focus on microaggressions as they pertain to race but acknowledge the varied ways people can experience microaggressions in relation to other personal factors.

The term **microaggressions** was coined during the 1970s by Chester Pierce, a Harvard University professor, but it has grown in mainstream consciousness throughout the 2000s. The term is often misunderstood by those unfamiliar with the lived experiences of people of color, often assuming that it is a stand-in term for calling someone racist or an overly sensitive reaction for a minor event. And among those in opposition to DEI movements, the term itself has become weaponized to minimize the very real effects that microaggressions have. To someone unfamiliar with the term, microaggression may come off as an oxymoron. How can an aggressive act be considered micro? Often, the microaggressions instance may not be explicitly egregious, such as many of the examples that Dr. Harper references. And as he explains, the issue with microaggressions is the consistency resulting in a "straw breaking the camel's back" racial experience.

Unfortunately, these different understandings of the word have become part of the problem. For those working against racial equity and justice, the prefix micro lends itself to minimizing the message the word is communicating. Its popularization in the American lexicon has undermined the meaning of the word, resulting in less-impactful responses when people work to address the microaggressed experience. The path forward to addressing these racialized instances is to call a spade a spade. Microaggressions are harmful, exclusionary behaviors. As Dr. Harper mentions, it is not intent but impact that matters. And the impact of microaggressions should not be understated or given space to be purposely misinterpreted. Dr. Harper himself notes that it is common to feel microaggressions for hours or days, not a short time for something many currently consider trivial. Continued usage of the word allows it to be further co-opted by those seeking to minimize the lived experiences of people of color.

The fried chicken example Dr. Harper addresses in his article is a nuanced scenario based on the reconciliation of two different lived experiences. While this specific instance may not be considered intentionally exclusionary, many of Dr. Harper's other examples are. Examples like referring to Black folks as ghetto, white women being visibly frightened and clutching their purses when Black men enter elevators with them, or assuming that Black shoppers are going to steal something are very real racist and exclusionary actions—they should be called out as such.

PRODUCTIVE RESPONSE FROM SEAN'S PROFESSOR

Chester Middlebrook Pierce was a Black man. He also was a longtime distinguished professor at Harvard Medical School and the Harvard Graduate School of Education. Sean indicated that Chet (as Dr. Pierce was affectionately known) coined the term microaggressions. As a Black academician, I am very intentional about honoring the originality of works that Black scholars who came before me gifted to their fields and disciplines. There's a very real chance that I do this with scholars across all racial groups, but I know for sure that I'm especially mindful about doing so with pioneering Black intellectual icons. Chet was a psychiatrist. The term that he ascribed to racialized experiences that Black and other people of color were enduring five decades ago felt right to him at that time. As Sean alludes, it's possible that the term microaggressions is no longer appropriate. I don't feel this way, despite my respect for Sean's stance. I still find the term to be a useful way of helping people understand the everydayness of racism, racial harm, racial stereotypes, and encounters with racially offensive statements and experiences. Unfortunately, too many Americans have been socialized to acknowledge only extreme acts of violence as racist. In my opinion, Professor Pierce's term, when used properly, remains useful in categorizing other kinds of racially injurious confrontations, those that are not so apparent to most people. I do agree with Sean, though, that microaggressions shouldn't be dismissed as trivial and inconsequential. They aren't.

CHAPTER 35

Remote Work Can Boost Diversity Yet Undermine Equity for Employees of Color

Facebook has doubled the number of women as well as Black and Latino employees since 2019, the company, now called Meta, said in its 2022 annual diversity report.[1] Maxine Williams, Meta's chief diversity officer, partly attributes the increase in people of color to the flexibility of hybrid and remote work options. This makes sense. Being able to work from anywhere does not require diverse employees to relocate themselves and their families to places in which they will be severely underrepresented. The COVID-19 pandemic created a solution to this problem for Meta and other companies. The reported increases—from 6.3% to 6.7% Latino and 3.9% to 4.9% Black—in the diversity of Facebook employees between 2020 and 2022 are not sizable enough to confirm that work location flexibility is a significant, sustainable solution to the tech industry's longstanding diversity problem. And then there is the question of whether this increased diversity is equitably distributed across all levels, or if it is most heavily concentrated in entry-level and low-compensated roles. Nevertheless, working from home seems to be making some demographic difference at Meta.

Eliminating stressful commutes, avoiding $6 per-gallon gas prices, being able to work in comfy pajama bottoms, and having more flexibility to spend time with kids and pets are some well-known reasons why many professionals, regardless of their race, still have no interest in returning to noisy cubicles and too hot/too cold office spaces. Also, they and their supervisors now have years of evidence to show that working from home negatively affects neither their productivity nor their performance. In addition to these somewhat universal rationales, employees of color say remote work provides much-appreciated shelter from the racist stereotypes, microaggressions, racial tensions, and overt racism that many of them experienced in on-site workplace settings prior to the pandemic.[2] For some, finding a new job that affords remote work is a more appealing alternative to returning to places in which they previously encountered tremendous racial stress.

A few years ago, I conducted a workplace racial climate assessment for a company. This entailed facilitating several racially homogeneous focus groups with white employees and their racially diverse colleagues. In interviews with

Black professionals, women repeatedly talked about white coworkers touching their hair. While some were at least polite enough to ask before violating these Black women, audacious others occasionally did so without seeking consent. A few weeks after the interviews, the CEO closed the headquarters for a daylong all-employee learning day with me—presenting and discussing findings of the workplace climate assessment was the centerpiece of our time together. I asked all white attendees to raise their hands. They did. I then instructed them to keep their hands raised if anyone had ever touched their hair at work. All hands went down. I then invited Black women to do the same. All but one hand remained raised (that one woman said she had only been at the company a short while). I have not been back since the pandemic began, but I am guessing that Black women who work there have not been eager to return to what one of them referred to as "a petting zoo." This is just one of numerous racialized experiences from which Black women and other employees of color are protected as they work from home.

Location flexibility has been good for diversity at Facebook and other organizations. Notwithstanding that, leaders have a responsibility to do something about the racism and racial stress that too many employees of color experience in on-site work settings. If left unaddressed, many loyal colleagues who make offices diverse may opt to switch to remote work. Also noteworthy is that remote work does not fully protect professionals of color from microaggressions and other racially harmful experiences. Asking the one Indigenous team member to speak on behalf of all Indigenous persons, for example, can just as easily occur in a virtual setting as it often does in on-site office meetings. Inclusion requires more data about how diverse employees, regardless of where their work is performed, experience the racial climate, and then using those findings to fix racist and otherwise problematic cultures, policies, structures, and systems.

There is at least one other important set of cautions about relying too heavily on remote workers of color to increase diversity numbers. Leaders must be mindful about providing opportunities for these professionals to lead, be seen, and showcase their advancement potential. While this is important for employees across all races, it seems especially essential for Asian American, Black, Indigenous, Latino, Pacific Islander, and multiracial people. In my interviews with them over the past 2 decades, these employees have consistently talked about how their managers invest more into their less qualified, quantifiably less accomplished white counterparts. Reportedly, white coworkers are also afforded more leadership audition opportunities and get tapped more often for promotions to higher-paying roles. These inequities will surely be exacerbated if disproportionately higher numbers of white employees work in the office and people of color work mostly from home.

Cultivating meaningful, professionally profitable relationships likely occurs more easily for those with whom leaders spend face-to-face time in offices. It seems plausible that executives and managers will promote employees whose offices they can drop into to ideate and solve problems, colleagues whom they see thinking and leading in real time. Rotation and leadership acceleration programs have to be intentionally inclusive of remote workers. Also, leaders must deliberately facilitate opportunities for colleagues at their level and above to be exposed to talented people of color whom they will never bump into in the office or see make in-person presentations.

Having clear promotion policies and processes that are inclusive of employees who work from home is imperative. Furthermore, written HR plans and DEI strategy documents ought to specify how racial equity will be ensured for remote workers; how people leaders will be held accountable for demonstrating fairness in promotion processes; and proactive steps the business can take to strategically poise diverse, extraordinarily talented in-office and offsite colleagues for career ascension. Remote work at Facebook and elsewhere could set up employees of color to contribute to the company's demographic bottom line, but diverse professionals will ultimately remain underrepresented in mid-level, senior, and executive roles if virtual-only interactions deny them equitable opportunities to display their advancement readiness.

LIZ'S PRODUCTIVE DISAGREEMENT

I enjoyed reading this article, and my own perspective aligns with the point that eliminating common workplace stressors and reducing instances of negative interactions (such as microaggressions) has the potential to benefit diversity for certain companies. I also agree that companies who see this increase must approach it with caution—they could risk proximity bias or inequities if not all employees are provided with the same opportunities in a remote or hybrid setting. However, I would like to offer an additional viewpoint on the matter.

The diversity report that much of this discussion stems from was released by Meta, which has seen an increase in employees of color hired after implementing flexible work policies. I believe that certain nuances to Meta itself as a company may be influencing these outcomes. Thus, companies should be cautious about making the assumption that remote work can translate to improved diversity for themselves. Meta is consistently ranked on top employer lists. Also, online salary transparency tools show that the average estimated annual salary of a Meta employee is around $140k. This shows that remote work at Meta, a relatively progressive technology company, does not represent the realities of remote work at many other companies. When researching remote jobs currently listed on Indeed .com, I found that many offer only a low hourly wage and require employees to provide their own computers. Some job seekers may not have the resources to own a computer, working Internet, dedicated office space, and other prerequisites.

These points show that Meta is already an attractive employer that is dedicated to diversity hiring efforts. The takeaways from its annual diversity report might be influenced by this factor. Most other companies need an additional line of caution when approaching hiring for remote jobs. Certain demands in job postings could ostracize communities of people, and the company must put in extra effort to show that they are committed to diversity. When potential employees cannot experience the culture in person, a company's reputation and brand are crucial for attracting candidates from diverse backgrounds. Meta, which is already well known as a big tech company that emphasizes diversity hiring, can afford to be more direct and might have an easier time increasing number of employees of color when candidates are offered flexibility on top of existing benefits and a positively perceived company culture.

Finally, as the article title highlights, remote work has the potential to undermine equity for employees of color. Colleagues are siloed and more likely to only interact with others through emails or virtual calls. In this environment, employees of color may find it hard to feel included or celebrated. These feelings of isolation are very detrimental to mental health. I would challenge Meta and all other companies releasing diversity reports to also share their attrition rate for employees of color. We should measure how long-lasting the impact of remote work on diversity within a firm is. Ultimately, diversity requires long-term, ongoing efforts that are both unbiased and adaptive.

PRODUCTIVE RESPONSE FROM LIZ'S PROFESSOR

Reading Liz's response helped me recognize a lopsided, potentially biased trend in my writings about workplace DEI topics. I've worked with more than 400 corporations, nonprofit and government agencies, educational institutions, and other organizations spanning a multitude of industries. At least half have been small places that employ 50 or fewer people. Yet most businesses I spotlight in articles are large, oftentimes global. I've not yet worked with Meta, but it more closely resembles the larger workplace contexts from which many of my written examples are drawn. I appreciate Liz's points about how Meta differs from many other companies. It likely has a more robust, well-funded infrastructure to support remote work. It's also large enough to have variation. Equity can be more easily achieved when there are both horizontal and vertical support systems, as well as when categories of employees (e.g., those who work from home) can be given customized support to ensure their wellness and professional advancement. This is much harder in organizations that are smaller, more flat, and relatively less wealthy than is Meta. Lastly, I really like Liz's notion of experiencing culture in person—as long as it isn't sexist, ableist, racist, transphobic, homophobic, or otherwise harmful to employees who make organizations diverse. Both in-office and remote work environments should be equitable and inclusive, which requires intentional strategies within both domains regardless of organizational size.

CHAPTER 36

Black Cops Upheld Institutional and Cultural Racism in Fatal Attack of Tyre Nichols

From the moment they pulled him over for what they claim was reckless driving, five Memphis police officers met Tyre Nichols with excessive force and disregard for his Black life. The City of Memphis released video footage of the cops slamming Nichols to the ground, kicking him in the head, punching him in the face, striking him with a baton, drenching him with pepper spray, tasing him, and cursing him out.[1] It's horrific, downright despicable. Nichols was approximately 80 yards from his home as he screamed repeatedly for his mom. He was unarmed. The 29-year-old Black man died three days after being so violently beaten.

All the officers who killed Nichols are Black. Derek Chauvin, the Minneapolis police officer who murdered George Floyd in 2020, is white. The Floyd tragedy forced a long-overdue grappling with racism in policing. Protests ensued all across the United States and around the world. The "white cop kills an unarmed Black man equals racism in policing" math was easy for most people to compute. But how could racism have anything to do with five Black cops killing an unarmed Black man given that all the people involved were Black?

Even though George Floyd's murderer was an individual, lots of people recognized that his death wasn't entirely attributable to the actions of one evil policeman. For many, it was their first introduction to systemic racism and anti-Blackness. They also learned that white supremacy isn't only embodied by individual racists hiding their faces under pointed hoods, but it's also upheld by police officers, health care providers, schoolteachers, business leaders, and others. Floyd was murdered at the end of May, uprisings occurred throughout the first couple weeks of June, and workplace conversations about systemic racism ended in most companies by the end of summer.

Institutional racism explains how five Black men could engage in police brutality, leading to the death of another Black man. They participated in the same trainings as white cops. They entered a profession that was born of anti-Blackness (slave catchers were America's original law enforcement officers). They worked in a place where decades of anti-Black policies and tactics were created. How a police department behaves, thinks about Black communities, and mistreats Black people informs how its employees engage with the Black citizens they were hired to protect and serve—even when they're Black. It doesn't matter if the police chief is Black, as is the case in Memphis. She inherited the leadership of an organization that has racism deeply embedded into its DNA.

It was also cultural racism that led those officers to beat Nichols so brutally. The five cops were all part of the "Scorpion Unit," which is an acronym for Street Crimes Operation to Restore Peace in Our Neighborhoods. In a press conference, civil rights attorney Ben Crump told the story of another unarmed Black man who was terrorized in Memphis five days prior to the Nichols beating.[2] "That same Scorpion Unit confronted him while he was in his car going to get pizza and he said that they used all kind of profanity against him, they threw him on the ground [asking], 'where are the drugs, where are the weapons' . . . and put a gun to his head."

According to Crump, after somehow surviving that potentially deadly ordeal, the man repeatedly called the Memphis Police Department's internal affairs unit to report what had happened to him. They were unresponsive; there was no accountability for the officers' gross misconduct. "If they would have responded to him, we might not be here today," Crump maintained. He went on to critique the culture of policing and argued that policy alone won't fix racism in law enforcement. "Policy means nothing if you have a culture that is rotten," he said. "You can make all the policy in the world, but culture does not respect policy. We have to make sure that the culture not only respects the policy, but the culture respects the community."

Here's how cultural racism in the policing profession works: New officers are inducted into a culture that doesn't value Black people; many become experienced cops and some stay long enough to become veterans who uphold the organization's cultural norms. The anti-Black culture is so pervasive that Black cops and other officers of color are often unable to escape it. Too many become unknowingly or unintentionally complicit in its sustainability and exacerbation. While assaulting Nichols, one officer yelled, "I'm going to baton the fuck out of you." Threatening to baton the fuck out of somebody (and then actually doing it) is a behavior learned within a specific cultural context. It's a cultural byproduct of the abuse of power.

Although the culture of the organizations in which many cops work is often bad and the institution of policing itself is racist, I don't believe every individual police officer is bad and racist. Some are able to resist the hypermasculine culture that gives them and their colleagues permission to cuss out and beat up people like the five officers did Nichols. Some resist the culture of cover-up and corruption when their colleagues act in ways that are so obviously wrong. Unless their lives or the lives of others are undeniably in serious danger, those cops resist the cultural norm of aggressively approaching harmless Black people with their guns drawn. We need more of *those* cops.

Officer training alone (especially a one-time workshop on implicit bias) will be insufficient. Furthermore, simply hiring a Black police chief and more Black police officers won't be enough to undo a racial crisis that has persisted for centuries. Law enforcement is in need of massive systemic, institutional, and cultural change. Police abolitionists disagree with me on this. They believe the only solution is to completely eliminate policing and law enforcement. While this isn't my stance, I can at least understand theirs. I can see why they have no faith that racist, low-accountability systems, cultures, and corrupt institutions can be reformed. I care less about which of us has the right philosophical position on this—I just want police officers to stop killing Black people.

OBIANEZE'S PRODUCTIVE DISAGREEMENT

On October 20, 2020, near the Lekki toll gate bridge in Lagos, Nigeria, Nigerian armed forces opened fire on a crowd of unarmed civilians protesting police brutality at the hands of the Special Anti-Robbery Squad (SARS). That shooting left around 25 people injured and 2 dead. I have always felt deep down that some Nigerians do not value the lives of other Nigerians. I feel that this sentiment exists among Black people worldwide, including the five murderers of Tyre Nichols. Dr. Harper, I agree with your stance that these officers entered into a profession that was created for the purpose of causing destruction and wreaking havoc in the lives of descendants of enslaved Africans and that that culture persists to this day. However, I wish you had spoken more about the anti-Blackness that these cops themselves might have harbored, even before entering the police force.

"You're Black, you're poor. . . . You're nothing at all!" These words angrily left Albert "Mister" Johnson's lips as Celie finally stood up to him in *The Color Purple*. Mister's sentiments are not unique to him, and I find that more Black people than we realize, for many reasons, also hate Black people. Maybe some of them experienced so much shame, humiliation, and pain from their Blackness that they swore to remove themselves from it as much as possible. Others might have grown up as one of few Black people in their communities and assimilated to their environment. Too, others may just hate Black people, plain and simple. Irrespective of the reason, I find it important to note that although these murderers were trained and molded to uphold a culture of anti-Blackness in their occupation, perhaps they also held these biases prior to joining the ranks of other officers.

I was especially excited to start my medical education and see others who look like me, grew up like me, think like me, and experience life like me pursuing a medical career. I was consistently disappointed to realize that many of these same people wouldn't even look at me twice in the wings of the hospital. Another memorable experience was when I excitedly reached out to a Black dermatologist to share my interest in conducting research and their unwillingness to provide me any assistance or mentorship, on top of insinuating that my research question was nonsensical without any feedback about how to improve it. These experiences do not prove that these physicians harbor anti-Blackness, but they make me question how much they value that aspect of their identity, especially as we all navigate this anti-Black world. I bring these personal experiences up because I wanted to highlight that beyond the culture of racism that exists within the environment of policing that may have influenced these five Black men to participate in murdering Tyre Nichols, they could have equally carried out this horrendous act on account of their own anti-Blackness, and the power and ability to act on it. I plead to those Black individuals who make it into positions of power and authority to please see value in your Blackness and use your positions to do right in the world. That is all I ask.

PRODUCTIVE RESPONSE FROM OBIANEZE'S PROFESSOR

Obianeze isn't wrong. But I honestly wish he were. Anti-Blackness is indeed a global phenomenon. Some of it is exported from the United States to other places around the world, but much of it was also locally manufactured within countries, towns, and cities on continents far beyond North America. Obianeze accurately acknowledges that some Black people (including but not limited to those in the Americas) possess anti-Black views and behave in anti-Black ways. Like their counterparts from other racial/ethnic groups, too many Black people were socialized to think negatively of other Black people. Obianeze is therefore right that Tyre Nichols's murderers may have entered the law enforcement profession with racist views about Black people and predominantly Black communities— this is called internalized racism. As indicated in Chapter 14 of this book, I'm staunchly opposed to flimsy, one-time implicit bias trainings. They aren't enough. Let's imagine that at least one of the Memphis cops was in his 30s; an hour-long workshop on unconscious bias, no matter how well designed, wouldn't have been sufficient to undo 3 decades of derogatory messages he'd previously received about Black people. One lesson on implicit bias won't help a 22-year-old new Black teacher recognize all the internalized messages he's bringing into his classroom or stop a 55-year-old doctor from inflicting harm on Black patients in the same ways as white physicians.

CHAPTER 37

What Executives Should Say to Employees When Police Officers Kill Unarmed Black People

America was on high alert just before the release of video footage of five Memphis police officers beating and killing Tyre Nichols, a 29-year-old unarmed Black man they pulled over for reckless driving.[1] Memphis braced itself for protests. Its public school system proactively canceled after-school programs, and a local community college abruptly shifted to online learning on the day the footage was publicly shared. Other cities also anticipated outrage and protests.

All five Memphis Police Department "Scorpion Unit" cops had already been fired and subsequently indicted on several criminal charges, including second-degree murder, two counts of official misconduct, two counts of aggravated kidnapping, one count of official oppression, and one count of aggravated assault. Memphis police chief Cerelyn "CJ" Davis had seen the video before it was released to the public. In comparing it to the police beating of Rodney King in 1992, "it is about the same, if not worse," she exclaimed in a CNN interview.[2] Davis said she hadn't personally witnessed anything worse in all her years of law enforcement.

Davis warned, "you're gonna see acts that defy humanity, you're going to see a disregard for life and the duty of care that we're all sworn to. Individuals watching will feel what the family felt, and if you don't, then you're not a human being." In a press conference, FBI director Christopher Wray said he'd also seen the video.[3] "I'm struggling to find a stronger word, but I will just tell you that I was appalled." Evidently, so too was President Joe Biden, who spoke with the Nichols family on the phone just hours before the video footage was released; *Washington Post* reporter Emily Davies tweeted a snippet of the conversation.[4]

In tragic moments like this, business leaders feel disgusted when they see similar video evidence of police officers killing Black people, but they don't know what to say or do. Unfortunately, some don't care enough to do anything. In June 2020, many executives sent company-wide emails to employees following Minneapolis police officer Derek Chauvin's murder of George Floyd, an unarmed Black man. As I noted in a *Washington Post* article at the height of global protests in response to Floyd's murder, those messages frustrated many Black employees who doubted their leaders' authenticity because of longstanding demonstrations of carelessness for Black lives.[5]

As the nation prepared to react to the fatal attack of Tyre Nichols, I anticipated that some executives would feel compelled to write to their employees. At the time, I felt they should've. Here are five things I recommended for inclusion in those messages:

1. A genuine expression of how the video personally made them feel. This requires leaders to actually watch the video in its entirety once it's released. It also demands that they replace the usual sanitized, corporatized language that ultimately says nothing with more honest and authentic reactions to what they saw in the video.
2. An acknowledgment that Nichols's homicide isn't an isolated incident but a continuation of the longstanding practice of police killings of unarmed Black Americans. Leaders might also strongly consider calling for more to be done to stop racial profiling, police brutality, and the killings of unarmed Black people.
3. An acknowledgment that while all employees who've seen the video or heard about Nichols's killing are likely negatively affected, Black colleagues are undoubtedly more devastated because Nichols was Black; because they, too, are susceptible to being pulled over and similarly terrorized; and because this latest fatality compounds generations of trauma that Black communities have experienced as a result of police brutality.
4. Encouragement to engage in self-care, including but not limited to taking time off to recover from the trauma of this most recent racial crisis. For companies that can afford to do so, these should be paid wellness days.
5. An affirmation of the value of Black lives. Doing this will be challenging for some executives who believe that all lives matter. They do. But in this instance (and in far too many others like it), it was a Black person's life that tragically ended as a result of police brutality. Hence, this particular message at this particular time should focus on Black lives.

As was the case in June 2020, some Black employees and other colleagues will read emails from their executives with understandably high levels of skepticism and doubt, especially if the fifth point that I recommended is grossly inconsistent with their everyday workplace realities. Given this, I argue that leaders must do all they can to consistently demonstrate their deep commitments by equitably hiring and promoting Black employees, ensuring workplaces are fair and inclusive, fixing structures and systems that cyclically disadvantage Black workers, and investing portions of their corporate social responsibility dollars into Black communities. They must also hold everyone else in the organization accountable for doing the same. On their own, one-time executive messages following tragedies like the murders of Tyre Nichols and George Floyd aren't enough.

SHIVANI'S PRODUCTIVE DISAGREEMENT

As a responsible and empathetic executive, it is important to address the recent fatal police beating of Tyre Nichols and its impact on our Black colleagues, friends, and partners. Professor Harper's *Forbes* article is an important wake-up call to all executives, reminding them of the importance of being a support system to their employees during such difficult times and also supporting them in doing so.

While I agree with the content of the article, I understand the concerns that an executive might have while addressing this issue. In my opinion, it is very important to address these issues proactively in the article and make recommendations while addressing those concerns. By understanding and addressing the concerns that an executive might have while addressing this issue, we can help ensure that this message is well received and acted on.

The article suggests taking a stance that this homicide isn't an isolated incident but a continuation of longstanding practices of police officers killing unarmed Black Americans. While I agree with this and even the executive might, it is important to understand that not everyone might hold the same views on this topic. Some might have opposing views (however incorrect), some might think that a workplace is not a place to discuss such issues and that discussing them can lead to tensions and conflict inside the workplace. Hence it is crucial for executives to explain why they are taking a stance against systemic racism, not just because it is the right thing to do but also to bring everyone on the same page and fight against the issue together. It also might be a good idea to guide employees to resources that could help them better understand this issue so that everyone can get together and take necessary steps to fight systemic racism.

The executives might also be concerned about the impact this message might have on their relationships with clients and partners. If an executive is reading this article, they might think, "I agree with the message but I can't do it because I will lose these many clients and ultimately hamper my employees financially." The concern is valid and can be addressed beforehand. The article could have said that although you risk losing some partners or clients that don't have the same views or values that you do, it is a good opportunity for executives to reevaluate their association with these partners. It is important for an organization to have a clear culture and values, and choosing partners who share those values is crucial for long-term success. Choose those values and then choose your partners rather than not being able to support your employees just because your partners won't like it.

At the end, the article suggests investing in Black communities and investing corporate social responsibility dollars in Black communities. I agree with this, but some other minority groups might feel they are being overlooked. So instead, I would suggest adding an emphasis on the support that we need to provide our Black friends and colleagues first and foremost so that everyone feels included and supported.

PRODUCTIVE RESPONSE FROM SHIVANI'S PROFESSOR

Shivani has me thinking about the need for multidimensionality, depth, and specificity in executive correspondence, as well as in corporate professional learning experiences. I agree that some employees will react negatively to an email that is grounded entirely in a leader's personal opinion. An anti-police message is the example Shivani provides. To avoid being misunderstood as a too-woke attack on all law enforcement officers, executives should include stats and facts that would help educate employees on the systemic durability of this problem. The email itself provides an opportunity for teaching and learning, and so too do professional learning experiences that are focused on racism and anti-Blackness. Data, not just philosophical stances, could be viewed as less polarizing. To be sure, I think it's fine for leaders and workshop facilitators to courageously articulate their own personal viewpoints but recognize that doing so will inevitably invite resistance from employees who have opposing opinions. Put differently, there absolutely should be space for emotions in executive correspondence and in learning experiences—but it shouldn't start and stop there. In my work with hundreds of organizations over the years, I have found that coupling feelings with data is far more effective. This may also help address Shivani's caution about some groups feeling overlooked because of an organization's emphasis on Black people. Plenty of evidence also exists that shows how racism disadvantages Indigenous, Asian American, Latino, and other people of color groups. Those issues deserve their own stand-alone executive messages and professional learning experiences.

CHAPTER 38

ChatGPT Threatens Authenticity of DEI Communications From Leaders

ChatGPT could make leaders sound like they *really* care about diversity, equity, and inclusion—even if they *really* don't. It'll be especially troubling when the messages being communicated are on DEI topics about which leaders know very little and aren't sufficiently invested. This poses one of the biggest threats to the integrity of DEI work in organizations. It's also one of the most significant risks to leaders' relationships with diverse employees whom AI-generated words deceptively affirm.

DEI communications from many C-suites are already plagued with authenticity problems. Statements from the CEO about the tragic police shootings of unarmed Black Americans, as well as the seemingly obligatory history/heritage month emails to celebrate LGBTQ+ Pride and various ethnic groups each year, are typically written by someone else. Employees can sometimes detect the artificiality. Ghostwriting therefore undermines executive integrity on DEI. ChatGPT will exacerbate this.

Women employees would surely be disappointed to learn that ChatGPT wrote the email they received from their CEO stressing the importance of ending sexism and advancing more of them to leadership roles within the company. Many would feel lied to. This would weaken the CEO's credibility with women and other colleagues who are seriously committed to women's workplace success. Future executive-level communications about gender equity and other DEI topics would likely be read through the prisms of skepticism and doubt—or altogether ignored.

ChatGPT could be seemingly useful to leaders who don't quite know what to say to their employees about specific racial, social justice, and DEI issues. I instructed this publicly available AI resource to write a statement from a CEO to employees about the recent fatal beating of Tyre Nichols by police officers in Memphis. Here's what it says:

> Dear Employees,
> It is with deep sorrow and regret that I must inform you of the senseless beating of Tyre Nichols on Tuesday night. This is an outrage and a tragedy, and we all send our thoughts and prayers to Tyre and his family. This incident is a

heartbreaking reminder of the racism, discrimination, and violence that still exist in our world today. We must all stand together in solidarity and not allow this hatred to take over our society. We must take action and fight against injustice, violence, and bigotry in any way we can.

At this time, our main focus is ensuring that Tyre and his family have all the support they need to get through this difficult time. We are doing everything we can to assist in their healing process.

We cannot and will not stand for any sort of hatred or violence in our community. We are all in this together and must work together to create a better and safer world for everyone.

Sincerely,
[Your Name]
CEO

Even though it doesn't include all the components I recommended to executives in Chapter 37 of this book, I must admit that the ChatGPT-crafted CEO message sounds quite authentic. That's the problem. But it isn't entirely a new problem. Words being communicated by executives that executives themselves didn't write isn't new.

American presidents rely heavily on speechwriters. Many listeners are aware that Mr. President didn't write the words he's reading off the teleprompter (by the way, the gendering here is intentional because all 46 U.S. presidents have been men). For better or worse, it was usually clear when President Donald Trump wasn't reading words that had been written on his behalf.[1] In companies and universities, communications officers often draft or fully construct statements, emails, and speeches for presidents who understandably don't have enough time to write everything themselves. This explains how and why those messages usually sound so empty, sanitized, and corporatized. It also helps partially explain why executive leaders' DEI-related actions often fail to match the words expressed in messages sent under their signatures.

As I explained in my *Washington Post* article following the murder of George Floyd in summer 2020, many Black professionals doubted the seriousness of messages they and coworkers were receiving from their executive leaders addressing the tragedy and declaring the value of Black lives.[2] In many companies, Black employees could tell that the comms team, not the CEO, wrote those words. It disappointed some and infuriated others.

Here's one longstanding truth of which many executives are probably unaware: A lot of Latino professionals in an audience can tell when the leader's Hispanic Heritage Month event remarks were written by someone else. The words sound hollow and it's painfully apparent that those leaders haven't spent much time immersing themselves in Latino culture or talking with the company's Latino employees. There's a chance that a ChatGPT speech would sound better—especially if it's instructed to make the second and third drafts sound more personal and compassionate. But is this the right thing to do? No.

Because ChatGPT is so new, I and other DEI researchers haven't yet had an opportunity to study how women, employees of color, and colleagues who are queer, Muslim, Jewish, or otherwise diverse would feel about receiving a caring-sounding email focused on their communities from a leader who used ChatGPT to write it. I comfortably predict that the overwhelming majority of them would deem it improper, inexcusably dishonest, and in some instances, typical.

Some K–12 school districts—including the New York City Department of Education, our nation's largest public school system—have already banned students' use of ChatGPT because it's considered plagiarism (as are other ways of misrepresenting something that someone else wrote as one's own work).[3] Higher education leaders and faculty members also are grappling with the tech tool's ethical implications. *Forbes* contributor Chris Westfall recently wrote about a survey in which nearly three-fourths of professors indicated they were concerned about collegians using the AI tool to cheat.[4]

ChatGPT shouldn't be banned in businesses, but corporate leaders must resist using it to voice their perspectives on and commitments to DEI. They have to be mindful of what the first letter in AI stands for—employees neither want nor deserve artificiality in the DEI communications they receive.

SHEHAB'S PRODUCTIVE DISAGREEMENT

In this article, Dr. Harper claims that the use of ChatGPT and other generative AI tools in the composition of DEI-related correspondences from leaders will undermine the integrity of the messaging, potentially damaging relationships with diverse audiences. The subject of "authenticity" is one that is especially challenging in the context of DEI. The majority of corporate DEI efforts were born or reignited during a period of relatively extreme social unrest triggered by a series of brutal murders—tragedies that brought into the spotlight many deeply disturbing structural flaws in our institutions. Corporate America being home to many, if not most, of those problematic institutions, the reaction of businesses defined how the public perceives DEI today.

Unfortunately, corporate crisis management mechanisms are not designed to deliver structural change but rather to protect shareholder value through strategic communications that delay, obfuscate, and distract. This is where public relations professionals step in: They are highly trained in managing outrage and limiting liability in the most cost-effective manner possible. As such, a fundamental lack of authenticity is woven into the fiber of many, if not most, corporate approaches to DEI.

The problem of authenticity has nothing to do with ChatGPT, it has to do with the existing design features of many corporate DEI initiatives. It is extremely rare that any executive drafts their own messaging. Even as a legal operative at a beauty start-up with 40 employees, I was often the one drafting press releases on behalf of the CEO.

Authenticity has nothing to do with the tools used to generate the messaging; it is born in incentive structures, then lives in commitments and KPIs. This is why, in the panorama of modern corporate strategies, the growth of "social impact" teams represents a fascinating evolution. I've found that corporates often consider their "impact" goals to interact more closely with their respective core businesses than they do goals associated with "DEI," which is often seen as a cost rather than an investment. This is problematic, of course, because we need both DEI and social impact programs in order to drive societal progress.

The branding effort that is necessary in order for DEI communications to be widely recognized as "authentic" presents a meaningful challenge, one that is far greater than simple avoidance of generative AI. I would argue that focusing on AI as the culprit constitutes a misidentification of the core challenges associated with DEI messaging. Admittedly, Dr. Harper does address those challenges in a compelling and fairly comprehensive manner in several other *Forbes* articles he has published.

PRODUCTIVE RESPONSE FROM SHEHAB'S PROFESSOR

What Shehab describes is disappointingly consistent with experiences I've had with several companies. It's clear to me when pleasing shareholders and board members is a higher priority than is ensuring that corporate communications deeply affirm diverse customers, employees, and partners. Is it really so hard to concurrently achieve both aims? Or is it that executives and communications professionals who ghostwrite on their behalf are too afraid? Or do they not know how? Or could it be that they don't care as much about DEI as they should? Demographic stratification also presents another plausible explanation. Executive-level and senior-level leadership teams tend to not be as diverse as other parts of the organization. Also, communications departments aren't particularly well known for being among the most racially diverse within organizations (even though the representation of women is usually higher). All these considerations compel me to agree with Shehab that the use of ChatGPT isn't the biggest problem here. Without it and other generative AI resources, corporate communications about DEI would still be insufficient and disappointing because of other factors that he and I identified in our exchanges. Notwithstanding my and Shehab's alignment on these points, I still feel strongly that leaders should write their own messages, especially those in which they are conveying personal and organizational commitments to DEI. If they don't know how, then they should get coaching and feedback.

CHAPTER 39

Rite Aid Facial Recognition Lawsuit Shows AI Risks of Shopping While Black

As a condition of a legal settlement with the Federal Trade Commission, Rite Aid has agreed to discontinue its reliance on AI-powered facial recognition technology in its shoplifting prevention efforts.[1] The retail drugstore chain allegedly profiled Black, Latino, and Asian shoppers at higher rates than whites. Specifically, stores began using AI-powered technology in 2012 to identify customers who were deemed likely to steal products, according to the FTC complaint.[2] Employees reportedly received faulty match alerts when those "Be on the Look Out" consumers entered stores. Trend data presented in the legal documents show that people of color were disproportionately and wrongly followed, harassed, and embarrassed in front of others.

"Shopping while black" is a longstanding phenomenon that usually entails greeting Black shoppers with suspicion the moment they enter stores, following them around the entire time, and wrongly accusing them of stealing. Locking Black haircare and beauty products in glass cabinets while placing similar goods aimed at white buyers on open shelves, as Walmart did for many years,[3] is another example of how retail stores discriminate against Black patrons. Rite Aid's misuse of facial recognition technology is a troubling case example of how AI further exposes Black people and other shoppers of color to what Michelle Dunlap and other scholars call retail racism.[4]

Rashawn Ray, a sociology professor at the University of Maryland and senior fellow at the Brookings Institution, explains: "AI technologies often replicate existing inequalities because they are created by people and in spaces that lack diversity and inclusion to make the technology equitable. If the same stereotypes used to profile Black people in everyday encounters are put in algorithms, then we get facial recognition that stereotypes Black people just like another human would."

Implicit biases are largely informed by implicit associations—mental shortcuts that compel people to unconsciously associate particular groups with particular characteristics, expectations, and behaviors. Implicit bias often plays out quite explicitly in retail environments. Problem is, store employees too often wrongly associate shoppers of color with trends that shoplifting data don't support. Most shoplifters in the United States are white, notes Shaun L. Gabbidon, author of the book *Shopping While Black: Consumer Racial Profiling in America*.[5] Despite this fact, "the racist deployment of the technology in mostly minority communities continues to perpetuate the false narrative around who the majority of shoplifters are."

Costs associated with theft of goods pose serious financial risks to businesses. Given this, it would seem that store owners and managers would want to be sure they're monitoring the right people. While they and their employees are unnecessarily surveilling and otherwise harassing shoppers of color, white shoplifters often get away with in-store crimes without interference. AI privileges them. Meanwhile, profits are forfeited from humiliated shoppers of color who would've spent money in those same stores on those same days had they not been treated like criminals. It's worth noting that in some communities, namely those that are food and retail deserts, low-income residents of color don't have a choice but to patronize establishments in which they're routinely subjected to such racism and abuse.

"Retailers need to think carefully and cautiously before utilizing AI to implement security measures in their stores," says Cassi Pittman Claytor, associate professor of sociology at Case Western Reserve University. "Heightened surveillance never makes people want to spend their money. Time and time again, research has illustrated that AI is not only capable but quite competent in perpetuating racial inequities and reflecting racial biases that are endemic to our society. It is extremely naive to think that AI is 'race-neutral' or that adopting new technologies will eliminate persistent and society-wide problems like retail racism."

AI also has the likelihood of exacerbating racial profiling in other domains, such as policing. There is the highly publicized example of Porsha Woodruff, an 8-months pregnant Black woman in Detroit whom facial recognition technology erroneously matched with someone who committed a robbery and carjacking.[6] Police wrongly arrested Woodruff at home in front of her two young daughters. Examples like this help explain why many Black Americans worry about and doubt the trustworthiness of AI-powered surveillance systems.

Pew Research Center data show that among all racial groups surveyed, Black respondents were least trusting of facial recognition technology in policing.[7] Nearly half (48%) of Black people predicted that officers would misuse AI-powered technologies to surveil predominantly Black and Latino neighborhoods more often than they would residential contexts with different racial demographics. Being misidentified by police on the streets and then mistakenly accused of stealing in stores doubly exposes people of color to extremely consequential technology-enabled dangers.

Safiya U. Noble, the David O. Sears Presidential Endowed Chair at UCLA, is one of the world's foremost experts on racist and sexist algorithmic harms. She contends, "racial profiling technologies like facial recognition and other pattern-recognition systems are marketed by Silicon Valley as hyper-convenient, but they are trained on historically racist and sexist data, and that, on its face, means that these technologies will continue to discriminate." Noble, who directs the UCLA Center on Race and Digital Justice, predicts "companies will continue to face serious consequences as they adopt these faulty systems that threaten both their bottom line and their brands." She also says we should expect the FTC to continue protecting consumers from dangerous technologies.

"Because it is notoriously less accurate when used on women and people of color, retailers should be incredibly cautious about deploying facial recognition technology in any situation—but at the very least, it is imperative that the technology not be unequally deployed in certain neighborhoods," advises Nicol Turner Lee, director of the Center for Technology Innovation at the Brookings Institution. "Generally speaking, retailers should shy away from ever using facial recognition technology as a predictive measure, like Rite Aid did, because the risk of biased inaccuracies makes racial profiling all too likely."

Earlier this year, five U.S. senators cosigned a letter opposing the Transportation Security Administration's (TSA) use of facial recognition technology at U.S. airports.[8] In it, they cited a National Institute of Standards and Technology study based on 18 million photos of more than 8 million Americans.[9] Results showed that in comparison to white men, Black and Asian people were up to 100 times more likely to be misidentified by facial recognition technology. As part of its settlement with the FTC, Rite Aid agreed to suspend its use of AI-powered surveillance systems for 5 years. Other retailers should do the same until racial biases that are embedded in those technologies are rigorously and repeatedly tested, then ultimately eliminated.

PAWAN'S PRODUCTIVE DISAGREEMENT

The article raises crucial questions about racial profiling and the use of AI in retail environments. Further, the FTC complaint raises valid concerns about "retail racism" amplified by AI. While the article effectively addresses the troubling use of AI racial profiling, it's crucial to recognize it as just one aspect of a larger issue: systemic racial bias.

As the article points out, retail racism is a manifestation of implicit biases held by employees, discriminatory store policies, training data, and targeting of minority communities with surveillance. Focusing solely on AI risks obscures the broader context and perpetuates the myth of technology as the sole culprit. AI itself isn't inherently biased. Biases in AI stem from the training data and human decisions guiding development and deployment. Overemphasizing bias in AI overlooks the human responsibility inherent in these technologies. AI can and should be designed and implemented to mitigate bias, not exacerbate it.

The article advocates for a ban on AI-powered surveillance in retail environments until biases are eliminated. This solution may be overly simplistic. As technology evolves at an incredible pace, and given its potential for positive applications, business owners and communities cannot afford to dismiss it altogether. Instead, the focus should be on developing and implementing equitable solutions. This means rethinking processes and governance practices. This requires a multipronged approach. Here are some aspects to consider:

Inclusive Data Collection and AI Algorithm Design—Surveillance AI algorithms need to be designed, trained, and tested by diverse teams.

Additionally, they should incorporate datasets that are diverse, and they should be audited regularly for bias.

Transparency and Accountability—The use of AI surveillance should be clearly communicated to guests along with its purpose. Retailers should review potential risks and put in safeguards. Additionally, an independent oversight mechanism should be established to ensure accountability.

Engaging Community and Employees—Communities that are disproportionately impacted by AI surveillance technologies should be involved in their development and implementation. Additionally, to mitigate unintended harm, employees of such stores should be trained in cultural competence, conflict de-escalation, and ethical use of these AI tools.

Addressing Systemic Biases—Regulatory agencies need to step in with clear guidelines on addressing systemic racism. These agencies can compel retailers to put in safeguards and to disclose adverse incidences.

Rite Aid's use of AI surveillance and their failings are a stark reminder to all stakeholders of the dangers of unchecked use of AI. It also underscores AI's ability to exacerbate inequities and perpetuate racism. At the same time, developing AI technologies is crucial for the future of businesses and communities. Some of the steps discussed earlier can mitigate the harm while enabling equitable development of AI solutions.

PRODUCTIVE RESPONSE FROM PAWAN'S PROFESSOR

I'm grateful that Pawan didn't just present a critique of my positions but also furnished a list of potential solutions. I agree that the AI train has left the station. Therefore, retailers and other organizational leaders really ought to take seriously the recommendations that Pawan and experts I interviewed for this article offered. I would add to their list the need to massively increase state, federal, and corporate investments into the creation and expansion of AI-focused degree programs at historically Black colleges and universities, Hispanic-serving institutions, tribal colleges, Asian American and Native American Pacific Islander-serving institutions, and community colleges that enroll comparatively higher numbers of students of color. The current and future generation of technologists must be more racially, ethnically, culturally, and linguistically diverse than prior cohorts. Until the people themselves who are making the technologies are more diverse, algorithmic biases and other technological harms will persist and multiply. Simply having more people of color among technologists isn't enough. Educational institutions that prepare them and companies that hire them have a responsibility to ensure they aren't bringing the same biases as their white counterparts to the development of new innovations. To be sure, the responsibility ought not rest entirely on technologists of color. Educational institutions that prepare them and companies that hire them have a responsibility to ensure that white professionals and AI engineers who've come to America from other parts of the world also are presented opportunities to discover and correct their implicit and explicit biases.

CHAPTER 40

Ways Philanthropic Foundations Can Respond to Costly Attacks on DEI

Philanthropic foundations have invested billions of dollars into programs, research, partnerships, and other initiatives that help reduce racial, gender, and socioeconomic disparities. Those efforts have been in response to longstanding, well-documented inequities in wealth, health, juvenile and criminal justice, and education, to name a few. Reckless, politicized attacks on diversity, equity, and inclusion threaten to undo much of the progress that has resulted from those foundation investments. The anti-DEI movement is well funded and masterfully coordinated. And it's working, as evidenced by the banning of DEI-focused books and lessons, the discontinuation of DEI-related resources in K–12 schools and higher education institutions, the firings of chief diversity officers and their teams, and the defunding of professional development experiences for educators. The movement has picked up steam in education over the past 4 years and is now swiftly making its way into corporations, our nation's military, and other workplaces. Money is needed to stop it.

Philanthropic support will help save our democracy from one of its biggest, most unnecessary threats. Secondarily, it will help foundations protect their past, current, and future financial investments. More inequity is guaranteed to ensue as DEI activities go away. Hence, much of the money that foundations have already committed to addressing inequities will be wasted. Furthermore, when this ridiculous movement ends, foundations will be left to help clean up the mess of inequities it produced. Recovery will be far costlier than would bold, preemptive attempts to decelerate the movement now.

Beyond grantmaking, many foundations have explicitly declared commitments to equity in their mission statements and elsewhere. Remaining silent and doing too little to expressly fight back against politicized attacks on DEI call into question the depth and integrity of those espoused values. Some program officers of color and other employees who make foundations diverse are wondering whether their workplace, which has so proudly and repeatedly pronounced a commitment to equity, is going to contradict itself during this horrifyingly consequential time. At this point, awarding grants to support DEI-focused projects while remaining silent on politicized attacks against the aims of those very projects isn't what our nation needs from its philanthropic investors. In addition to awarding and renewing grants to support difference-making DEI work, here are at least a few additional ways foundations can step up at this moment.

Leverage Influence to Help People Understand Why DEI Is Essential—Attackers often make bold, overwhelmingly false generalizations about DEI. Foremost, they claim it's divisive. Foundations know better. They understand that DEI efforts aim to unite people, right past wrongs, eliminate disparities between groups, and make organizations and communities stronger. They've invested in thousands of high-quality initiatives that have advanced DEI across the United States and around the globe. Foundations are therefore perfectly poised to disrupt misinformation and disinformation pertaining to DEI.

Unite Previous and Current Grantees—Foundations have enormous convening power. They also know who they've invested in and which of those organizations used their grants to effectively address racial, gender, and socioeconomic inequities. Those grantees could be brought together to identify ways they might collaboratively fight back against politicized attacks on DEI. Foundation dollars could support the DEI sustainability agendas that previous and current grantees coconstruct. If funders set the right tables, organizations that do high-quality DEI work could easily furnish evidence that disproves the lies exaggerators are effectively spreading.

Invest in DEI Defense Efforts—Foundations ought to seek out and award their largest grants to organizations that are actively fighting back against politicized efforts to dismantle DEI. Most funders try to stay out of politics and may therefore convince themselves that investing in DEI defense movements is a form of political side-taking. They should pick the right side. One side is using divisive partisan politics to trick as many Americans as possible into believing that DEI is what it isn't; the other side is simply defending the work that rigorous foundation vetting processes previously deemed worthy of investment. They're also responding to credible research that shows persistent and pervasive racial, gender, and socioeconomic inequities. They're defending democracy. These high-trust organizations ought to be given the resources needed not only to defend DEI but also to greatly expand longstanding work that has helped communities, organizations, and professions begin to correct problematic histories, cultures, mindsets, structures, systems, practices, and policies. These organizations need money to finance their defense activities, especially since the destructive anti-DEI movement is so well funded.

Adapt Rapid Emergency Funding Processes—In the early stages of the pandemic, many foundations impressively evolved their grantmaking processes to rapidly fund research on the coronavirus, including its higher rates of infection and mortality in communities of color. Grants were also awarded to study the impact of COVID-19 on educational outcomes for students. In addition to research, foundations awarded grants to organizations that were providing COVID testing, hotspots to schoolchildren in Internet deserts, vaccine promotion campaigns, and other programmatic responses to the public health crisis. Politicized attacks on DEI are sure to produce catastrophic levels of inequities that will negatively affect millions of Americans. It's an urgent national crisis at this point. Surely, there are lessons that foundations learned as they awarded rapid emergency grants as part of their COVID responses. The DEI crisis necessitates a reboot of the best of what worked well within and across foundations 4–5 years ago.

Join With Other Foundations to Collectively Respond—Despite some inescapable bureaucratic challenges and maneuverable cross-organizational tensions, much about funders' collaboratives works well. Groups of funders already pool funds to make a collective impact on a pressing issue or opportunity about which each individual foundation cares. Again, many foundations say equity is among their highest priorities, and they annually award numerous grants to organizations that are working on DEI-focused projects. These shared priorities set those funders up for successful co-investment partnerships during this highly consequential moment in American history.

These aren't the only ways that foundations can help rescue our democracy from one of its biggest cross-sector threats. But these five actions would undoubtedly help them enact their espoused values while supporting grantees who are fighting back against politicized attacks on DEI. It would be a real shame if a 4–5-year senseless, misguided movement reversed decades of progress that philanthropic dollars helped achieve. Individually and collectively, foundations must protect their investments.

DEVON'S PRODUCTIVE DISAGREEMENT

Philanthropic foundations must be engaged in the fight against politicized attacks on DEI. With combined assets of more than $1.5 trillion,[1] foundations in the United States have not only the funds to enact change but also the power and social capital to influence our culture. However, some of the suggestions made by Shaun Harper may not be feasible or the most effective.

Before we can determine how foundations can best support DEI, we must have an honest assessment of where the philanthropic sector stands in its own understanding of these efforts. In response to false claims about DEI, Harper states that "foundations know better." Unfortunately, while one might hope or assume that is the case, this generalization is not fully accurate. Many foundations today are still perpetuating colonialism, white saviorism, and paternalism. The pervasive system of "Global North philanthropy" reflects philanthropy's roots in colonial power dynamics and the notion that one community, historically white, must "save" the others.[2] Following the murder of George Floyd in 2020, many private foundations made pledges to support organizations fighting for racial justice and racial equity. However, over a third of the top 20 grant recipients in this category were founded by white people in power.[3]

Harper's call for foundations to embrace the DEI movement and influence the public to join in is helpful to explore further. Some alternative methods foundations should consider include adding DEI questions to grant applications, highlighting grantees and partners who are exemplary in implementing DEI practices both internally and externally, and funding DEI efforts directly. Adding questions to grant applications about DEI practices and considerations will allow foundations to both evaluate nonprofits based on their commitment to DEI and signal to applicants and other organizations in the sector that DEI is important and essential. This signaling can also occur if foundations make an effort to highlight where DEI is going well. This will not only showcase the benefits and positive effects of DEI practices but also contribute to the conversation as a whole. Finally, the most direct way foundations can support DEI is to fund it. This can take a few different forms—grants to organizations that are supporting diverse communities, grants to organizations to build internal DEI programming, and grants to organizations that are advocating for DEI on a larger scale.

As agents of change, it is clear that philanthropic foundations must play a role in the fight for DEI. Harper's call to action for these foundations is timely and critical. However, we must be realistic in our approach and understand the historical limitations of philanthropy.

PRODUCTIVE RESPONSE FROM DEVON'S PROFESSOR

Devon respectfully called attention to an inadvertent overstatement of mine: "foundations know better." I definitely didn't mean that so universally. Some know better, but I have no evidence that all or even most do. Devon's critique was also a reminder that foundation leaders and employees need consciousness-raising and skill-building professional learning opportunities on a range of racial equity and DEI-focused topics. They also would benefit from reading syntheses of research on inequities and injustices, and then discussing what they learned with other colleagues within and beyond their foundations. Their familiarity with these issues cannot be isolated to their readings of applications from prospective grantees. Devon's recommendation to add DEI-focused questions to grant applications is good but with a couple of caveats. First, program officers have to actually read and take seriously what applicants write. In other words, simply adding these questions to forms because it's trendy to do so isn't helpful. Second, weak demonstrations of organizational commitment to DEI should be disqualifying. Questions shouldn't invite mere philosophical articulations of why DEI is important to the applicant's work. Instead, they should require the furnishing of specific and meaningful examples of how DEI has been advanced and sustained, as well as honest explanations about why and how the work remains underachieved along with descriptions of efforts the organization is taking to improve its DEI-related outcomes. While I appreciate Devon's recommendations, I still advocate for the five categorical actions presented in my article.

Endnotes

Preface

1. Turning Point USA. "Professor Watchlist." Accessed February 23, 2025. https://www.professorwatchlist.org
2. U.S. Congress. Senate. Dismantle DEI Act of 2024. S.4516. 118th Cong., 2nd sess. Introduced in Senate June 12, 2024. https://www.congress.gov/bill/118th-congress/senate-bill/4516/text
3. Hess, Frederick M., and Pedro A. Noguera. *A Search for Common Ground: Conversations About the Toughest Questions in K-12 Education*. Teachers College Press, 2021.

Chapter 1

1. "Parents Demanding Answers After Upland Students Receive Racist Drawings." YouTube. February 20, 2023. Video, https://www.youtube.com/watch?v=OQ9FlUn7BeY
2. California Department of Education. "2021–22 Enrollment by Ethnicity, Pepper Tree Elementary Report (36-75069-6109573)." Accessed February 23, 2025. https://dq.cde.ca.gov/dataquest/dqcensus/EnrEthLevels.aspx?cds=36750696109573&agglevel=School&year=2021-22&ro=y
3. Harper, Shaun R., and James Bridgeforth. "Why We Weren't Surprised to See Teachers Holding a Noose." *Education Week*, May 14, 2019. https://www.edweek.org/leadership/opinion-why-we-werent-surprised-to-see-teachers-holding-a-noose/2019/05
4. Bridgeforth, James C. "'This Isn't Who We Are': A Critical Discourse Analysis of School and District Leaders' Responses to Racial Violence in Schools." *Journal of School Leadership* 31, no. 1–2 (2021): 85–106.
5. Modereger, Becki. "Letter to Pepper Tree Elementary School Families." Accessed February 23, 2025. https://www.dropbox.com/scl/fi/s5kae56f5kisysh9bm6g4/Pepper-Tree-Principal-Modereger-Letter.pdf
6. Smith, Edward J., and Shaun R. Harper. *Disproportionate Impact of K-12 School Suspension and Expulsion on Black Students in Southern States*. University of Pennsylvania, Center for the Study of Race and Equity in Education, 2015.

Chapter 2

1. Dellatto, Marisa. "Unprecedented Book Ban Attempts in 2021—Many With LGBTQ Themes—Library Group Reports." *Forbes*, April 4, 2022. https://www.forbes.com/sites/marisadellatto/2022/04/04/unprecedented-book-ban-attempts-in-2021-many-with-lgbtq-themes-library-group-reports/

2. Waxman, Olivia B. "Why Toni Morrison's Books Are So Often the Target of Book Bans." *TIME*, January 31, 2022. https://time.com/6143127/toni-morrison-book-bans

3. Schwartz, Sarah. "Map: Where Critical Race Theory Is Under Attack." *Education Week*, June 11, 2021. https://www.edweek.org/policy-politics/map-where-critical-race-theory-is-under-attack/2021/06

4. "The Debate Over LGBTQ+ Topics in Schools." Fox11 Los Angeles, June 5, 2023. Video, https://www.foxla.com/video/1230635.amp

5. Faguy, Ana. "DeSantis Signs Bill Banning Public Colleges From Funding Diversity Programs." *Forbes*, May 15, 2023. https://www.forbes.com/sites/anafaguy/2023/05/15/desantis-signs-bill-banning-public-colleges-from-funding-diversity-programs/

6. Burch, Audra D. S. "Texas Lawmakers Pass Ban on D.E.I. Programs at State Universities." *The New York Times*, May 29, 2023. https://www.nytimes.com/2023/05/29/us/texas-dei-program-ban.html

7. McWhorter, John. "Racism in America Is Over." *Forbes*, December 30, 2008. https://www.forbes.com/2008/12/30/end-of-racism-oped-cx_jm_1230mcwhorter.html

8. Ryan, Josiah. "'This Was a Whitelash': Van Jones' Take on the Election Results." CNN, November 9, 2016. https://www.cnn.com/2016/11/09/politics/van-jones-results-disappointment-cnntv/index.html

9. Pew Research Center. "An Examination of the 2016 Electorate, Based on Validated Voters." Accessed February 23, 2025. https://www.pewresearch.org/politics/2018/08/09/an-examination-of-the-2016-electorate-based-on-validated-voters

10. The White House. "Executive Order on Combating Race and Sex Stereotyping." September 22, 2020. https://trumpwhitehouse.archives.gov/presidential-actions/executive-order-combating-race-sex-stereotyping

11. Fuchs, Hailey. "Trump Attack on Diversity Training Has a Quick and Chilling Effect." *The New York Times*, October 13, 2020. https://www.nytimes.com/2020/10/13/us/politics/trump-diversity-training-race.html

12. Guynn, Jessica. "President Joe Biden Rescinds Donald Trump Ban on Diversity Training About Systemic Racism." *USA Today*, January 20, 2021. https://www.usatoday.com/story/money/2021/01/20/biden-executive-order-overturns-trump-diversity-training-ban/4236891001

13. Harper, Shaun. "Why It's Important to Say George Floyd Was Murdered." *Forbes*, October 14, 2022. https://www.forbes.com/sites/shaunharper/2022/10/14/why-its-important-to-say-george-floyd-was-murdered/

14. Beer, Tommy. "Darnella Frazier—Teen Who Recorded George Floyd's Final Moments—Praised by Biden, Oprah and More." *Forbes*, April 21, 2021. https://www.forbes.com/sites/tommybeer/2021/04/21/teen-who-recorded-george-floyds-final-moments-praised-for-her-bravery/?sh=5a66c977c545

15. Webb, M. L. *The GayBCs*. Quirk, 2019.

Chapter 3

1. State of Washington, Office of Governor Jay Inslee. "Executive Order 22-02: Achieving Equity in Washington State Government." https://governor.wa.gov/sites/default/files/exe_order/22-02%20-%20Equity%20in%20State%20Government%20%28tmp%29.pdf

2. Trounson, Rebecca. "A Startling Statistic at UCLA." *The Los Angeles Times*, June 3, 2006. https://www.latimes.com/archives/la-xpm-2006-jun-03-me-ucla3-story.html

3. Lumpkin, Lauren, Nick Anderson, and Danielle Douglas-Gabriel. "Amid Nationwide Enrollment Drops, Some HBCUs Are Growing. So Are Threats." *The Washington Post*, February 16, 2022. https://www.washingtonpost.com/education/2022/02/11/hbcu-enrollment-growth-bomb-threats

4. Harper, Shaun R. *Black Male Student-Athletes and Racial Inequities in NCAA Division I Revenue-Generating College Sports: 2018 Edition*. University of Southern California Race and Equity Center, 2018.

5. Harper, Shaun R. "COVID-19 and the Racial Equity Implications of Reopening College and University Campuses." *American Journal of Education* 127 (2020), 153–162.

6. Wood, Sarah. "What the End of Race-Conscious College Admissions Could Mean for HBCUs." *U.S. News & World Report*, September 1, 2023. https://www.usnews.com/education/best-colleges/articles/what-the-end-of-race-conscious-college-admissions-could-mean-for-hbcus

Chapter 4

1. Harper, Shaun. "Supreme Court Ends Affirmative Action in College Admissions—Here's What Will Happen On Campuses." *Forbes*, June 29, 2023. https://www.forbes.com/sites/shaunharper/2023/06/29/supreme-court-ends-affirmative-action-in-college-admissions---heres-what-will-happen-on-campuses/

2. Harper, Shaun. "Presidents Say Their Colleges Will Uphold Diversity Commitments Regardless of Supreme Court Affirmative Action Ruling." *Forbes*, May 4, 2023. https://www.forbes.com/sites/shaunharper/2023/05/04/presidents-say-their-colleges-will-sustain-diversity-commitments-regardless-of-supreme-court-affirmative-action-ruling

3. Harper, Shaun. "Legacy Admissions at Harvard and Other Elite Institutions Advantage White Applicants, New Evidence Shows." *Forbes*, July 5, 2023. https://www.forbes.com/sites/shaunharper/2023/07/05/legacy-admissions-at-harvard-and-other-elite-institutions-privilege-white-applicants-new-evidence-reveals/

4. Nietzel, Michael T. "University of California Reaches Final Decision: No More Standardized Admission Testing." *Forbes*, November 19, 2021. https://www.forbes.com/sites/michaeltnietzel/2021/11/19/university-of-california-reaches-final-decision-no-more-standardized-admission-testing/

5. ETS. "Best Practices for Admissions with GRE Scores." Accessed February 23, 2025. https://www.ets.org/pdfs/gre/gre-holistic-admissions-infographic.pdf

6. Posselt, Julie R. *Inside Graduate Admissions: Merit, Diversity, and Faculty Gatekeeping*. Harvard University Press, 2016.

7. Grieder, Erica. "The Top 10 Percent Rule on Trial." *Texas Monthly*, December 11, 2015. https://www.texasmonthly.com/burka-blog/the-top-10-percent-rule-on-trial

Chapter 5

1. 42 U.S.C. §§ 2000d to 2000d-7; Complaint Under Title VI of the Civil Rights Act of 1964 at 2–3, 5–6, Chica Project, African Community Economic Development of New England, and Greater Boston Latino Network v. President and Fellows of Harvard College. Office for Civil Rights, U.S. Department of Education, July 3, 2023. https://assets.bwbx.io/documents/users/iqjWHBFdfxIU/rKHUM_KThEyQ/v0

2. Harper, Shaun. "Supreme Court Ends Affirmative Action in College Admissions—Here's What Will Happen on Campuses." *Forbes*, June 29, 2023. https://www.forbes

.com/sites/shaunharper/2023/06/29/supreme-court-ends-affirmative-action-in-college-admissions---heres-what-will-happen-on-campuses/

3. Fuesting, Melissa. "The Higher Ed Admissions Workforce: Pay, Diversity, Equity, and Years in Position." College and University Professional Association for Human Resources. Accessed February 23, 2025. https://www.cupahr.org/surveys/research-briefs/the-higher-ed-admissions-workforce-april-2023

4. Nietzel, Michael T. "Amherst College Will End Legacy Admissions." *Forbes*, October 20, 2021. https://www.forbes.com/sites/michaeltnietzel/2021/10/20/amherst-college-will-end-legacy-admissions/

5. Merkley, Jeff, and Jamaal Bowman. "Fair College Admissions for Students Act Bill Summary." Accessed February 23, 2025. https://www.merkley.senate.gov/merkley-bowman-no-more-legacy-admissions-at-colleges-and-universities/

6. Patel, Vimal. "Why Legacy Admissions Are at the Center of a Dispute in Higher Education." *The New York Times*, July 26, 2023. https://www.nytimes.com/2023/07/26/us/legacy-admissions-colleges-universities.html

7. University of Southern California. "Facts and Stats." Accessed February 23, 2025. https://www.usc.edu/we-are-usc/the-university/facts-and-stats

8. University of Southern California, Ibid.

Chapter 6

1. The Harvard Gazette. "Harvard Names Claudine Gay 30th President." Accessed February 23, 2025. https://news.harvard.edu/gazette/story/2022/12/harvard-names-claudine-gay-30th-president

2. Mochkofsky, Graciela. "Why Lorgia García Peña Was Denied Tenure at Harvard." *The New Yorker*, July 27, 2021. https://www.newyorker.com/news/annals-of-education/why-lorgia-garcia-pena-was-denied-tenure-at-harvard

Chapter 7

1. Harper, Shaun. "Harvard University's Next President Is a Black Woman." *Forbes*, December 15, 2022. https://www.forbes.com/sites/shaunharper/2022/12/15/harvard-universitys-next-president-is-a-black-woman/

2. Gay, Claudine. "What Just Happened at Harvard Is Bigger Than Me." *The New York Times*, January 3, 2024. https://www.nytimes.com/2024/01/03/opinion/claudine-gay-harvard-president.html

3. American Council on Education. "The American College President, 2023 edition." Accessed February 23, 2025. https://www.acenet.edu/Documents/American-College-President-IX-2023.pdf

4. Skipworth, William. "Penn President Liz Magill Resigns After Backlash Over Antisemitism Hearing Testimony." *Forbes*, December 9, 2023. https://www.forbes.com/sites/willskipworth/2023/12/09/penn-president-liz-magill-resigns-after-backlash-over-antisemitism-hearing-testimony

5. Congress of the United States. "Letter to the Members of the Governing Boards of Harvard University, Massachusetts Institute of Technology, and University of Pennsylvania." Accessed February 23, 2025. https://stefanik.house.gov/_cache/files/1/d/1d0473f2-23a9-464b-9d22-f36eb428cd59/48410627924DF6929544B83E3F9AA1AE.letter-to-university-governing-boards-47-26-.pdf

6. Gay, Claudine. "Personal News." Accessed February 23, 2025. https://www.harvard.edu/president/news/2024/personal-news

7. The Fellows of Harvard College. "Statement from the Harvard Corporation: President Gay." Accessed February 23, 2025. https://www.harvard.edu/blog/2024/01/02/statement-from-the-harvard-corporation-president-gay

8. Stefanik, Elise. "Stefanik Statement on the Resignation of the University of Pennsylvania President Liz Magill." Accessed February 23, 2025. https://stefanik.house.gov/2023/12/stefanik-statement-on-the-resignation-of-the-university-of-pennsylvania-president-liz-magill

9. Drezner, Daniel W. "You Could Not Pay Me Enough to Be a College President." *Chronicle of Higher Education*, December 14, 2023. https://www.chronicle.com/article/you-could-not-pay-me-enough-to-be-a-college-president

Chapter 8

1. Plati, David. "Deion 'Coach Prime' Sanders Named Head Football Coach at Colorado." Colorado Buffaloes, December 3, 2022. https://cubuffs.com/news/2022/12/3/deion-coach-prime-sanders-named-head-football-coach-at-colorado.aspx

2. Fornelli, Tom, and Barrett Sallee. "Colorado Offers Deion Sanders More Than $5 Million Annually as Coach Mulls Landing Spot." *CBS Sports*, December 3, 2022. https://www.cbssports.com/college-football/news/colorado-offers-deion-sanders-more-than-5-million-annually-as-coach-mulls-landing-spot

3. Kasabian, Paul. "Deion Sanders, Jackson State Go Undefeated in Regular Season for 1st Time in History." *Bleacher Report*, November 19, 2022. https://bleacherreport.com/articles/10056214-deion-sanders-jackson-state-go-undefeated-in-regular-season-for-1st-time-in-history

4. "Deion Sanders Will Donate Half of Salary to Jackson State to Complete Football Facility." *ESPN News Services*, July 18, 2022. https://www.espn.com/college-football/story/_/id/34264209/deion-sanders-donate-half-salary-jackson-state-complete-football-facility

5. Chavkin, Daniel. "Deion Sanders Owes $300,000 Contract Buyout to Jackson State, per Report." *Sports Illustrated*, December 4, 2022. https://www.si.com/college/2022/12/04/deion-sanders-jackson-state-buyout-contract-colorado

6. Harper, Shaun R. *Black Male Student-Athletes and Racial Inequities in NCAA Division I Revenue-Generating College Sports: 2018 Edition*. University of Southern California Race and Equity Center, 2018.

7. Harper, Shaun R. "Brian Flores's Lawsuit Shows How Empty the NFL's Anti-Racism Messaging Is." *The Washington Post*, February 11, 2022. https://www.washingtonpost.com/outlook/2022/02/08/nfl-brian-flores-lawsuit-race

8. Schrotenboer, Brent. "Colorado Hires Deion Sanders as Its New Head Football Coach." *USA Today*, December 3, 2022. https://www.usatoday.com/story/sports/ncaaf/pac12/2022/12/03/deion-sanders-hiring-colorado-football-coach/10827197002

9. "NCAA Demographics Database." National Collegiate Athletic Association. Accessed February 23, 2025. https://www.ncaa.org/sports/2018/12/13/ncaa-demographics-database.aspx

Chapter 9

1. Harper, Shaun R. "Corporations Say They Support Black Lives Matter. Their Employees Doubt Them." *The Washington Post*, June 16, 2020. https://www.washingtonpost.com/outlook/2020/06/16/corporations-say-they-support-black-lives-matter-their-employees-doubt-them

2. Harper, Shaun. "Where Is the $200 Billion Companies Promised After George Floyd's Murder?" *Forbes*, October 17, 2022. https://www.forbes.com/sites/shaunharper/2022/10/17/where-is-the-200-billion-companies-promised-after-george-floyds-murder/

3. Lowery, Wesley. *American Whitelash: A Changing Nation and the Cost of Progress*. HarperCollins, 2023.

4. Kane, Paul. "House Narrowly Passes Divisive Pentagon Policy Bill." *The Washington Post*, July 14, 2023. https://www.washingtonpost.com/national-security/2023/07/13/pentagon-abortion-policy-house-republicans

5. Raikes, Jeff. "Is The 'War on Woke' a War on Our Country's Future?" *Forbes*, July 17, 2023. https://www.forbes.com/sites/jeffraikes/2023/07/17/is-the-war-on-woke-a-war-on-our-countrys-future/

6. "Republican Attorneys General Letter for Fortune 100 CEOs." Accessed February 23, 2025. https://s.wsj.net/public/resources/documents/AGLetterFortune100713.pdf

Chapter 10

1. Musk, Elon (@ElonMusk). 2023. "DEI must DIE. The point was to end discrimination, not replace it with different discrimination." Twitter, December 14, 2023, 11:54 p.m. https://twitter.com/elonmusk/status/1735821713688940843?s=46

2. Brown, Abram. "Twitter Accepts Elon Musk's $44 Billion Deal." *Forbes*, April 25, 2022. https://www.forbes.com/sites/abrambrown/2022/04/25/twitter-elon-musk-takeover-bid-deal-43-billion-54-20/

3. Cineas, Fabiola. "How Republicans Are Weaponizing Antisemitism to Take Down DEI." *Vox*, December 21, 2023. https://www.vox.com/24010858/republicans-antisemitism-dei-diversity-equity-inclusion-jewish-students

4. Dobbin, Frank, and Alexandra Kalev. "Why Diversity Programs Fail." *Harvard Business Review*, July-August 2016. https://hbr.org/2016/07/why-diversity-programs-fail

5. D&I Leaders. "Inspirational D&I Leaders—Diversity and Inclusion Leaders—Accelerating Workplace Inclusion." Accessed February 23, 2025. https://dileaders.com/inspirational

Chapter 11

1. Wexler, Natalie. "Democrats Can't Keep Dismissing Complaints About 'Critical Race Theory.'" *Forbes*, November 4, 2021. https://www.forbes.com/sites/nataliewexler/2021/11/04/democrats-cant-keep-dismissing-complaints-about-critical-race-theory/

2. Cillizza, Chris. "This Is Exactly How Dumb Our Politics Have Gotten." CNN, November 4, 2021. https://www.cnn.com/2021/11/02/politics/critical-race-theory-virginia-governor-youngkin-mcauliffe/index.html

3. Schwartz, Sarah. "Map: Where Critical Race Theory Is Under Attack." *Education Week*, June 11, 2021. https://www.edweek.org/policy-politics/map-where-critical-race-theory-is-under-attack/2021/06

4. The White House. "Executive Order on Combating Race and Sex Stereotyping." September 22, 2020. https://trumpwhitehouse.archives.gov/presidential-actions/executive-order-combating-race-sex-stereotyping

5. Fortin, Jacey. "Critical Race Theory: A Brief History." *The New York Times*, November 8, 2021. https://www.nytimes.com/article/what-is-critical-race-theory.html

6. Crenshaw, Kimberlé, Neil T. Gotanda, Gary Peller, and Kendall Thomas. *Critical Race Theory: The Key Writings That Formed the Movement*. The New Press, 1996.

Chapter 13

1. "Republican Attorneys General Letter for Fortune 100 CEOs." Accessed February 23, 2025. https://s.wsj.net/public/resources/documents/AGLetterFortune100713.pdf
2. "Democratic Attorneys General Letter for Fortune 100 CEOs." Accessed February 23, 2025. https://aboutblaw.com/9pR
3. Levenson, Michael. "Jury Awards $10 Million to White Male Executive in Discrimination Case." *The New York Times*, October 28, 2021. https://www.nytimes.com/2021/10/28/us/david-duvall-firing-lawsuit-diversity.html
4. Riess, Rebekah. "A White Hospital Executive Says He Was Fired and Replaced by 2 Women as Part of a Diversity Push. He Sued and Was Just Awarded $10 Million." CNN, October 28, 2021. https://www.cnn.com/2021/10/28/us/novant-health-wrongful-termination-white-executive-fired/index.html
5. Zahn, Max. "Starbucks Discrimination Lawsuit Awarded White Employee $25 Million: Legal Experts Weigh In." *ABC News*, June 16, 2023. https://abcnews.go.com/Business/starbucks-discrimination-lawsuit-awarded-white-employee-25-million/story?id=100104620
6. Stevens, Matt. "Starbucks C.E.O. Apologizes After Arrests of 2 Black Men." *The New York Times*, April 15, 2018. https://www.nytimes.com/2018/04/15/us/starbucks-philadelphia-black-men-arrest.html

Chapter 14

1. Champagne Tiō (@champagne_tio_). 2022. "Na we aint letting @sesameplace off the hook that easy!! Your characters have something against black kids period!!" Instagram, July 18, 2022. https://www.instagram.com/tv/CgKPoXzlk-E/?igshid=YmMyMTA2M2Y=
2. CBS News Philadelphia. "New Sesame Place Video, Incident Emerges as Civil Rights Leaders Meet to Discuss Discrimination Allegations." July 29, 2022. Video, https://philadelphia.cbslocal.com/2022/07/29/new-sesame-place-video-incident-emerges-as-civil-rights-leaders-meet-to-discuss-discrimination-allegations
3. __jodiii__ (@__jodiii__). 2022. "I'm going to keep posting this, because this had me hot. We were on our way out of sesame place and the kids wanted to stop to see the characters." Instagram, July 16, 2022. https://www.instagram.com/tv/CgGAHtyFoHg/?utm_source=ig_embed&utm_campaign=loading
4. Chan, Anna. "Kelly Rowland Is 'So Mad' After Seeing Video of Muppet Appearing to Ignore 2 Black Girls at Sesame Place." *Billboard*, July 18, 2022. https://www.billboard.com/music/music-news/kelly-rowland-reacts-sesame-place-viral-video-1235115370
5. Reshamwala, Saleem. "Peanut Butter, Jelly and Racism." *The New York Times*, December 16, 2016. Video, https://www.nytimes.com/video/us/100000004818663/peanut-butter-jelly-and-racism.html?playlistId=video/who-me-biased
6. Slovak, Julianne. "Starbucks Attacks Thorny Problem of Unconscious Bias." *Forbes*, May 29, 2018. https://www.forbes.com/sites/julianneslovak/2018/05/29/starbucks-attacks-thorny-problem-of-unconscious-bias/
7. Giammona, Craig. "Starbucks Investors Question Cost of Bias Training, Howard Schultz Says." *Bloomberg*, May 29, 2018. https://www.bloomberg.com/news/articles/2018-05-29/starbucks-investors-question-cost-of-bias-training-schultz-says
8. Goldenstein, Taylor. "Texas to Require All Police Officers Receive Implicit Bias Training, in First George Floyd-Inspired Reform." *Houston Chronicle*, June 9, 2020.

https://www.houstonchronicle.com/politics/texas/article/Texas-to-require-all-police-officers-receive-15327779.php

9. Sesame Workshop (@SesameWorkshop). 2022. "Sesame Workshop is aware of the recent incident at Sesame Place Philadelphia, which we take very seriously. What these children experienced is unacceptable." Twitter, July 18, 2022, 4:26 p.m. https://twitter.com/SesameWorkshop/status/1549173873010266112

10. Reshamwala, Saleem. "Snacks and Punishment." *The New York Times*, December 16, 2016. Video, https://www.nytimes.com/video/us/100000004818677/snacks-and-punishment.html?playlistId=video/who-me-biased

11. Karimi, Faith. "Sesame Place Announces Diversity Initiatives After Accusations of Racial Bias." CNN, August 10, 2022. https://www.cnn.com/2022/08/10/us/sesame-place-diversity-efforts-cec/index.html

12. Atewologun, Doyin, Tinu Cornish, and Fatima Tresh. "Unconscious Bias Training: An Assessment of the Evidence for Effectiveness." Equality and Human Rights Commission. Accessed February 23, 2025. https://www.equalityhumanrights.com/sites/default/files/research-report-113-unconcious-bais-training-an-assessment-of-the-evidence-for-effectiveness-pdf.pdf

13. Legault, Lisa, Jennifer N. Gutsell, and Michael Inzlicht. "Ironic Effects of Antiprejudice Messages: How Motivational Interventions Can Reduce (but Also Increase) Prejudice." *Psychological Science* 22, no. 12 (2011): 1472–1477.

14. Kaste, Martin. "NYPD Study: Implicit Bias Training Changes Minds, Not Necessarily Behavior." NPR, September 10, 2020. https://www.npr.org/2020/09/10/909380525/nypd-study-implicit-bias-training-changes-minds-not-necessarily-behavior

15. Lawrence, Andrew. "Theme Parks Were Not Meant for Black Families: Why Racism at Sesame Place Is Part of a Shameful Tradition." *The Guardian*, July 30, 2022. https://www.theguardian.com/travel/2022/jul/30/sesame-place-theme-parks-black-families-racism

Chapter 15

1. Musk, Elon (@ElonMusk). 2022. "Should I step down as head of Twitter? I will abide by the results of this poll." Twitter, December 18, 2022, 3:20 p.m. https://twitter.com/elonmusk/status/1604617643973124097

2. Musk, Elon (@ElonMusk). 2022. "I will resign as CEO as soon as I find someone foolish enough to take the job! After that, I will just run the software & servers teams." Twitter, December 20, 2022, 5:20 p.m. https://twitter.com/elonmusk/status/1605372724800393216

3. Musk, Elon (@ElonMusk). 2022. "The question is not finding a CEO, the question is finding a CEO who can keep Twitter alive." Twitter, December 18, 2022, 3:34 p.m. https://twitter.com/elonmusk/status/1604621101245419520

4. Nieva, Richard. "Twitter to Begin Layoffs, Will Notify Workers Over Email." *Forbes*, November 3, 2022. https://www.forbes.com/sites/richardnieva/2022/11/03/twitter-to-begin-layoffs-will-notify-workers-over-email/

5. O'Sullivan, Donie, and Clare Duffy. "Elon Musk Has Taken Control of Twitter and Fired Its Top Executives." CNN, October 28, 2022. https://www.cnn.com/2022/10/27/tech/elon-musk-twitter/index.html

6. Porterfield, Carlie. "New Lawsuit Claims Elon Musk's Twitter Layoffs Targeted Women." *Forbes*, December 8, 2022. https://www.forbes.com/sites/carlieporterfield/2022/12/08/new-lawsuit-claims-elon-musks-twitter-layoffs-targeted-women/

Endnotes

7. Harper, Shaun. "Hate Speech Rises on Twitter After Elon Musk Takes Over, Researchers Find." *Forbes*, October 31, 2022. https://www.forbes.com/sites/shaunharper/2022/10/31/elon-musk-twitter-takeover-leads-to-n-word-and-hate-speech-increase-lebron-james-calls-for-action/

8. Ray, Siladitya. "Twitter Shuts Down Its Trust and Safety Council—Here's What You Need to Know." *Forbes*, December 13, 2022. https://www.forbes.com/sites/siladityaray/2022/12/13/twitter-shuts-down-its-trust-and-safety-council-heres-what-you-need-to-know/

9. Ray, Siladitya. "Elon Musk Reinstates Donald Trump's Twitter Account After Asking Users to Vote." *Forbes*, November 20, 2022. https://www.forbes.com/sites/siladityaray/2022/11/20/elon-musk-reinstates-donald-trumps-twitter-account-after-users-vote-to-bring-him-back/

10. Adgate, Brad. "Twitter Suspends the Accounts of Tech Journalists, Creating an Uproar." *Forbes*, December 16, 2022. https://www.forbes.com/sites/bradadgate/2022/12/16/twitter-suspends-the-accounts-of-journalists-creating-an-uproar

11. Mier, Tomás. "All the Celebrities Who've Quit Twitter Because of Elon Musk." *Rolling Stone*, December 19, 2022. https://www.rollingstone.com/culture/culture-lists/elon-musk-twitter-celebrities-quit-1234634670

12. Ryan, Michelle K., and S. Alexander Haslam. "The Glass Cliff: Evidence That Women Are Over-Represented in Precarious Leadership Positions." *British Journal of Management* 16 (2005): 81–90.

13. Burns, Ursula. "How I Saved Xerox from a Near-Death Experience." Accessed February 23, 2025. https://builtin.com/corporate-innovation/xerox-ursula-burns

14. Tempest, Lynsey. "How Indra Nooyi Changed the Face of PepsiCo." Accessed February 23, 2025. https://www.worldfinance.com/special-reports/how-indra-nooyi-changed-the-face-of-pepsico

15. Huang, Georgene. "Men And Women Aren't Promoted by the Same People—Here's the Difference." *Forbes*, May 10, 2018. https://www.forbes.com/sites/georgenehuang/2018/05/10/men-and-women-arent-promoted-by-the-same-people-heres-the-difference/

16. Zenger, Jack, and Joseph Folkman. "Research: Women Are Better Leaders During a Crisis." *Harvard Business Review*, December 30, 2020. https://hbr.org/2020/12/research-women-are-better-leaders-during-a-crisis

17. Balingit, Moriah, Nick Anderson, and Susan Svrluga. "USC Names Its Next President: Former UNC Chancellor Carol Folt." *The Washington Post*, March 20, 2019. https://www.washingtonpost.com/local/education/usc-names-its-next-president-former-unc-chancellor-carol-folt/2019/03/20/8b008306-4b3c-11e9-93d0-64dbcf38ba41_story.html

Chapter 16

1. Bank of America. "Bank of America Introduces Community Affordable Loan Solution to Expand Homeownership Opportunities in Black/African American and Hispanic-Latino Communities." Accessed February 23, 2025. https://newsroom.bankofamerica.com/content/newsroom/press-releases/2022/08/bank-of-america-introduces-community-affordable-loan-solution--t.html

2. National Fair Housing Alliance. "Using Special Purpose Credit Programs to Expand Equality." Accessed February 23, 2025. https://nationalfairhousing.org/resource/using-special-purpose-credit-programs-to-expand-equality

3. Bank of America. "Community Homeownership Commitment." Accessed February 23, 2025. https://promotions.bankofamerica.com/homeloans/homeowner?subCampCode=60518&scsCampCode=60518&sourceCd=18189&dmcode=18097607837

4. Holt, Brianna. "'We Don't Fit the Demographic': A Community in Dallas Grapples With Gentrification." *The Guardian*, September 11, 2021. https://www.theguardian.com/cities/2021/sep/11/dallas-texas-oak-cliff-gentrification

5. U.S. Department of Justice, Office of Public Affairs. "Justice Department Reaches $335 Million Settlement to Resolve Allegations of Lending Discrimination by Countrywide Financial Corporation." Accessed February 23, 2025. https://www.justice.gov/opa/pr/justice-department-reaches-335-million-settlement-resolve-allegations-lending-discrimination

Chapter 17

1. McDonnell, Isabelle, and Teny Sahakian. "Riley Gaines Urges Female Athletes to Boycott Competing Against Trans Girls: 'Don't Run . . . Don't Swim.'" Fox News, May 7, 2023. https://www.foxnews.com/sports/riley-gaines-urges-female-athletes-boycott-competing-trans-girls-run-swim

2. Riley Gaines (@Riley_Gaines_). 2023. "I dont understand why companies are voluntarily doing this to themselves. They could have at least said the suit is 'unisex,' but they didn't because its about erasing women. Ever wondered why we hardly see this go the other way?" Twitter, May 17, 2023, 8:46 a.m. https://x.com/Riley_Gaines_/status/1658861624768225280

3. Rep. Nancy Mace (@RepNancyMace). 2023. "I'm old enough to remember when women actually modeled women's bathing suits, not men." Twitter, May 17, 2023, 9:48 a.m. https://x.com/RepNancyMace/status/1658877270138683415

4. Marjorie Taylor Greene (@mtgreenee). 2023. "Who is telling these major corporations to alienate women, half the population, in order to market to trans which are less than 1%?" Twitter, May 17, 2023, 1:42 p.m. https://x.com/mtgreenee/status/1658936166538772482

5. Jewell, Zach. "Here Are the Men Who Have Dominated Women's Sports." *The Daily Wire*, February 2, 2024. https://www.dailywire.com/news/here-are-the-men-who-have-dominated-womens-sports

6. Guynn, Jessica. "Is Adidas Having a Bud Light Moment? Transgender Pride Swimsuit Touches Off Controversy." *USA Today*, May 19, 2023. https://www.usatoday.com/story/money/2023/05/19/adidas-pride-transgender-swimsuit-controversy/70237256007

7. Guynn, Ibid.

8. Holpuch, Amanda. "Behind the Backlash Against Bud Light." *The New York Times*, November 21, 2023. https://www.nytimes.com/article/bud-light-boycott.html

Chapter 18

1. Ms. Frizzle's Twin (msfizzletwin). 2023. "Idk who needs to correct it but it needs to be pulled off the shelves notheless. Any person could have missed the mistake but it just takes one person to point it out and ask for corrections #blackhistory #blackhistorymonth #blacktiktok." TikTok. https://www.tiktok.com/t/ZTYG4FDu2

2. Woodson, Carter Goodwin. *The Mis-education of the Negro*. Associated Publishers, 1933.

3. Harper, Shaun. "Companies Are Trying to Cash In on Juneteenth. Here's Why That's a Problem." *Reader's Digest*, June 16, 2023. https://www.rd.com/article/commercialization-juneteenth

Chapter 19

1. Schwartz, Sarah. "Map: Where Critical Race Theory Is Under Attack." *Education Week*, June 11, 2021. https://www.edweek.org/policy-politics/map-where-critical-race-theory-is-under-attack/2021/06
2. Chronicle of Higher Education. "DEI Legislation Tracker." Accessed February 23, 2025. https://www.chronicle.com/article/here-are-the-states-where-lawmakers-are-seeking-to-ban-colleges-dei-efforts
3. Dorn, Sara. "Rare Moment of Bipartisanship: Congress Passes Defense Bill with Military Pay Raise and No Abortion, Trans Crackdown." *Forbes*, December 14, 2023. https://www.forbes.com/sites/saradorn/2023/12/14/rare-moment-of-bipartisanship-congress-passes-defense-bill-with-military-pay-raise-and-no-abortion-trans-crackdown/
4. Harper, Shaun. "Elon Musk Articulates What Many DEI Opponents Think, but Are Too Afraid to Publicly Say." *Forbes*, December 19, 2023. https://www.forbes.com/sites/shaunharper/2023/12/19/elon-musk-articulates-what-many-dei-opponents-think-but-are-too-afraid-to-publicly-say/
5. Elias, Jennifer. "Tech Companies Like Google and Meta Made Cuts to DEI Programs in 2023 After Big Promises in Prior Years." CNBC, December 22, 2023. https://www.cnbc.com/2023/12/22/google-meta-other-tech-giants-cut-dei-programs-in-2023.html
6. Harper, Shaun R. "Corporations Say They Support Black Lives Matter. Their Employees Doubt Them." *The Washington Post*, June 16, 2020. https://www.washingtonpost.com/outlook/2020/06/16/corporations-say-they-support-black-lives-matter-their-employees-doubt-them

Chapter 20

1. Frum, David. "What Could Turn Biden's Reelection Upside Down." *The Atlantic*, May 9, 2023. https://www.theatlantic.com/ideas/archive/2023/05/joe-biden-health-versus-donald-trump-indictments/673989
2. Langer, Gary. "Broad Doubts About Biden's Age and Acuity Spell Republican Opportunity in 2024." *ABC News*, May 6, 2023. https://abcnews.go.com/Politics/broad-doubts-bidens-age-acuity-spell-republican-opportunity/story?id=99109308
3. Murray, Mark. "NBC News Poll: Nearly 70% of GOP Voters Stand Behind Trump Amid Indictment and Investigation." *NBC News*, April 23, 2023. https://www.nbcnews.com/politics/2024-election/nbc-news-poll-nearly-70-gop-voters-stand-trump-indictment-investigatio-rcna80917
4. "Stephanie Ruhle of MSNBC Interviews Joe Biden for 'The 11th Hour.'" YouTube. May 5, 2023. Video, https://www.youtube.com/watch?v=g5xIkluPmvk
5. Silver, Laura. *As Biden and Trump Seek Reelection, Who Are the Oldest—and Youngest—Current World Leaders?* Pew Research Center, May 1, 2024. https://www.pewresearch.org/short-reads/2024/05/01/as-biden-and-trump-seek-reelection-who-are-the-oldest-and-youngest-current-world-leaders
6. United States Census Bureau. *America Is Getting Older: New Population Estimates Highlight Increase in National Median Age.* Accessed February 23, 2025. https://www.census.gov/newsroom/press-releases/2023/population-estimates-characteristics.html
7. World Health Organization. "Ageing: Ageism." Accessed February 23, 2025. https://www.who.int/news-room/questions-and-answers/item/ageing-ageism

8. Reilly, Ryan J., Ken Dilanian, and Megan Lebowitz. "Biden Won't Be Charged in Classified Docs Case; Special Counsel Cites Instances of 'Poor Memory.'" *NBC News*, February 8, 2024. https://www.nbcnews.com/politics/joe-biden/special-counsel-says-evidence-biden-willfully-retained-disclosed-class-rcna96666

Chapter 21

1. "MSNBC Host Goes After Nikki Haley, Gets Fiery Response." YouTube. January 16, 2024. Video, https://www.youtube.com/watch?v=3lT8DtKiMjI
2. "Hear DeSantis' Answer on Whether the US Has Been a Racist Country." *CNN*. Video, https://www.cnn.com/videos/politics/2024/01/17/ron-desantis-haley-us-not-racist-gop-presidential-town-hall-vpx.cnn
3. Durkee, Alison. "Rejecting AP Studies, Restricting Libraries: Here's How DeSantis and His 'Anti-Woke' Policies Are Impacting Florida Education." *Forbes*, January 20, 2023. https://www.forbes.com/sites/alisondurkee/2023/01/20/rejecting-ap-studies-restricting-libraries-heres-how-desantis-and-his-anti-woke-policies-are-impacting-florida-education/
4. Hartig, Hannah, Andrew Daniller, Scott Keeter, and Ted Van Green. *Demographic Profiles of Republican and Democratic Voters*. Pew Research Center, July 12, 2023. https://www.pewresearch.org/politics/2023/07/12/demographic-profiles-of-republican-and-democratic-voters
5. Langer, Gary, Christine Filer, and Steven Sparks. "Trump Trounces in Iowa, and Election Deniers and MAGA Got Him There: Entrance Poll Analysis." *ABC News*, January 15, 2024. https://abcnews.go.com/Politics/conservative-iowa-caucus-electorate-minds-made-analysis/story?id=106395184

Chapter 22

1. Harper, Shaun. "Hakeem Jeffries to Replace Nancy Pelosi as House Democratic Leader—Why His Blackness Matters." *Forbes*, November 30, 2022. https://www.forbes.com/sites/shaunharper/2022/11/30/why-it-matters-that-hakeem-jeffries-will-be-the-first-black-leader-of-any-congressional-party/
2. "BREAKING: House Chamber Stunned When Chip Roy Votes for Byron Donalds for Speaker." YouTube. January 3, 2023. Video, https://www.youtube.com/watch?v=0uuyYwWMAng
3. Harper, Shaun. "If George Santos Were Black, There'd Be Harsher Consequences for the Newly Elected Congressman's Lies." *Forbes*, December 29, 2022. https://www.forbes.com/sites/shaunharper/2022/12/29/if-george-santos-were-black-thered-be-harsher-consequences-for-the-newly-elected-congressmans-lies/
4. Lavietes, Matt. "In Historic House Race Between Gay Candidates, Republican Defeats Democrat, NBC News Projects." *NBC News*, November 5, 2022. https://www.nbcnews.com/nbc-out/out-politics-and-policy/historic-house-race-gay-candidates-republican-defeats-democrat-nbc-new-rcna55951
5. Congressional Research Service. "Membership of the 117th Congress: A Profile." Accessed February 23, 2025. https://crsreports.congress.gov/product/pdf/R/R46705
6. Zanona, Melanie, and Lauren Fox. "Inside McCarthy's Struggle to Lock Down the House Speakership." CNN, January 2, 2023. https://www.cnn.com/2023/01/02/politics/kevin-mccarthy-house-speaker-struggle/index.html
7. Lukas, Carrie. "One Type of Diversity Never Seems to Matter." *Forbes*, July 23, 2019. https://www.forbes.com/sites/carrielukas/2019/07/23/one-type-of-diversity-never-seems-to-matter/

Endnotes

8. Dixon-Fyle, Sundiatu, Vivian Hunt, Kevin Dolan, and Sara Prince. "Diversity Wins: How Inclusion Matters." *McKinsey & Company*, May 19, 2020. https://www.mckinsey.com/featured-insights/diversity-and-inclusion/diversity-wins-how-inclusion-matters

9. Lukas, Ibid.

Chapter 23

1. Ashford, Grace, and Michael Gold. "Who Is Rep.-Elect George Santos? His Résumé May Be Largely Fiction." *The New York Times*, December 19, 2022. https://www.nytimes.com/2022/12/19/nyregion/george-santos-ny-republicans.html

2. *Powell v. McCormack*, 395 U.S. 486 (1969).

3. Nick LaLota (@nicklalota). 2022. "New Yorkers deserve the truth and House Republicans deserve an opportunity to govern." Twitter, December 27, 2022, 12:16 p.m. https://x.com/nicklalota/status/1607832712836009989

4. Harper, Shaun. "Herschel Walker's Loss in Georgia Senate Runoff Shows Why Tokenizing Black People Usually Fails." *Forbes*, December 7, 2022. https://www.forbes.com/sites/shaunharper/2022/12/07/herschel-walkers-loss-in-georgia-senate-runoff-shows-why-tokenizing-black-people-usually-fails/

5. Bushard, Brian. "2nd Woman Accuses Herschel Walker of Paying for an Abortion." *Forbes*, October 26, 2022. https://www.forbes.com/sites/brianbushard/2022/10/26/new-woman-claims-herschel-walker-drove-her-to-abortion-clinic/

6. Blake, Aaron. "The Scale of George Santos's Deceit—and the Remaining Questions." *The Washington Post*, December 27, 2022. Video, https://www.washingtonpost.com/politics/2022/12/27/george-santos-explanations-questions

7. "Police Off the Cuff After Hours # 37 with Congressional Candidate George Santos." YouTube. October 29, 2020. Video, https://www.youtube.com/watch?v=P2IF-5bUsksQ

8. George Santos (@MrSantosNY). 2022. "Tonight I joined Rabbi Lau, the Chief Ashkenazi Rabbi of Israel, in a special event held by the Chabad of Great Neck. We stand strong as Antisemitism and violent crime shakes us to the core. It was an honor to address fellow members of the Jewish community in #NY03." Twitter, November 3, 2022, 5:53 p.m. https://x.com/MrSantosNY/status/1588333599413108738

9. Levin, Bess. "George Santos Says He Only Pretended to Be Jewish as 'a Joke.'" *Vanity Fair*, February 21, 2023. https://www.vanityfair.com/news/2023/02/george-santos-jewish-for-the-jokes

10. Brown, Pamela, Carolyn Sung, and Jack Forrest. "Federal Prosecutors Are Investigating Rep.-Elect George Santos' Finances." CNN, December 28, 2022. https://www.cnn.com/2022/12/28/politics/george-santos-investigating-federal-nassau-county/index.html

11. Vakil, Caroline. "Nassau County DA Announces Probe into George Santos." *The Hill*, December 28, 2022. https://thehill.com/homenews/house/3791113-nassau-county-da-announced-probe-into-george-santos

12. "George Santos on 'Tucker Carlson Tonight': 'I Made a Mistake.'" YouTube. December 27, 2022. Video, https://www.youtube.com/watch?v=k3sC1Ha2JwU

13. Smith, Edward J., and Shaun R. Harper. *Disproportionate Impact of K-12 School Suspension and Expulsion on Black Students in Southern States*. University of Pennsylvania, Center for the Study of Race and Equity in Education, 2015.

14. Blair, Samone. "Protesters Injured by Police Before Trump Photo-Op Testify: 'It Hurts.'" *TheGrio*, June 29, 2020. https://thegrio.com/2020/06/29/protesters-lafayette-square-trump

15. Slodysko, Brian, and James Laporta. "Ohio GOP House Candidate Has Misrepresented Military Service." *Associated Press*, September 22, 2022. https://apnews.com/article/2022-midterm-elections-afghanistan-ohio-campaigns-e75d2566635f11f49332b-d1c46711999

16. Congressional Research Service. "Expulsion of Members of Congress: Legal Authority and Historical Practice." Accessed February 23, 2025. https://crsreports.congress.gov/product/pdf/R/R45078

Chapter 24

1. Wick, Julia. "Caruso on Track to Exceed $100 Million in Campaign Spending." *The Los Angeles Times*, October 28, 2022. https://www.latimes.com/california/story/2022-10-28/caruso-on-track-to-exceed-100-million-in-campaign-spending

2. Smith, Doug, and Benjamin Oreskes "Can Bass or Caruso Solve the L.A. Homeless Housing Crisis? Here Are Their Divergent Plans." *The Los Angeles Times*, September 4, 2022. https://www.latimes.com/california/story/2022-09-04/homelessness-plans-la-mayor-candidates-karen-bass-rick-caruso-explainer

3. "Mayoral Candidate Rick Caruso Calls for 1,500 More LAPD Officers." *KCAL News*, February 15, 2022. https://www.cbsnews.com/losangeles/news/mayoral-candidate-rick-caruso-calls-for-1500-more-lapd-officers

4. Oreskes, Benjamin. "Rick Caruso Changes Registration to Democrat as He Weighs a Run for L.A. Mayor." *The Los Angeles Times*, January 24, 2022. https://www.latimes.com/california/story/2022-01-24/prospective-la-mayoral-candidate-rick-caruso-registers-as-democrat

5. Lee, MJ, Jeff Zeleny, and Jasmine Wright. "Joe Biden Narrows Down his VP List, with Karen Bass Emerging as One of Several Key Contenders." CNN, July 31, 2020. https://www.cnn.com/2020/07/31/politics/joe-biden-running-mate/index.html

6. Truffaut-Wong, Olivia. "Celebrities Can't Stop Endorsing Rick Caruso for L.A. Mayor." *The Cut*, November 8, 2022. https://www.thecut.com/2022/11/celebrities-endorsing-rick-caruso-for-la-mayor.html

7. Li, David K. "Los Angeles Mayoral Candidate Rick Caruso Declares He's Not White Because He's Italian." *NBC News*, October 12, 2022. https://www.nbcnews.com/news/us-news/los-angeles-mayoral-candidate-rick-caruso-declares-not-white-italian-rcna51852

8. Murray, Andrew, and Paul Steinhauser. "Los Angeles Mayor Race: Caruso Brushes Off Trump Comparisons from Rep. Bass, Touts Law-and-Order Policies." Fox News, June 9, 2022. https://www.foxnews.com/politics/los-angeles-mayor-race-caruso-trump-comparison-rep-karen-bass

Chapter 25

1. "JUST IN: Biden Announces Prisoner Swap with Russia, Freeing Brittney Griner For 'Merchant Of Death.'" YouTube. December 8, 2022. Video, https://www.youtube.com/watch?v=DhbqEVEEcAk

2. "Blinken on Griner, Whelan: Choice Was 'One or None.'" YouTube. December 8, 2022. Video, https://www.youtube.com/watch?v=kyw2QOMMN38

3. The White House. "Press Briefing by Press Secretary Karine Jean-Pierre, December 8, 2022." Accessed February 23, 2025. https://bidenwhitehouse.archives.gov/briefing-room/press-briefings/2022/12/08/press-briefing-by-press-secretary-karine-jean-pierre-december-8-2022/

Endnotes

4. Reimann, Nicholas. "'Unpatriotic Embarrassment': Republicans Slam Biden's Deal to Free Brittney Griner as Paul Whelan Stays in Russia." *Forbes*, December 8, 2022. https://www.forbes.com/sites/nicholasreimann/2022/12/08/unpatriotic-embarrassment-republicans-slam-bidens-deal-to-free-brittney-griner-as-paul-whelan-stays-in-russia/

5. Saul, Derek. "U.S. Marine Veteran Trevor Reed Released from Russian Prison." *Forbes*, April 27, 2022. https://www.forbes.com/sites/dereksaul/2022/04/27/us-marine-veteran-trevor-reed-released-from-russian-prison/

6. Harper, Shaun. "Brittney Griner Freed, Fight for Wrongly Incarcerated Black Women Must Continue." *Forbes*, December 8, 2022. https://www.forbes.com/sites/shaunharper/2022/12/08/brittney-griner-freed-fight-for-wrongly-incarcerated-black-women-must-continue/

Chapter 26

1. Harper, Shaun. "Diversity, Inclusion and Dance Overflow in Renaissance, New Beyoncé Album." *Forbes*, July 29, 2022. https://www.forbes.com/sites/shaunharper/2022/07/29/diversity-inclusion-and-dance-overflow-in-renaissance-new-beyonc-album/

Chapter 27

1. Associated Press. "Tory Lanez Convicted in Megan Thee Stallion's Shooting." *TheGrio*, December 23, 2022. https://thegrio.com/2022/12/23/tory-lanez-convicted-in-megan-thee-stallions-shooting

2. Morino, Douglas, and Joe Coscarelli. "Tory Lanez Is Sentenced to 10 Years for Shooting Megan Thee Stallion." *The New York Times*, August 8, 2023. https://www.nytimes.com/2023/08/08/arts/tory-lanez-megan-thee-stallion-sentence.html

3. "Appeal Tory Lanez Verdict Immediately." Change.org. Accessed February 23, 2025. https://www.change.org/p/appeal-tory-lanez-verdict-immediately

4. France, Lisa Respers. "Megan Thee Stallion Says Tory Lanez Shot Her." CNN, August 21, 2020. https://www.cnn.com/2020/08/21/entertainment/megan-thee-stallion-tory-lanez-shooting/index.html

5. Haylock, Zoe. "Megan Thee Stallion Shuts Down Rumors with Gunshot-Wound Photo." *New York Magazine*, August 19, 2020. https://www.vulture.com/2020/08/megan-thee-stallion-ig-gunshot-wound-photo.html

6. Madarang, Charisma, and Tomás Mier. "From 'Broke Boys' to 'Privileged Rappers,' Drake and 21 Savage Announce 'Her Loss' Tracklist." *Rolling Stone*, November 3, 2022. https://www.rollingstone.com/music/music-news/drake-21-savage-her-loss-cover-art-1234623701

7. Soteriou, Stephanie. "Drake Is Facing Serious Backlash After He Rapped That Megan Thee Stallion Lied About Being Shot and She's Being Praised For Her Response." *BuzzFeed News*, November 4, 2022. https://www.buzzfeednews.com/article/stephaniesoteriou/drake-backlash-megan-thee-stallion-shot

8. Tina Snow (@theestallion). 2022. "Stop using my shooting for clout bitch ass Niggas! Since when tf is it cool to joke abt women getting shot ! You niggas especially RAP NIGGAS ARE LAME! Ready to boycott bout shoes and clothes but dog pile on a black woman when she say one of y'all homeboys abused her." Twitter, November 3, 2022, 10:13 p.m. https://x.com/theestallion/status/1588398931381088256

9. "'I Was Really Scared.' Megan Thee Stallion on 2020 Shooting Allegedly Involving Rapper Tory Lanez." YouTube. April 24, 2022. Video, https://www.youtube.com/watch?v=AtjzVI5bFao

10. Bailey, Moya. *Misogynoir Transformed: Black Women's Digital Resistance*. NYU Press, 2021.

11. Lindsey, Treva B. *America, Goddam: Violence, Black Women, and the Struggle for Justice*. University of California Press, 2022.

Chapter 28

1. Sakoui, Anousha, and Wendy Lee. "Hollywood Talent Agency CAA Cuts Ties with Kanye West After Antisemitic Tirade." *The Los Angeles Times*, October 24, 2022. https://www.latimes.com/entertainment-arts/business/story/2022-10-24/hollywood-talent-agency-caa-cuts-ties-with-ye-after-anti-semitic-tirade

2. Walcott, David. "How Kanye West Is Helping to Destigmatize Mental Illness." *Forbes*, August 4, 2020. https://www.forbes.com/sites/davidwalcott/2020/08/04/how-kanye-west-is-helping-to-destigmatize-mental-illness/

3. Levitz, Eric. "Mental Illness Does Not Excuse Kanye's Antisemitism, Even If It Explains It." *New York Magazine*, October 12, 2022. https://nymag.com/intelligencer/2022/10/kanye-west-anti-semitism-mental-illness-bipolar-jews-white-lives-matter.html

4. Dellatto, Marisa. "Kanye West Wears 'White Lives Matter' Shirt at Yeezy Fashion Show." *Forbes*, October 3, 2022. https://www.forbes.com/sites/marisadellatto/2022/10/03/kanye-west-wears-white-lives-matter-shirt-at-yeezy-fashion-show/

5. Morin, Rebecca. "Kanye West Says Trump Hat Makes Him 'Feel Like Superman.'" *Politico*, October 11, 2018. https://www.politico.com/story/2018/10/11/kanye-west-donald-trump-meeting-894725

6. Shapiro, Ariel. "Kanye West Sticks by Trump: 'We Know Who I'm Voting On.'" *Forbes*, April 15, 2020. https://www.forbes.com/sites/arielshapiro/2020/04/15/kanye-west-sticks-by-trump-we-know-who-im-voting-on/

7. McIntyre, Hugh. "Kanye West Announces He's Running for President." *Forbes*, July 4, 2020. https://www.forbes.com/sites/hughmcintyre/2020/07/04/kanye-west-announces-hes-running-for-president/

8. Di Placido, Dani. "Kanye West Condemned for Music Video Depicting Pete Davidson Being Buried Alive." *Forbes*, March 3, 2022. https://www.forbes.com/sites/danidiplacido/2022/03/03/kanye-west-condemned-for-music-video-depicting-pete-davidson-being-buried-alive/

9. Porterfield, Carlie. "Twitter Locks Kanye West's Account After Post About Jewish People." *Forbes*, October 9, 2022. https://www.forbes.com/sites/carlieporterfield/2022/10/09/twitter-deletes-kanye-west-post-about-jewish-people/

10. Dellatto, Marisa. "George Floyd's Family Will Sue Kanye West for $250 Million Over False Comments About Death." *Forbes*, October 18, 2022. https://www.forbes.com/sites/marisadellatto/2022/10/18/george-floyds-family-will-sue-kanye-west-for-250-million-over-false-comments-about-death/

11. "Ye (Kanye West) Calls Biden "F—ing Retarded" for Not Taking Advice from Elon Musk." YouTube. October 19, 2022. Video, https://www.youtube.com/watch?v=MHZf17fQdw4

12. Ray, Siladitya. "Kanye West Is Buying Right-Wing Social Media Platform Parler." *Forbes*, October 17, 2022. https://www.forbes.com/sites/siladityaray/2022/10/17/kanye-west-is-buying-right-wing-social-media-platform-parler/

13. "jeen-yuhs: A Kanye Trilogy." Netflix. Accessed February 23, 2025. https://www.netflix.com/title/81426972

14. Greenburg, Zack O'Malley. "Kanye West Is Now Officially a Billionaire (and He Really Wants the World to Know)." *Forbes*, April 30, 2022. https://www.forbes.com/sites/zackomalleygreenburg/2020/04/24/kanye-west-is-now-officially-a-billionaireand-he-really-wants-the-world-to-know/

15. Debter, Lauren, and Lisette Voytko-Best. "The House of Ye: Chaos, Anti-Semitism, 'White Lives Matter'—and Steady, Unbothered Sales." *Forbes*, October 20, 2022. https://www.forbes.com/sites/laurendebter/2022/10/20/the-house-of-ye-chaos-antisemitism-white-lives-matter—and-steady-unbothered-sales/

16. Golden, Jessica. "Adidas Says Its Relationship with Kanye West Is Under Review." CNBC, October 6, 2022. https://www.cnbc.com/2022/10/06/adidas-says-its-relationship-with-kanye-west-is-under-review.html

17. Voytko-Best, Lisette. "What's Eating Kanye West? Leaving Adidas Would Drop the Volatile Superstar from Billionaire Status." *Forbes*, September 15, 2022. https://www.forbes.com/sites/lisettevoytko/2022/09/15/whats-eating-kanye-west-leaving-adidas-would-drop-the-volatile-superstar-from-billionaire-status/

18. Dellatto, Marisa. "Kanye West Dropped by Balenciaga—First Company to Sever Ties Amid Controversy." *Forbes*, October 21, 2022. https://www.forbes.com/sites/marisadellatto/2022/10/21/balenciaga-severs-ties-with-kanye-west/

19. Coleman, Oli. "Vogue Says It Has 'No Intention' of Working with Kanye West in Future." *Page Six*, October 21, 2022. https://pagesix.com/2022/10/21/vogue-has-no-intention-of-working-with-kanye-west-again

20. Associated Press. "Banking Breakup Between Ye, JPMorgan Planned for Weeks." *Bloomberg*, October 13, 2022. https://www.bloomberg.com/news/articles/2022-10-13/kanye-west-jpmorgan-banking-breakup-planned-for-weeks

21. Halpert, Madeline. "Kanye Tells Gap He's Ending Contract." *Forbes*, September 15, 2022. https://www.forbes.com/sites/madelinehalpert/2022/09/15/kanye-reportedly-tries-to-end-10-year-gap-deal/

22. Bhasin, Kim. "Gap Brand CEO Tells Staff the Kanye West Partnership Is Over." *Bloomberg*, September 15, 2022. https://www.bloomberg.com/news/articles/2022-09-15/gap-ends-partnership-with-kanye-west-s-yeezy-after-public-fight?leadSource=uverify%20wall

23. Swanson, Jeffrey W., E. Elizabeth McGinty, Seena Fazel, and Vickie M. Mays. "Mental Illness and Reduction of Gun Violence and Suicide: Bringing Epidemiologic Research to Policy." *Annals of Epidemiology* 25, no. 5 (2015): 366–376.

24. Amenabar, Teddy. "What Does Bipolar Disorder Feel Like? Can It Explain Kanye's Behavior?" *The Washington Post*, October 11, 2022. https://www.washingtonpost.com/wellness/2022/10/11/bipolar-disorder-symptoms-treatment

25. Harper, Shaun. "Businesses Ended Their Relationships with Kanye West—I Must, Too." *Forbes*, December 3, 2022. https://www.forbes.com/sites/shaunharper/2022/12/03/businesses-ended-their-relationships-with-kanye-west---i-must-too/

Chapter 29

1. Roeloffs, Mary Whitfill. "'The Color Purple' Rakes in Biggest Christmas Box Office Debut in Over a Decade—Beating 'Aquaman' and 'Wonka.'" *Forbes*, December 26, 2023. https://www.forbes.com/sites/maryroeloffs/2023/12/26/the-color-purple-rakes-in-biggest-christmas-box-office-debut-in-over-a-decade-beating-aquaman-and-wonka/?sh=2002dc136d40

Chapter 30

1. Solly, Meilan. "The Real Warriors Behind 'The Woman King.'" *Smithsonian Magazine*, September 15, 2022. https://www.smithsonianmag.com/history/real-warriors-woman-king-dahomey-agojie-amazons-180980750

2. "Viola Davis Discusses Her New Movie, 'The Woman King.'" Facebook. September 15, 2022. Video, https://www.facebook.com/CBSMornings/videos/viola-davis-discusses-her-new-movie-the-woman-king/769539484331822

3. Consumer Reports. "Is Bias Keeping Female, Minority Patients from Getting Proper Care for Their Pain?" *The Washington Post*, July 29, 2019. https://www.washingtonpost.com/health/is-bias-keeping-female-minority-patients-from-getting-proper-care-for-their-pain/2019/07/26/9d1b3a78-a810-11e9-9214-246e594de5d5_story.html

4. U.S. Centers for Disease Control and Prevention. "Working Together to Reduce Black Maternal Mortality." Accessed February 23, 2025. https://www.cdc.gov/womens-health/features/maternal-mortality.html?CDC_AAref_Val=https://www.cdc.gov/healthequity/features/maternal-mortality/index.html

5. Walsh, Savannah. "Michelle Obama Speaks Out About Facing Racism as First Lady." *Elle*, August 27, 2020. https://www.elle.com/culture/career-politics/a33823373/michelle-obama-racism-first-lady-black-womanhood-podcast

6. Desmond-Harris, Jenée. "Despite Decades of Racist and Sexist Attacks, Serena Williams Keeps Winning." *Vox*, January 28, 2017. https://www.vox.com/2017/1/28/14424624/serena-williams-wins-australian-open-venus-record-racist-sexist-attacks

Chapter 31

1. Robb, Michael B., and Supreet Mann. "Teens and Pornography." Common Sense Media. Accessed February 23, 2025. https://www.commonsensemedia.org/sites/default/files/research/report/2022-teens-and-pornography-final-web.pdf

2. Ballester-Arnal, Rafael, Marta García-Barba, Jesús Castro-Calvo, Cristina Giménez-García, and Maria Dolores Gil-Llario. "Pornography Consumption in People of Different Age Groups: An Analysis Based on Gender, Contents, and Consequences." *Sexuality Research and Social Policy* 20 (2023): 766–779.

3. Hsu, Tiffany. "When Mortal Kombat Came Under Congressional Scrutiny." *The New York Times*, March 8, 2018. https://www.nytimes.com/2018/03/08/business/video-games-violence.html

Chapter 32

1. "Why Does John Cena Say You Can't See Me?" YouTube. February 2, 2023. Video, https://www.youtube.com/watch?v=y3ThnX9ghuo

2. Keith Olbermann (@KeithOlbermann). 2023. "What a fucking idiot." Twitter, April 2, 2023, 3:05 p.m. https://x.com/KeithOlbermann/status/1642649593140637706

3. Dave Portnoy (@stoolpresidente). 2023. "Classless piece of shit." Twitter, April 2, 2023, 3:02 p.m. https://x.com/stoolpresidente/status/1642648843010428931

4. John Cena (@JohnCena). 2023. "Even if they could see you . . . they couldn't guard you! Congrats on the historic performance @CaitlinClark22 and to @IowaWBB on advancing to the Final Four! @MarchMadnessWBB #WFinalFour." Twitter, March 28, 2023, 10:56 a.m. https://x.com/JohnCena/status/1640774822626992139

5. Bailey, Moya. *Misogynoir Transformed: Black Women's Digital Resistance*. NYU Press, 2021.

6. Rafat, Misbah. "Social Role Theory: Stereotyped Expectations of Gendered Toys and Its Implications in a Society." *American Journal of Gender and Development Studies* 1, no. 1 (2022): 1–14.

Chapter 33

1. Parrott, Dominic J., and Christopher I. Eckhardt. "Effects of Alcohol on Human Aggression." *Current Opinion in Psychology* 19 (2018): 1–5.
2. Sundin, Erica, Maria Rosaria Galanti, Jonas Landberg, and Mats Ramstedt. "Severe Harm from Others' Drinking: A Population-Based Study on Sex Differences and the Role of One's Own Drinking Habits." *Drug and Alcohol Review* 40, no. 2 (2021): 263–271.
3. Heinz, Adrienne, Anne Beck, Andreas Meyer-Lindenberg, Philipp Sterzer, and Andreas Heinz. "Cognitive and Neurobiological Mechanisms of Alcohol-Related Aggression." *Neuroscience* 12, no. 7 (2011): 400–413.
4. Giancola, Peter R. 2015. "Development and Evaluation of Theories of Alcohol-Related Violence: Covering a 40-Year Span." *Substance Use & Misuse* 50, no. 8–9 (2015): 1182–1187.
5. Parrott and Eckhardt, Ibid.
6. Sundin et al., Ibid.

Chapter 34

1. Sue, Derald Wing, and Lisa Spanierman. *Microaggressions in Everyday Life*, 2nd ed.. Wiley, 2020.

Chapter 35

1. Williams, Maxine. "Embracing Change Through Inclusion: Meta's 2022 Diversity Report." *Meta*, July 19, 2022. https://about.fb.com/news/2022/07/metas-diversity-report-2022
2. Miller, Karla L. "Microaggressions at the Office Can Make Remote Work Even More Appealing." *The Washington Post*, May 13, 2021. https://www.washingtonpost.com/business/2021/05/13/workplace-microaggressions-remote-workers

Chapter 36

1. "New Videos Released from Night of Tyre Nichols' Fatal Traffic Stop." YouTube. January 30, 2024. Video, https://www.youtube.com/watch?v=IU4Rd0nK1R8
2. "Tyre Nichols' Family, Attorney Ben Crump Speak to Reporters After Arrest of 5 Officers." YouTube. January 27, 2023. Video, https://www.youtube.com/watch?v=4djA-JGvuOA0

Chapter 37

1. Rojas, Rick. "Who Was Tyre Nichols?" *The New York Times*, January 26, 2023. https://www.nytimes.com/2023/01/26/us/who-was-tyre-nichols.html
2. "Memphis Police Chief Explains What Public Should Expect From Nichols' Arrest Footage." YouTube. January 27, 2023. Video, https://www.youtube.com/watch?v=OmTpfTOCz_4
3. "BREAKING: FBI Director Christopher Wray Reacts to Video Showing Fatal Beating of Tyre Nichols." YouTube. January 27, 2023. Video, https://www.youtube.com/watch?v=GDuRinvCeps

4. Emily Davies (@ELaserDavies). 2023. "President Biden just called Tyre Nichols' parents. He talked to them for more than 10 minutes." Twitter, January 27, 2023, 12:04 p.m. https://x.com/ELaserDavies/status/1619063942705455104

5. Harper, Shaun R. "Corporations Say They Support Black Lives Matter. Their Employees Doubt Them." *The Washington Post*, June 16, 2020. https://www.washingtonpost.com/outlook/2020/06/16/corporations-say-they-support-black-lives-matter-their-employees-doubt-them

Chapter 38

1. "On Script vs. Off the Cuff: Comparing Trump's Speaking Styles." YouTube. August 23, 2017. Video, https://www.youtube.com/watch?v=wGrQYoJEi1c

2. Harper, Shaun R. "Corporations Say They Support Black Lives Matter. Their Employees Doubt Them." *The Washington Post*, June 16, 2020. https://www.washingtonpost.com/outlook/2020/06/16/corporations-say-they-support-black-lives-matter-their-employees-doubt-them

3. Eliot, Lance. "Those Schools Banning Access to Generative AI ChatGPT Are Not Going to Move the Needle and Are Missing the Boat, Says AI Ethics and AI Law." *Forbes*, January 20, 2023. https://www.forbes.com/sites/lanceeliot/2023/01/20/those-schools-banning-access-to-generative-ai-chatgpt-are-not-going-to-move-the-needle-and-are-missing-the-boat-says-ai-ethics-and-ai-law/

4. Westfall, Chris. "Educators Battle Plagiarism as 89% of Students Admit to Using OpenAI's ChatGPT for Homework." *Forbes*, January 28, 2023. https://www.forbes.com/sites/chriswestfall/2023/01/28/educators-battle-plagiarism-as-89-of-students-admit-to-using-open-ais-chatgpt-for-homework/

Chapter 39

1. Bohannon, Molly. "Rite Aid Banned from Using AI Facial Recognition Technology for 5 Years After False Shoplifting Match Allegations." *Forbes*, December 19, 2023. https://www.forbes.com/sites/mollybohannon/2023/12/19/rite-aid-banned-from-using-ai-facial-recognition-technology-for-5-years-after-false-shoplifting-match-allegations/

2. "Rite Aid Banned from Using AI Facial Recognition After FTC Says Retailer Deployed Technology Without Reasonable Safeguards." Federal Trade Commission, December 19, 2023. https://www.ftc.gov/system/files/ftc_gov/pdf/2023190_riteaid_complaint_filed.pdf

3. Vigdor, Neil, and Elisha Brown. "Walmart Says It Will No Longer Lock Up African-American Beauty Products." *The New York Times*, June 10, 2020. https://www.nytimes.com/2020/06/10/business/walmart-black-hair-beauty-products.html

4. Dunlap, Michelle R. *Retail Racism: Shopping While Black and Brown in America*. MIT Press, 2023.

5. Gabbidon, Shaun, and George E. Higgins. *Shopping While Black: Consumer Racial Profiling in America*. Routledge, 2020.

6. Benedicto, Irene. "Detroit Woman Sues City Police After Being Wrongfully Arrested Due to AI Facial Recognition." *Forbes*, August 7, 2023. https://www.forbes.com/sites/irenebenedicto/2023/08/07/detroit-woman-sues-city-police-after-being-wrongfully-arrested-due-to-ai-facial-recognition/

7. Vogels, Emily A., and Andrew Perrin. "How Black Americans View the Use of Face Recognition Technology by Police." Pew Research Center, July 14, 2022. https://www

.pewresearch.org/short-reads/2022/07/14/how-black-americans-view-the-use-of-face-rec
ognition-technology-by-police

8. United States Senate. "Letter to David Pekoske, Transportation Security Administration." Accessed February 23, 2025. https://www.merkley.senate.gov/wp-content/uploads/imo/media/doc/tsa_facial_recognition_technology_letter.pdf

9. U.S. Department of Commerce. "NIST Study Evaluates Effects of Race, Age, Sex on Face Recognition Software." National Institute of Standards and Technology, December 19, 2019. https://www.nist.gov/news-events/news/2019/12/nist-study-evaluates-effects-race-age-sex-face-recognition-software

Chapter 40

1. Kavate, Michael. "Foundation Assets Reach a Record $1.5 Trillion, Propelled by Investment Gains and Big Donors." *Inside Philanthropy*, January 29, 2024. https://www.insidephilanthropy.com/home/2024-1-29-foundation-assets-reach-a-record

2. Naylor, Nicolette, and Nina Blackwell. "Freeing Ourselves from Colonial, White Savior Models of Philanthropy." *Nonprofit Quarterly*, June 16, 2022. https://nonprofitquarterly.org/freeing-ourselves-from-colonial-white-savior-models-of-philanthropy

3. Tomkin, Anastasia Reesa. "Philanthropic Pledges for Racial Justice Found to Be Superficial." *Nonprofit Quarterly*, October 7, 2021. https://nonprofitquarterly.org/philanthropic-pledges-for-racial-justice-found-to-be-superficial

Credits

Harper, Shaun. "Actions Educational Leaders Must Take When Kids Do Racist Things at School." *Forbes*, February 26, 2023.
Harper, Shaun. "Why Politicized Attacks on DEI in Schools Are Occurring, and How They're Bad for America." *Forbes*, June 9, 2023.
Harper, Shaun. "Supreme Court Ends Affirmative Action in College Admissions—Here's What Will Happen on Campuses." *Forbes*, June 29, 2023.
Harper, Shaun. "Eliminating Standardized Tests to Achieve Racial Equity in Post-Affirmative Action College Admissions." *Forbes*, July 9, 2023.
Harper, Shaun. "Legacy Admissions at Harvard and Other Elite Institutions Advantage White Applicants, New Evidence Shows." *Forbes*, July 5, 2023.
Harper, Shaun. "Harvard University's Next President Is a Black Woman." *Forbes*, December 15, 2022.
Harper, Shaun. "What It Means That a Black Woman Survived Only Six Months as Harvard's President." *Forbes*, January 4, 2024.
Harper, Shaun. "What Deion Sanders' Departure From Jackson State Could Mean for the Business of HBCU Athletics." *Forbes*, December 5, 2022.
Harper, Shaun. "Why Business Leaders Are Pulling the Plug On DEI." *Forbes*, July 18, 2023.
Harper, Shaun. "Elon Musk Articulates What Many DEI Opponents Think, but Are Too Afraid to Publicly Say." *Forbes*, December 19, 2023.
Harper, Shaun. "Your Company's DEI Training Isn't Critical Race Theory, No Need to Ban It." *Forbes*, August 8, 2022.
Harper, Shaun. "12 Ways CEOs and Companies Fail Chief Diversity Officers." *Forbes*, February 14, 2023.
Harper, Shaun. "Discrimination Against White Job Applicants and Employees, or Is It Racial Equity?" *Forbes*, July 23, 2023.
Harper, Shaun. "Repeated Snubbing of Black Kids at Amusement Parks Shows Need for More Complex Bias Trainings." *Forbes*, August 2, 2022.
Harper, Shaun. "Elon Musk Says He's Hiring a New Twitter CEO—Women Beware of the Glass Cliff." *Forbes*, December 21, 2022.
Harper, Shaun. "New Bank of America Loan Could Further Push Black and Latino Families Out of Communities." *Forbes*, September 6, 2022.
Harper, Shaun. "Adidas Gets Transphobic Backlash for 'Woke' Pride Month Swimsuit Marketing." *Forbes*, May 18, 2023.
Harper, Shaun. "Target Fumbles Black History Month, Pulls Offensive Item From Stores." *Forbes*, February 2, 2024.
Harper, Shaun. "Why a 'Lay Low' DEI Strategy Is Especially Bad Right Now." *Forbes*, January 15, 2024.

Harper, Shaun. "They're Saying He's Too Old: Ageism in Media Discourse About Biden's Reelection." *Forbes*, June 3, 2023.
Harper, Shaun. "Who Told Nikki Haley and Ron DeSantis That America Has Never Been Racist?" *Forbes*, January 17, 2024.
Harper, Shaun. "Kevin McCarthy's Failed Bids for House Speaker Expose the Ironies of Ideological Diversity and Homogeneity in the GOP." *Forbes*, January 4, 2023.
Harper, Shaun. "If George Santos Were Black, There'd Be Harsher Consequences for the Newly Elected Congressman's Lies." *Forbes*, December 29, 2022.
Harper, Shaun. "How Karen Bass Beat a Billionaire to Become First Woman and Second Black LA Mayor." *Forbes*, November 17, 2022.
Harper, Shaun. "Brittney Griner, Paul Whelan or Nothing? Why the Biden Administration Chose the Black Woman." *Forbes*, December 9, 2022.
Harper, Shaun. "Beyoncé Wins the Most Grammy Awards, Becomes the Actual G.O.A.T." *Forbes*, February 6, 2023.
Harper, Shaun. "Megan Thee Stallion Supporters Call Out Misogynoir in Hip-Hop Industry—What It Is and Where Else It Exists." *Forbes*, December 26, 2022.
Harper, Shaun. "Kanye West Could Lose Everything If Someone Doesn't Help Him." *Forbes*, October 23, 2022.
Harper, Shaun. "'The Color Purple' Cinematic Remix Expands Cultural Contribution and Financial Impact." *Forbes*, December 27, 2023.
Harper, Shaun. "Viola Davis Makes Compelling Case for Darker Skin Black Women in 'The Woman King.'" *Forbes*, September 15, 2022.
Harper, Shaun. "Porn Teaches Teens, Especially Guys, How to Have Sex: New Evidence and Long-Term Risks." *Forbes*, January 10, 2023.
Harper, Shaun. "NCAA Basketball Champ Angel Reese Is Being Called 'Classless' Because She's Black." *Forbes*, April 3, 2023.
Harper, Shaun. "What to Do When Drunk Fans Say Inexcusably Offensive Things at Sporting Events." *Forbes*, November 27, 2022.
Harper, Shaun. "White Guy Says He'll Bring Fried Chicken to the Black Cookout—How to Recover From Racial Microaggressions." *Forbes*, February 21, 2023.
Harper, Shaun. "Remote Work Can Boost Diversity yet Undermine Equity for Employees of Color." *Forbes*, July 22, 2022.
Harper, Shaun. "5 Black Memphis Cops Upheld Institutional and Cultural Racism in Fatal Attack of Tyre Nichols." *Forbes*, January 27, 2023.
Harper, Shaun. "What Execs Should Say to Employees About the Fatal Police Beating of Tyre Nichols." *Forbes*, January 27, 2023.
Harper, Shaun. "ChatGPT Threatens Authenticity of DEI Communications From Leaders." *Forbes*, February 19, 2023.
Harper, Shaun. "Rite Aid Facial Recognition Lawsuit Shows AI Risks of Shopping While Black." *Forbes*, December 21, 2023.
Harper, Shaun. "Ways Philanthropic Foundations Can Respond to Costly Attacks On DEI." *Forbes*, January 31, 2024.

Index

ACT tests, 17–20
Adgate, Brad, 68n10
Adidas (apparel corporation), 75–78, 127
Affirmative action
   corporate hiring practices, 58–62
   interpreted as discriminatory, 15
   Students for Fair Admissions (SFFA) cases, 12–16
   white women as beneficiaries, 16
African American Film Critics Association, 131
African Community Economic Development of New England (ACEDONE), 21
Ageism, 89–92
Agojie Warriors, 134
Aguilar, Pete, 97
Amenabar, Teddy, 128n24
America, Goddam (Lindsey), 122
American Council on Education, 29
American Journal of Education, 14
Americans with Disabilities Act, 126
American Whitelash (Lowery), 40
Amherst College, 22
Amusement parks, 63–66
Anderson, Nick, 13n3, 70n17
Anheuser-Busch (brewing company), 78
Anti-Semitism, 29–32, 128–129
   Kanye West, 126–127
Arbery, Ahmaud, 49
Artificial intelligence (AI)
   ChatGPT, 169–172
   facial recognition, 173–176
Ashford, Grace, 101n1
Associated Press, 121n1, 128n20
Atewologun, Doyin, 66n12
Athletics
   college football, 33–36
   in higher education, 13
   intoxication among sports fans, 147–150
   transgender athletes, 75–78
   women's basketball, 110–114, 143–146

The Atlantic, 89
Authenticity of messaging, 169–172

Bailey, Halle, 132
Bailey, Moya, 122, 122n10, 144
Balenciaga (fashion brand), 127
Balingit, Moriah, 70n17
Ballester-Arnal, Rafael, 139n2
Bank of America, 71–74
Barrino, Fantasia, 131
Basketball, women's
   NCAA Tournament, 143–146
   WNBA, 110–114
Bass, Karen, 106–109
Beck, Anne, 149n3
Beer, Tommy, 9n14
Bell, Derrick, 51
Bendon Publishing, 80
Benedicto, Irene, 174n6
Benenson Strategy Group, 138
Beyoncé, 117–120
Bhasin, Kim, 128n22
Bias training, 63–66
Biden, Joe, 9, 89–92, 107, 127, 165
   prisoner releases from Russia, 110–114
Bipolar disorder, 126–129
Black History Month, 79–82
   Pepper Tree Elementary School, 3–7
Black Lives Matter, 119–120
Black trauma, 137
Blackwell, Nina, 179n2
Blair, Samone, 103n14
Blake, Aaron, 102
Blinken, Antony, 110
Boebert, Lauren, 97
Bohannon, Molly, 173n1
Book banning, 8
Bout, Viktor, 111
Bowman, Jamaal, 22
Breitbard, Mark, 128

Index

Bridgeforth, James, 4
Brooks, Danielle, 132
Brown, Abram, 44n2
Brown, Elisha, 173n3
Brown, Jay, 77
Brown, Jodi, 63
Brown, Pamela, 102n10
Brown, Sharon, 131
Bryant, Kobe, 145
Burch, Audra D. S., 8n6
Burleson, Nate, 153
Burns, Ursula, 69
Bushard, Brian, 101n5
Businesses
    chief diversity officers (CDOs), 52–57
    corporate hiring practices, 58–62
    DEI practices, 39–43
    racial equity actions, 59–60

California Department of Education, 4
Cammack, Kat, 97
Carlson, Tucker, 111
Carter Andrews, Dorinda, 144
Caruso, Rick, 106–109
Carville, James, 111
Castro-Valva, Jesús, 139n2
CBS Mornings (television program), 122, 134, 135, 153, 155
CBS News Philadelphia, 63n2
Cena, John, 143, 145
Center for Technology Innovation (Brookings Institution), 175
Chan, Anna, 63n4
ChatGPT, 169–172
Chauvin, Derek, 9, 39, 161, 165
Chavkin, Daniel, 33n5
Chica Project, 21–22
Chief diversity officers (CDOs), 52–57
Christian, Jade Holmes, 132
Chronicle of Higher Education, 31, 83
Cillizza, Chris, 49n2
Cineas, Fabiola, 46n3
Clark, Caitlin, 143–146
Claytor, Cassi Pittman, 174
Clinton, Hillary, 64
CNN (news organization), 98, 99
Cole, Eddie R., 25, 26
Coleman, Oli, 127n19
College admissions, 12–16. *See also* Higher education
College and University Professional Association for Human Resources, 22

Colorism, 134–137
The Color Purple (1985 film), 130
The Color Purple (2023 film), 130–133
The Color Purple (Broadway show), 130
The Color Purple (Walker), 130, 163
Common Sense (nonprofit organization), 138–141
Communication
    authenticity and ChatGPT, 169–172
    and CDO roles, 53
The Community Affordable Loan Solution (TCALS), 71, 74
Community Homeownership Commitment, 71–74
Congressional Black Caucus, 107
Congressional Research Service, 98, 104n16
"Consequence inequities," 103–104
Consumer Reports, 134n3
Cornish, Tinu, 66n12
Corporate climate. *See* Businesses
Corporate Equality Index, 81
Coscarelli, Joe, 121n2
COVID-19 pandemic, 157. *See also* Remote work
Crenshaw, Kimberlé, 48, 51, 145–146
Critical Race Theory (Crenshaw et al.), 51
Critical race theory (CRT), 48–51
    legislation against, 8, 48–49
    misunderstandings of, 48
Crump, Ben, 162
Culture wars, 41

The Daily Wire, 77
Daniller, Andrew, 94n4
Davidson, Pete, 127
Davidson, Warren, 97
Davies, Emily, 165
Davis, Cerelyn "CJ," 165
Davis, Viola, 134–137
Debter, Lauren, 127n15
DEI (diversity, equity, inclusion)
    in business contexts, 39–43
    ChatGPT and authentic communication, 169–172
    chief diversity officers (CDOs), 52–57
    as divisive topic, xx–xxi
    "lay low" strategies, 83–86
    misunderstandings of, 44–47
    responses to attacks on, 177–180
    in schools, politicized attacks on, 8–11
Dellatto, Marisa, 8n1, 126n4, 127n10, 127n18
Democratic Party, 98
    Democratic vs. Republican attorneys general, 58–59

De Placido, Dani, 127n8
DeSantis, Ron, 8, 41, 93, 94
Desmond-Harris, Jenée, 135n6
Dilanian, Ken, 91n8
Disinformation, 40–41
Dismantle DEI Act, xx–xxi
Dissociative amnesia, 124
Diversity. *See also* DEI (diversity, equity, inclusion)
   lack of, in higher education, 14
   and remote work, 157–160
Dixon-Fyle, Sundiatu, 98n8
Dobbin, Frank, 46n4
Dokoupil, Tony, 153, 154–155
Dolan, Keven, 98n8
Domingo, Colman, 131
Donalds, Byron, 97
Donnelly, Anne, 102
Dorn, Sara, 83n3
Douglas, Maylana, 3
Douglas, Rome, 3
Douglas-Gabriel, Danielle, 13n3
Douglass, Frederick, 98
Drake (rapper/singer), 119, 121, 124
Drezner, Daniel, 31
Drink Champs (podcast), 127
Du Bois, W. E. B., 79
Duffy, Claire, 68n5
Duncan, Jericka, 153, 154
Dunlap, Michelle, 173
Durkee, Alisa, 93n3
Duvall, David, 59

Eckhardt, Christopher I., 149
Education Week, 4, 8, 83
The 11th Hour (news program), 90
Elias, Jennifer, 83n5
Eliot, Lance, 171n3
Elvir, Dunia, 107
Employee resource groups (ERGs), 60
Equal Credit Opportunity Act, 71
Equality and Human Rights Commission, 65
Equity. *See also* DEI (diversity, equity, inclusion)
   philanthropic support for, 177–180
   and remote work, 157–160
Erikson, Erik, 6
Expulsion as disciplinary measure, 4

Facebook (Meta), 157, 159–160
facial recognition, 173–176
Faguy, Ana, 8n5
Fair College Admissions for Students Act (2022), 22

Faust, Drew Gilpin, 25, 28, 29
Fazel, Seena, 128n23
Female Quotient, 69
50 Cent, 124
Filer, Christine, 94n5
Fisher, Abigail, 20
Fitzpatrick, Brian, 98
Fleming, Nathan, 63
Floyd, George, 9, 13, 39, 49, 84, 126, 127, 161, 165
Folkman, Joseph, 69n16
Folt, Carol, 70
Football, college, 33–36
Forbes, 76, 98, 112, 127
Fornelli, Tom, 33n2
Forrest, Jack, 102n10
Fortin, Jacey, 50n5
Fox, Lauren, 98n6
Fox News, 111
France, Lisa Respers, 121n4
Franklin, Aretha, 118
Frazier, Darnella, 9
Freedom Caucus, 98
Frum, David, 89
Fuchs, Hailey, 9n11
Fuesting, Melissa, 22n3

Gabbard, Tulsi, 102
Gabbidon, Shaun L., 173–174
Gaines, Riley, 75, 76
Galanti, Maria Rosaria, 149n2, 149n6
Gap (apparel company), 128
Garces, Liliana, 18
García-Barba, Marta, 139n2
García Peña, Lorgi, 27
Garnett, Kevin, 145
Gay, Claudine, 25–28
   plagiarism, accusations of, 32
   short tenure of, 29–32
The GayBCs (Webb), 9
Gayles, Joy Gaston, 143–144
Gender disparities in CEO positions, 67–70
Gender inclusivity, 75–78
Generational wealth, 18, 19, 23
Gentrification, 71–72
Giammona, Craig, 64n7
Giancola, Peter R., 149
GI Bill, 11
Gil-Llarno, Maria Dolores, 139n2
Giménez-García, Cristina, 139n2
Givens, Jarvis R., 26
"Glass ceiling," 67–70
Glover, Danny, 131

Index

GOAT status, 117–120
Gold, Michael, 101n1
Goldberg, Whoopi, 131
Golden, Jessica, 127n16
Goldenstein, Taylor, 64n8
GOP. See Republican Party
Gotanda, Neil T., 51n6
Graham-Barnes, AnnMarie, 93
Grammy Awards, 117–120
Greater Boston Latino Network (GBLN), 21
Greenburg, Zack O'Malley, 127n14
Greene, Marjorie Taylor, 75, 111
GRE tests, 17–20
Grieder, Erica, 20n7
Griner, Brittney, 110–114, 145
Grutter v. Bollinger, 12
The Guardian, 66
Gutsell, Jennifer N., 66n13
Guynn, Jessica, 9n12, 77nn6–7

Haley, Nikki, 93–94
Halpert, Madeline, 128n21
Harris, Frank, III, 139, 140
Harris, Kamala, 28, 79, 92, 107
Hartig, Hannah, 94n4
Harvard Business Review, 69
Harvard University, 21–24
   Claudine Gay's presidency, 25–32
Haslam, S. Alexander, 69
Hate speech, 68
Haylock, Zoe, 121n5
HBCUs (historically Black colleges and universities), 13, 15, 72
   athletics, 33–36
Heinz, Adrienne, 149
Heinz, Andreas, 149
Henson, Taraji P., 131
Hern, Kevin, 98
Hess, Rick, xxi
Higgins, George E., 173n5
Higher education
   admissions, nuanced approaches, 15
   admissions processes, post–affirmative action, 17–20
   admissions processes, race-conscious, 12–16
   anti-Semitism on campus, 29–32
   diversity, lack of, 14
   elite institutions, 21–24
   faculty/administrators of color, 13–14
   HBCUs (historically Black colleges and universities), 13, 15, 33–36, 72
   legacy admissions, 21–24
   polarization vs. productive debate, xix–xxi
   predominantly white institutions (PWIs), 12–13, 15
   race-focused campus initiatives, 13
   U.S. News & World Report rankings, 17
Hill, Marc Lamont, 122–123
Hip-hop industry, 121–125
Hispanic Heritage Month, 170
Hispanic/Latino Organization for Leadership & Advancement (HOLA), 73
History: erasure of racism, 93–96
Holpuch, Amanda, 78n8
Holt, Brianna, 72n4
Houston, Whitney, 118
Hsu, Tiffany, 142n3
Huang, Georgene, 69n15
Human lifespan development, 5–6
Human resources, 53
Hunt, Vivian, 98n8
Hur, Robert, 91
Hurtado, Sylvia, 18

Implicit bias, 63–66, 173–174
Individuals with Disabilities Education Act (1975), 11
Inequality in America Initiative (Harvard University), 25
Inside Graduate Admissions (Posselt), 18–19
Inslee, Jay, 12
Intersectionality
   Claudine Gay's leadership, 29
   concept of, 48
   for darker-skin Black women, 134–137
   misogynoir, 121–125, 145–146
   in the workplace, 50
Intoxication among sports fans, 147–150
Inzlicht, Michael, 66n13
Ivy League institutions, 21, 30

Jackson, DeSean, 36
Jackson, Michael, 118
Jackson State University, 33–36
James, LeBron, 118, 119
January 6 Capitol insurrection, 103, 105
Jay Z, 118
Jean-Pierre, Karine, 110, 112
jeen-yuhs: A Kanye Trilogy (Netflix docuseries), 127
Jeffries, Hakeem, 97
Jenner, Kylie, 121
Jewell, Zack, 77
Johns Hopkins University, 22
Johnson, Dusty, 98
Jones, Van, 8

Jordan, Michael, 118, 119
Journal of School Leadership, 4
Joyce, David, 98
JPMorgan Chase, 128

Kalev, Alexandra, 46n4
Kane, Paul, 41n4
Kardashian, Kim, 107, 127
Karimi, Faith, 65n11
Kasabian, Paul, 33n3
Kaste, Martin, 66n14
Kavanaugh, Brett, 104
Kavate, Michael, 179n1
Keeter, Scott, 94n4
King, Gayle, 122, 124
King, Martin Luther, Jr., 79, 97
King, Rodney, 165
Kornbluth, Sally, 30

LaBelle, Patti, 118
LaLota, Nick, 101
Lamar, Kendrick, 119
Landberg, Jonas, 149n2, 149n6
Lanez, Tory, 121–125
Langer, Gary, 89n2, 94n5
Laporta, James, 104n15
Lara Croft: Tomb Raider (film), 135
Latimer, Chris, 36
Lavietes, Matt, 98n4
Lawrence, Andrew, 66
Lebowitz, Megan, 91n8
Lee, MJ, 107n5
Lee, Nicol Turner, 175
Lee, Wendy, 126n1
Legacy admissions in higher education, 21–24
Legault, Lisa, 66
Levenson, Michael, 59n3
Levin, Bess, 102n9
Levitz, Eric, 126n3
LGBTQ+ communities
  porn use, 139–142
  Pride Month, 75
Li, David K., 107n7
Lindsey, Treva B., 122
Loan programs, 71–74
Los Angeles, California, 4, 106–109
Los Angeles Times, 106
Lowery, Wesley, 40
Lukas, Carrie, 98, 99
Lumpkin, Lauren, 13n3

Mace, Nancy, 75
Madarang, Charisma, 121n6
Magill, Liz, 29
Main Street Caucus, 98
Majewski, J. R., 103–104
Mann, Supreet, 138n1
Marshall, Thurgood, 79
Mays, Vickie M., 128n23
McAuliffe, Terry, 48
McCarthy, Kevin, 90, 97–100
McDowell, Isabelle, 75n1
McGinty, E. Elizabeth, 128n23
McIntyre, Hugh, 126n7
McKinsey reports, 98
McWhorter, John, 8n7
Megan Thee Stallion, 121–125
Memphis Police Department, 161–164, 165
Mental illness, 126–129
Merkley, Jeff, 22
Meta (Facebook), 157, 159–160
Metzger, Isha, 128
Meyer-Lindenberg, Andreas, 149n3
Microaggressions, racial, 153–156
Microaggressions in Everyday Life (Sue & Spanierman), 154
Mier, Tomás, 68n11, 121n6
Miller, Karla L., 157n2
The Mis-education of the Negro (Woodson), 79
Misinformation, 40–41
Misogynoir, 121–125, 144
Misogynoir Transformed (Bailey), 122
Mochkofsky, Graciela, 27n2
Modereger, Becki, 4
Morgan, Piers, 127
Morin, Rebecca, 126n5
Morino, Douglas, 121n2
Morrison, Toni, 8
Mortgage programs: Bank of America, 71–74
Mulvaney, Dylan, 78
Murray, Andrew, 109n8
Murray, Mark, 89n3
Musk, Elon, 61, 127
  DEI, misunderstandings of, 44–47, 83
  endorsement of Rick Caruso, 107
  Twitter CEO, 67–70

National Board for Education Sciences, 92
National Defense Authorization Act, 83
National Fair Housing Alliance, 71n2
National Institutes of Health, 128
Naylor, Nicolette, 179n2
NCAA athletics, 13, 33, 34

Women's Basketball, 143–146
Newman, Christopher, 3
New York Times, 101
   on chilling effect of Trump's policies, 9
   Claudine Gay's essay, 29
   on critical race theory (CRT), 50
   on legacy admissions, 22–23
Nichols, Tyre, 161–164, 165–168
Nietzel, Michael T., 17n4, 22n4
Nieva, Richard, 68n4
Nigeria, police brutality in, 163
Noah, Trevor, 118
Noble, Safiya U., 174
Noguera, Pedro, xxi
Nonbinary communities, 75–78
Nooyi, Indra, 69
NYPD (New York Police Department), 66

Obama, Barack, 8, 28, 79, 103, 104, 107
Obama, Michelle, 118, 135
O'Connor, Sandra Day, 12, 14
Olbermann, Keith, 143
Oreskes, Benjamin, 106n2, 106n4
O'Sullivan, Donie, 68n5

Paltrow, Gwyneth, 107
Parks, Rosa, 79
Parler (social media platform), 127
Parrott, Dominic J., 149
Patel, Vimal, 22n6
Patriot Front, 6
Patton Davis, Lori, 26, 28
Peller, Gary, 51n6
Pelosi, Nancy, 92, 97
Pepper Tree Elementary School (Upland, California), 3–4
PepsiCo., 69
Pérez Huber, Lindsay, 154
Perrin, Andrew, 174n7
Perry, Imani, 130
Perry, Katy, 107
Perry, Scott, 97–98
Pew Research Center, 9, 90, 94, 174
Philanthropic foundations, 177–180
Phillips, Shannon, 59
Piaget, Jean, 6
Pierce, Chester Middlebrook, 155, 156
Plagiarism, 32
Plati, David, 33n1
Police brutality
   executive responses to, 165–168, 169–170
   in Nigeria, 163
   Tyre Nichols' death, 161–164, 165–168

Police Off the Record (YouTube show), 102
Pornography industry, 138–142
Porterfield, Carlie, 68n6, 127n9
Portnoy, David, 143
Posselt, Julie, 18–19
"possibility confirmation," 34
"possibility models," 26, 28
Powell v. McCormack, 101
PragerU, 6
Pratt, Chris, 107
Predominantly white institutions (PWIs), 12–13, 15
Pride Month, 75–78
Prince (singer/songwriter), 118
Prince, Sara, 98n8
Problem Solvers, 98
Proposition 209 (California), 12, 13
Pryor, Richard, 118

Racial discrimination
   microaggressions, 153–156
   profiling, 64
   tokenism, 101
Racism
   amusement park incidents, 63–66
   anti-Blackness in business, 40
   cultural, 161–164
   darker-skin Black women, 134–137
   enduring nature of, 93–96
   implicit bias, 173–174
   incarceration rates, 112
   loan programs, 71–74
   Pepper Tree School Valentine's Day incident (2023), 3–4
   in political elections, 101–105
   in schools, 4–7
   "shopping while Black," 173–176
   systemic, 48
   women's basketball players, 143–146
Rafat, Misbah, 146n6
Raikes, Jeff, 41n5
Ramstedt, Mats, 148n6, 149n2
Ray, Rashawn, 173
Ray, Siladitya, 68nn8–9, 127n12
Real estate development, 71–74
Reed, Trevor, 111
Reese, Angel, 143–146
Regents of the University of California v. Bakke, 12
Reid, Joy, 93–94
The ReidOut (news program), 93–94
Reilly, Ryan, 91n8
Reimann, Nicholas, 111n4

Remote work, 157–160
Renaissance (Beyoncé album), 117
Replacement theory, 40
Republican Party, 97–100
   GOP Governance Group, 98
   Republican Study Committee, 98
   Republican *vs.* Democratic attorneys general, 58–59
   Rick Caruso's switch, 106–107
Reshamwala, Saleem, 64n5, 65n10
Retail racism, 174–176
"Reverse discrimination," 59–60
Rice, Jerry, 36
Riess, Rebekah, 59n4
Rite Aid and facial recognition lawsuit, 173–176
Robb, Michael B., 138n1
Robertson, Gil, IV, 131
Roeloffs, Mary Whitfill, 130n1
Roe v. Wade, 108
Rojas, Rick, 165n1
Rousseau, Julie, 144, 146
Rowland, Kelly, 63
Roy, Chip, 97
Rufo, Christopher, 46
Ruhle, Stephanie, 90, 91
Russia: release of U.S. prisoners, 110–114
Ryan, Josiah, 8n8
Ryan, Michelle, 69

Sahakian, Teny, 75n1
Sakoui, Anousha, 126n1
Sallee, Barrett, 33n2
Sanders, Bernie, 107
Sanders, Deion, 33–36
Santos, George, 98, 101–105
SAT tests, 17–20
Saul, Derek, 111n5
Scheller, Stuart, 111
Schrotenboer, Brent, 34n8
Schwartz, Sarah, 8n3, 49n3, 83n1
A Search for Common Ground (Hess & Noguera), xxi
Segregation, residential, 20
Servicemen's Readjustment Act (1944), 11
Sesame Place parks, 63–64
Sesame Street character mascots, 63
Sesame Workshop, 64n9
Sexual assault, 147–148
Sexuality Research and Social Policy, 139
Shapiro, Ariel, 126n6
Sharpe, Shannon, 36
Shopping While Black (Gabbidon), 173–174
"Shopping while Black," 173–176

Shotwell, Gwynne, 67
Silver, Adam, 113
Silver, Laura, 90n5
Simmons, Ruth, 26, 30
Skin tone and racism, 134–137
Skipworth, William, 29n4
Slodysko, Brian, 104n15
Slovak, Julianne, 64n6
Smith, Doug, 106n2
Smith, Edward J., 4, 102–103
Snoop Dogg, 107
Snow, Tina, 121n8
Social media
   algorithms, xix
   and misinformation, 9
Social Security Administration, 126
Solly, Meilan, 134n1
Solórzano, Daniel G., 154
Solti, Georg, 117
Soteriou, Stephanie, 121n7
SpaceX, 67
Spanierman, Lisa, 154
Sparks, Steven, 94n5
Special Purpose Credit Programs (SPCPs), 71
Speechwriting, 170
Sports. *See* Athletics
Sports Illustrated, 33
Standardized tests in college admissions process, 17–20
Starbucks workshops, 64
Stefanik, Elise, 30, 46
Steinhauser, Paul, 109n8
Sterzer, Philipp, 149n3
Stevens, Matt, 59n6
Stewart, Breanna, 113
Steyer, Jim, 138
Stop Asian hate movement, 40
Students for Fair Admissions (SFFA) cases, 12–16, 21
Study of Higher Education, 18
Sue, Derald Wing, 154
Sundin, Erica, 149
Sung, Carolyn, 102n10
Supreme Court decisions: admissions cases, 12–16
Surluga, Susan, 70n17
Suspension as school disciplinary measure, 4
Swanson, Jeffrey W., 128n23

Target (retail corporation), 79–82
Taylor, Breonna, 49
Tempest, Lynsey, 69n14
Texas A&M University, 22

Index

Thomas, Clarence, 104
Thomas, Kendall, 51n6
Thomas, Lia, 77
Title IX, 11
Tomkin, Anastasia Reesa, 179n3
Transgender athletes, 75–78
Transphobia, 40, 75–78
Transportation Security Administration (TSA), 175
Tresh, Fatima, 66n12
Trojan Transfer Plan, 23
Trounson, Rebecca, 13n2
Truffaut-Wong, Olivia, 107n6
Trump, Donald, 68
  on Brittney Griner release, 111
  classified documents, 91
  communication style, 170
  "consequence inequities," 103, 104
  election as reaction to Obama presidency, 10
  impact of first term, 107–108
  racism and offensive comments, 8–9, 113–114
  voters, motivation of, 11
  Ye's support of, 126
Truth Social (social media platform), 99
Tubman, Harriet, 79
Turning Point USA, xx, 6
21 Savage, 121
Twitter, 67–70

UCLA Center on Race and Digital Justice, 174
Unconscious bias, 64
Underground Railroad, 79
United States Senate, 175n8
University of California system, 17, 22
University of Georgia, 22
University of Southern California (USC), 23, 70
  Race and Equity Center, 34
USA Today, 77
U.S. Census Bureau, 91n6
U.S. Centers for Disease Control and Prevention, 134n4
U.S. Congress
  diversity within, 98
  "Five Families" in GOP, 98, 99
  George Santos and truth *vs.* lies, 101–105
  hearing concerning anti-Semitism, 29–30
  House of Representatives, 97–100
U.S. Department of Commerce, 175n9
U.S. Department of Justice, 72n5
"Us versus them" attitudes, 10

Vakil, Caroline, 102n11
Vance, J. D., xxi

Vandross, Luther, 118
Van Green, Ted, 94n4
Vick, Michael, 36
Vigdor, Neil, 173n3
Vogels, Emily, 174n7
Vogue, 127–128
Voytko-Best, Lisette, 127n15, 127n17

Walcott, David, 126n2
Walker, Alice, 130
Walker, Herschel, 101
Walsh, Savannah, 135n5
Washington, Booker T., 79
Washington, Denzel, 118
Washington Post, 33, 34, 70, 102
Waters, Maxine, 92
Waxman, Olivia B., 8n2
Webb, M. L., 9
West, Kanye, 68, 126–129
Westfall, Chris, 171
Wexler, Natalie, 48n1
Whelan, Paul, 110–114
The White House, 9n10, 49n4, 110n3
"Whitelash," 8, 10–11, 40
"White tears," 154
Wick, Julia, 106n1
Williams, Maxine, 157
Williams, Serena, 118, 135, 145
Williams, Venus, 135
Winfrey, Oprah, 118, 130, 131, 133
Wintour, Anna, 127–128
WNBA (Women's National Basketball Association), 110–114
The Woman King (film), 134–137
Wonder, Stevie, 118
Wood, Sarah, 15n6
Woodruff, Porsha, 174
Woods, Tiger, 118
Woodson, Carter G., 79
World Health Organization, 91
Wray, Christopher, 165
Wright, Jasmine, 107n5

Xerox Corporation, 69

Ye (Kanye West), 126–129
Youngkin, Glenn, 48

Zahn, Max, 59n5
Zanona, Melanie, 98n6
Zeleny, Jeff, 107n5
Zenger, Jack, 69n16

About the Author

Shaun Harper is a provost professor in the Rossier School of Education, Marshall School of Business, and Price School of Public Policy at the University of Southern California. In 2022, he was appointed university professor, a distinction bestowed on only 30 of 4,700 USC full-time faculty members. Harper also is the Clifford and Betty Allen Chair in Urban Leadership, as well as the USC Race and Equity Center's founder and chief research scientist. He served as the 2020–21 American Educational Research Association president and the 2016–17 Association for the Study of Higher Education president. He was inducted into the National Academy of Education in 2021.

More than 3.5 million people have read essays Harper has written for *The Washington Post*, *Forbes*, *The Los Angeles Times*, *Rolling Stone*, *Ebony*, and other major newspapers and magazines. His 13 books include *The Big Lie About Race in America's Schools* (Harvard Education Press, 2024). Harper also has published over 100 peer-reviewed journal articles and other academic papers. His research has been cited in more than 25,000 published studies spanning a vast array of disciplines. *The New York Times*, *Wall Street Journal*, *Sports Illustrated*, *The Atlantic*, *Diverse Issues in Higher Education*, *Inside Higher Ed*, and several hundred other news outlets have quoted Harper and featured his research. He has been interviewed on CNN, MSNBC, CNBC, ESPN, *PBS NewsHour*, NPR, and *The Dr. Phil Show*.

The U.S. Air Force, Nike, Google, Microsoft, T-Mobile, Anheuser-Busch, Hulu, the National Football League, Major League Baseball, Princeton University, and the New York City Department of Education are among the more than 400 organizations with which Harper has worked over the past 2 decades. The recipient of dozens of top awards in his profession and five honorary degrees, Harper has been repeatedly recognized in *Education Week* as one of the field's 10 most influential scholars; in 2025, he was ranked #1 in education policy.